BANESH HOFFMANN, who was educated at
Oxford and Princeton universities, is Professor
Emeritus of Mathematics at Queens College of the
City University of New York. He is the author of
a number of books, including *The Strange Story
of the Quantum*, considered a classic of science
writing for the layman, and *The Tyranny of
Testing*, which has caused a major stir of
controversy within the educational establishment.
Three times a member of the Institute for
Advanced Study, he collaborated in 1936 and
1937 with Albert Einstein and Leopold Infeld
on a fundamental contribution to the theory of
relativity. For a commemorative documentary
television program on the tenth anniversary of
Einstein's death, the BBC selected Dr. Hoffmann
to explain Einstein's theories of relativity to a
popular audience. In 1969, Dr. Hoffmann was
made the Honorary Patron of the Tensor Society of
Great Britain. He was awarded first prize by the
Gravity Research Foundation in 1964, and recently
received a patent for an Orthopedic Alphabet
for the teaching of reading. His latest book is
entitled *Albert Einstein: The Human Side*.

HELEN DUKAS was Albert Einstein's secretary
from 1928 until his death in 1955, when she became
a trustee of his literary estate.

Einstein, ca. 1946.

ALBERT EINSTEIN

CREATOR AND REBEL

Banesh Hoffmann

with the collaboration of
Helen Dukas

The
Collection of
BIOGRAPHY
and
AUTOBIOGRAPHY

The Collection of Biography and Autobiography

Published by New American Library
1633 Broadway
New York, NY 10019

First Printing 1986

PRINTED IN THE UNITED STATES OF AMERICA

One thing I have learned in a long life: that all our science, measured against reality, is primitive and childlike—and yet it is the most precious thing we have.

ALBERT EINSTEIN

Acknowledgments

Grateful acknowledgment is made to Dr. Otto Nathan, Trustee of the Estate of Albert Einstein, for permisson to quote from *Einstein on Peace*, edited by Otto Nathan and Heinz Norden (Schocken Books, 1968), and to quote or reproduce other material belonging to the Estate of Albert Einstein, including hitherto unpublished material in the Einstein Archives; and for ready and unfailing help on numerous other matters connected with this book.

Grateful acknowledgment is also made to Professor Paul Schilpp for permission to quote from *Albert Einstein: Philosopher-Scientist*, edited by Paul Schilpp (The Library of Living Philosophers, 1949); to Philippe Halsman, H. Landshoff, and others for the use of photographs as noted where these photographs appear; to Alvin Jaeggli, director of the rare books and manuscripts department of the Library of the Swiss Federal Polytechnic Institute in Zurich, for aid in securing documents and data; to Dr. Pierre Speziali, Professor of Mathematics at the Collège Voltaire de Genève, and to Madame Lydia Besso-Brönnimann, the widow of Michele Besso's son Vero Besso, for making available not only pictures of Michele Besso but also the unpublished biographical manuscript of Maja Winteler-Einstein; to Freeman Dyson, Professor of Theoretical Physics at the Institute for Advanced Study, to Martin J. Klein, Professor of the History of Physics at Yale University, and to Otto Nathan once more, for reading the manuscript in whole or in part and making valuable suggestions; and to Beatrice Rosenfeld, without whose editorial creativity this book would not have come into being.

Note to the Reader

Every biography is an act of selection, and in the case of a man like Einstein this fact is particularly relevant. Nothing approaching a definitive biography exists. This book does not pretend to be one. We have tried, in brief compass, to give an indication of the man, letting his image come through when possible in terms of his own writings and devoting much space to his science. For science was so much a part of the man, so central to his being, that no biography can be more than anecdotal and superficial that passes over it lightly. Enough is told of the science to show in depth the distinctive character that gave it greatness. Yet, unless the reader is particularly interested in science, he should not pause over subtle details. Our aim has been to present the story in such a way that, by regarding it as pure narrative, the reader can catch the essential flavor of the man and his science, and something of the tumultuous scientific and political era in which he lived and made his extraordinary contributions.

Contents

NOTE TO THE READER   *ix*

1
The Man and the Child   *3*

2
The Child and the Young Man   *15*

3
Prelude   *37*

4
Dawn of a New Light   *43*

5
Atomic Agitation   *55*

6
Better Times   *60*

7
From Bern to Berlin   *81*

8

From Principia *to Principe*   *103*

9

From Principe to Princeton   *134*

10

The Battle and the Bomb   *173*

11

A Broader Canvas   *211*

12

All Men Are Mortal   *221*

INDEX   *265*

Illustrations

Einstein, ca. 1946   *frontispiece*
Sketch of Einstein by Charlotte Behrend   4
Autograph-charity card used by Einstein   5
Einstein's parents   6
Einstein's paternal grandparents   8
Earliest photograph of Albert Einstein   13
The house in Ulm where Einstein was born   16
Ruins of the house in Ulm   16
Maja and Albert Einstein, about three and five   17
Class photograph, Munich, 1889   19
Maja and Albert Einstein, about twelve and fourteen   21
Albert Einstein, about fourteen   21
Title page of the "holy geometry book"   22
Page 76 of the "holy geometry book"   23
Graduating class, Aarau, 1896   29
Aarau class reunion, 1933   29
Einstein at the Zurich Polytechnic Institute   30
List of Einstein's class at the Zurich Poly   31
Advertisement of vacancy at the Patent Office   35
The Olympia Academy   38
Einstein with Mileva and Hans Albert, 1904   40
Michele and Anna Besso   42

Framed portraits of Faraday and Maxwell from Einstein's
    study   *46*
Max Planck   *49*
Einstein in the Patent Office   *50*
Title page of Newton's *Principia*   *62*
H. A. Lorentz   *65*
Page of lecture "Geometry and Experience"   *70*
Verso of lecture page   *71*
Einstein and Besso   *80*
Receipt for payment to Einstein for private lessons, 1905   *85*
The 1911 Solvay Congress   *97*
Mileva Einstein with Hans Albert and Eduard, 1914   *102*
Letter to George Hale   *112*
Marcel Grossmann   *118*
Einstein writing gravitation equation on the blackboard   *123*
Einstein, 1916   *125*
Introductory paragraph of manuscript on the general theory
    of relativity   *130*
Postcard from Einstein to his mother   *131*
Eddington and Einstein   *132*
Page of lecture notes at the time of the revolution in Berlin,
    1918   *136*
Photomontage of Wertheimer, Einstein, and Born   *137*
Einstein and fellow scientists in Leiden, 1920   *138*
Newton   *140*
Einstein's quatrain on Newton   *142*
Verso of quatrain on Newton   *142*
Academic procession, Princeton, 1921   *145*
Einstein and Weizmann   *146*
Ticket for Einstein's lecture at King's College, University of
    London   *147*
Einstein lecturing at the Collège de France, 1922   *148*
Einstein in Sweden for his Nobel lecture, 1923   *151*
Exterior of the Einsteins' apartment in Berlin   *153*
Music room of the Berlin apartment   *153*
Joseph Schwarz, Boris Schwarz, and Einstein   *154*
Nobel laureates in Berlin, 1931   *155*
Cartoon of Einstein by Low   *156*
Einstein receiving the Planck medal   *157*

Lithograph of Einstein by Emil Orlik   *158*
Einstein's couplet about the Orlik lithograph   *158*
The house at Caputh   *160*
Einstein's study at Caputh   *160*
Einstein sailing with his daughter and son-in-law   *161*
Einstein on his way to his sailboat   *161*
Einstein, his son, and his grandson, ca. 1930   *162*
Einstein and Elsa, 1931   *162*
Einstein with fellow scientists in Pasadena, ca. 1931   *162*
Planning group for the 1933 Solvay Congress   *165*
Photo of Einstein by Queen Elizabeth   *166*
Queen Elizabeth of Belgium   *166*
Einstein and King Albert of Belgium   *167*
Einstein and Churchill   *171*
Einstein just before final departure from Berlin   *172*
The 1913 Solvay Congress   *174*
The 1927 Solvay Congress   *187*
Three photographs of Bohr and Einstein taken by Ehrenfest *188–89*
Statue of Einstein in Montevideo   *194*
Sketch of Einstein by Leonid Pasternak   *204*
Einstein and Szilard   *208*
The Einsteins in Japan   *210*
Einstein's house in Princeton   *226*
Einstein at the Copernican Quadricentennial   *235*
Einstein and Otto Nathan   *238*
Einstein in his study in Princeton   *239*
Einstein with his secretary and Margot   *241*
Maja Winteler-Einstein   *242*
The "Olympia Academy" postcard   *243*
Einstein not "at home" in Philadelphia   *249*
Silhouettes made by Einstein of himself and his wife and
     daughters   *250*
Einstein in winter   *251*
Einstein at the seventieth-birthday symposium   *254–55*
The last photo of Einstein   *256*
Painting of Michele Besso   *258*
Einstein's last page of calculations   *260*
Halsman portrait of Einstein   *262*
Obituary cartoon by Herblock   *263*

ALBERT
EINSTEIN
CREATOR
AND REBEL

I

The Man and
the Child

We sketch in this book the story of a profoundly simple man.

The essence of Einstein's profundity lay in his simplicity; and the essence of his science lay in his artistry—his phenomenal sense of beauty. *"This was sometime a paradox, but now the time gives it proof,"* as Hamlet said in a different connection.

Already paradox is upon us waiting to be resolved. But there is more to come. As the story unfolds we shall discover that Hamlet's words, thus torn from their context, take on a new and unexpected aptness. For Einstein has strange things to tell about Time.

He is, of course, best known for his theory of relativity, which brought him world fame. But with fame came a form of near-idolatry that Einstein found incomprehensible. To his amazement, he became a living legend, a veritable folk hero, looked upon as an oracle, entertained by royalty, statesmen, and other celebrities, and treated by public and press as if he were a movie star rather than a scientist. When, in Hollywood's glittering heyday, Chaplin took Einstein to the gala opening of his film *City Lights*, the crowds surged around the limousine as much to gape at Einstein as at Chaplin. Turning in bewilderment to his host, Einstein asked, "What does it mean?" to which the worldly-wise Chaplin bitterly replied, "Nothing."

Though fame brought its inevitable problems, it had no power to spoil Einstein; vanity was no part of him. He showed no trace of pomposity or exaggerated self-importance. Journalists pestered him with irrelevancies and inanities. Painters, sculptors, and photographers, famous and obscure, came in a steady stream to make his portrait. Yet through it all he retained his simplicity and his sense of humor. When a passenger on a train, not recognizing him, asked him his occupation, he ruefully replied, "I am an artists' model." Harassed by requests for his autograph, he remarked to friends that autograph hunting was the last vestige of cannibalism: people used to eat people, but now they sought symbolic pieces of them instead. After being lionized at a social affair, he confided dolefully, "When I was young, all I wanted and expected from life was to sit quietly in some corner doing my work without the public paying attention to me. And now see what has become of me."

Long before the public heard of him, Einstein's importance had

Pencil sketch of Einstein by the artist Charlotte Behrend, 1944.

There was a time when Einstein used to send this printed card to people writing for his autograph. It starts: "I have decided to give autographs in the future only to those persons who are ready to make a modest charitable contribution." The autograph was given after a money order had been sent directly to a recipient designated by Einstein and Einstein had received the stub as evidence that this had been done. The card ends: "It is advisable not to give a return address on the money order so as to prevent annoyance by begging letters."

been recognized by physicists. His theory of relativity has two main parts, the special theory and the general. Not till just after World War I, when eclipse observations lent confirmation to a prediction of the general theory of relativity, did word leak out to the public that something momentous had happened in the world of science.

Einstein came at a time of unprecedented crisis in physics. Relativity was not the only revolutionary scientific development of the early twentieth century. The quantum revolution, which is also part of our story, developed more or less simultaneously and was even more radical than relativity. Yet it made no such public splash and produced no such popular hero as did the latter.

The myth arose that in the whole world only a half-dozen scientists were capable of understanding the general theory of relativity. When Einstein first propounded the theory this may well have been no great exaggeration. But even after dozens of authors had written articles and books explaining the theory, the myth did not die. It has had a long life and traces of it survive even now, when according to a recent estimate the year's output of significant published articles involving the general theory of relativity is somewhere in the neighborhood of seven hundred to a thousand.

The myth and the eclipse observations gave the theory an aura of mystery and cosmic serenity that must have caught the fancy of a war-weary public eager to forget the guilt and horror of World War I. Yet, even when looked at plain, the theory of relativity remains a towering achievement. In a letter written when he had just turned fifty-one, Einstein indicated that he regarded this theory as his true lifework and said of his other concepts that he looked on them more as *Gelegenheitsarbeit*—work performed as the occasion arose.

But the *Gelegenheitsarbeit* of an Einstein may not be lightly dismissed. Max Born, who won the Nobel Prize for physics, put

Einstein's parents, Hermann Einstein and Pauline Einstein, née Koch.

it well when he said that Einstein "would be one of the greatest theoretical physicists of all times even if he had not written a single line on relativity." What of Einstein's own Nobel Prize? Suppose we naively take the official citation at face value. Then we may well say that he was awarded the prize primarily for part of his *Gelegenheitsarbeit*. And all this in no way conflicts with the pre-eminence of his theory of relativity.

Carl Seelig, one of Einstein's chief biographers, once wrote to him asking whether he inherited his scientific gift from his father's side and his musical from his mother's. Einstein replied in all sincerity, "I have no special gift—I am only passionately curious. Thus it is not a question of heredity." In saying this, Einstein was not being coy. Rather, he was being careful. He was responding as best he could to an ill-conceived question. If we imagine that it referred to Einstein's scientific artistry, we read into it something that Seelig surely did not have in mind. Implicitly the question put Einstein's music on a par with his science. True, Einstein loved music and played the violin better than many an amateur. But was he, in music, comparable to his favorite composer, Mozart, as in science he was comparable to Newton, whom he revered?

In science Einstein was certainly no amateur. His talents were of thoroughly professional caliber. To the layman the talents of an outstanding professional in any field, whether theology or forgery, can well seem awe-inspiring. But talent is no great rarity, and by professional standards Einstein's scientific talent and technical skill were not spectacular. They were surpassed by those of many a competent practitioner. In this strict sense, then, Einstein indeed had no special scientific gift. What he did have that was special was the magic touch without which even the most passionate curiosity would be ineffectual: he had the authentic magic that transcends logic and distinguishes the genius from the mass of lesser men with greater talent.

This we shall be seeing for ourselves as we proceed. Einstein implicitly conceded it in his autobiography, though in words more consonant with the demands of modesty. After all, he could not, with good grace, say baldly, "I am a genius." This is what he wrote, telling why he became a physicist rather than a mathematician:

The fact that I neglected mathematics to a certain extent had its causes not merely in my stronger interest in science than in mathematics but also in the following strange experience. I saw that mathematics was split up into numerous specialties, each of which could easily absorb the short lifetime granted to us. Consequently I saw myself in the position of Buridan's ass, which was unable to decide upon any specific bundle of hay. This was obviously due to the fact that my intuition was not strong enough in the field of mathematics. . . . In [physics], however, I soon learned to scent out that which was able to lead to fundamentals and to turn aside from everything else, from the multitude of things that clutter up the mind and divert it from the essential.

Such powerful intuition can not be rationally explained. It is not something teachable or reducible to rule, else we might all be geniuses. It wells up spontaneously from within. Albert Einstein wrote his autobiography at the age of sixty-seven, and in it he reminisced about a major event that had occurred more than sixty years before. It is a story that he was fond of telling. Apparently,

Einstein's paternal grandparents, Abraham Einstein and Hindel Einstein. Hermann and Pauline, in memory of Abraham, chose for their son the name Albert, which begins with the same letter.

as a child of four or five, he had been ill in bed and his father had brought him a magnetic compass to play with. Many a child has played with such a toy. But the effect on young Albert was dramatic—and prophetic. In his autobiography the aging Einstein vividly recalled the sense of wonder that had overwhelmed him those many years before: here was a needle, isolated and unreachable, totally enclosed, yet caught in the grip of an invisible urge that made it strive determinedly toward the north. Never mind that the magnetic needle was no more wonderful—no less wonderful—than a pendulum striving toward the earth. Pendulums and falling objects were already familiar to the child. He took them as a matter of course. He could not realize at the time that they too presented a mystery, nor could he know that later in life he was to make his own great contribution to our understanding, such as it is, of gravitation. To young Albert the magnetic needle came as a revelation. It did not fit. It mocked his early, simple picture of an orderly physical world. In his autobiography he wrote, "I can still remember—or at least I believe I can remember—that this experience made a deep and abiding impression on me."

These are remarkable words in more ways than one. They tell of the sudden awakening of the passionate curiosity that was to be Einstein's lifelong companion—or, it may be, of the sudden crystallization of something inborn that had already been long in process of formation. Knowing what Einstein accomplished, we can see in these autobiographical words that he found his métier at an early age. Yet there is something strange about his words that will repay our scrutiny. Read them again: "I can still remember—*or at least I believe I can remember*—that this experience made a deep and abiding impression on me." Is there not an air of illogic about them? If the experience made a deep and abiding impression on him, surely he should have had no doubts that he remembered its doing so. Why then the precautionary phrase "or at least I believe I can remember"?

Have we caught the great Einstein in a contradiction? Superficially, yes. Yet in a deeper sense we have not. He had told the story often. He knew the frailties of memory. He knew that with repetition a story can become exaggerated, and the teller come to believe it nevertheless. He believed that the magnet had made an unforgettable impression on him. Yet perhaps the effect had not been quite as great as he had come to think. Note how artlessly he conveyed this thought that lay at the back of his mind. The words of caution are unpremeditated. They interrupt the logic. They burst in uninvited, like a Freudian slip, and reveal Einstein's instinctive striving after truth. And they do more. They show us Einstein deepening a truth by means of a paradox.

What of his autobiography? Twice already we have dipped into it. It must be a veritable treasure trove. It is indeed, yet not wholly of the sort we might expect. Einstein had strong views about biographies. A distinguished poet writing a notable biography of a major scientist of the nineteenth century asked Einstein in 1942 to contribute a foreword. He wrote in reply:

> In my view there is but one way to bring a great scientist to the attention of the larger public: it is to discuss and explain, in language which will be generally understood, the problems and the solutions which have characterized his lifework. This can only be done by someone who has a fundamental grasp of the material. . . . the external life and personal relations can only be, in the main, of secondary importance. Of course, in such a book, the personal side must be taken account of; but it should not be made the chief thing especially when no book exists dealing with the actual achievement. Otherwise, the result is a banal hero-worship, based on emotion and not on insight. I have learned by my own experience how hateful and ridiculous it is, when a serious man, absorbed in important endeavors, is ignorantly lionized.

> In any case, I cannot give my public endorsement to such an undertaking. It would seem to me less than honourable. That sounds harsh; I even fear that you will take my inability for unjustifiable unkindness. But so I am, and cannot be otherwise.

Only rarely did Einstein endorse biographies of himself. For one by his son-in-law, Rudolf Kayser,* he wrote a preface, saying in part:

> I found the facts of the book duly accurate, and its characterization, throughout, as good as might be expected of one who is perforce himself, and who can no more be another than I can.

* Writing under the pseudonym Anton Reiser.

What has perhaps been overlooked is the irrational, the inconsistent, the droll, even the insane, which nature, inexhaustively
operative, implants in an individual, seemingly for her own amusement. But these things are singled out only in the crucible of one's
own mind.

Surely, then, we should look more closely at Einstein's autobiography. Unfortunately, in speaking of his autobiography we
have been less than candid. If his words to the poet writing the
biography of the nineteenth-century scientist seemed harsh, we
shall see that they are as nothing compared to the biographical
standards he imposed on himself in this instance, which we owe
to the persistence and persuasiveness of Paul Arthur Schilpp, a
professor of philosophy. Schilpp had edited a series of books about
great living philosophers—men of the caliber of Dewey, Santa-
yana, Whitehead, and Russell—and, realizing that Einstein could
well be ranked as a major philosopher, he sought to add him to
his list. Each book was devoted to a single man. It contained his
specially written autobiography, followed by a series of essays by
authorities evaluating and criticizing his work. These essays were
then answered by the philosopher himself, who thus had a chance
to correct misunderstandings of his teachings and to clarify what
the experts had evidently found obscure.

Despite Schilpp's persuasiveness, Einstein refused to write his
autobiography for the book. Instead he consented to write his
scientific autobiography. With gallows humor, he spoke of it as
his obituary, and when it was done, it was entitled not "Autobiography" but "Autobiographical Notes"* (*"Autobiographisches"*
in the original German). It did not begin, as a conventional autobiography might, by saying, "I was born on the 14th of March
1879 in the town of Ulm in Germany." It did not even mention
such matters. Nor did it say such things as, "I had a younger sister
named Maja," or, "I had two sons by my first wife," or, "My
mother's name was Pauline." It did tell of the sense of wonder
that came over him when his father showed him the magnetic
compass needle, but emotional and intellectual events of this sort
could be deemed to have a rightful place in a scientific autobi-

* In *Albert Einstein: Philosopher-Scientist,* ed. Paul A. Schilpp. Library of
Living Philosophers. Evanston, Ill., 1949.

ography. They were not in the same category as such things as falling in love or grieving over a death. These last were private matters, and after long years in the limelight Einstein valued his privacy. Even so, would one not have expected Einstein to have mentioned somewhere in this scientific autobiography that his father, who had shown him the compass, was named Hermann? The only names that appear are those of scientists and philosophers. There is no mention of changes of domicile. No mention of positions held. Only the most fleeting reference to his being a Jew. None at all to the political effects of the world on him, or of him on the world. Barely is the "obituary" started before it is immersed in a profound discussion of science and philosophy, and at that level, for the most part, it remains. Well aware of his autobiographical shortcomings, Einstein suddenly interrupts his deep discussion to interject these words:

> "Is this supposed to be an obituary?" the astonished reader will likely ask. I would like to reply: essentially yes. For the essential in the being of a man of my type lies precisely in *what* he thinks and *how* he thinks, not in what he does or suffers. Consequently, the obituary can limit itself in the main to the communicating of thoughts that have played a considerable role in my endeavors.

And having said this, he is off again, his conscience eased, to discuss the nature of physical theories without so much as a pause for printed breath that he could have marked by at least starting a fresh paragraph.

Yet the "Autobiographical Notes," with their mathematical formulas and subtle concepts, are of endless fascination to the specialist—and to the layman too if he is prepared to skip whenever discretion takes precedence over valor. Even Einstein's omissions help to tell us what manner of man he was. Here he felt no need to say that such and such an idea came to him in Bern, or Zurich, or Berlin, or Princeton. The "Notes," though autobiographical, are in no sense geographical. They are essentially placeless. Wherever he went, his ideas went with him, and where he went was here irrelevant. The "Notes" are not wholly placeless, though. They tell of a unique adventure—and a world-shaking one—that took place within the ivory tower of a mind.

The earliest known photograph of Albert Einstein.

On 24 June 1881, when Einstein was two years and three months old, his maternal grandmother, Jette Koch, wrote this to relatives: "Little Albert is such a dear good child that I already feel very sad when I think that I shall not see him again for quite a time." And a week later she wrote, "We have fond recollections of little Albert. He was so dear and good, and we talk again and again of his droll ideas."

The testimony of grandparents about their grandchildren is notoriously biased. What gives these excerpts interest is not so much the effect little Albert had on his grandmother. Rather it is that they are the earliest surviving contemporary references to him as a personality. They make us wonder what the "droll ideas" were of this two-year-old who was destined to surpass the fondest dreams of even the fondest of grandparents. Were the ideas something more than droll? Was there in them an inkling of what was to come? Or, contrariwise, did his grandparents ever despairingly think, as his parents at one time thought, that the beloved Albert Einstein was a dullard? They had good reason to think so, and the thought must have been agonizing. As Einstein recalled in a letter he wrote in 1954: "My parents were worried because I started to talk comparatively late, and they consulted the doctor because of it. I cannot tell how old I was at that time, but certainly not younger than three."

This is indeed quite late to begin to talk. The ideas that his grandparents found droll could hardly have been verbal. In his letter Einstein did go on to say, "Also, I never exactly became an orator later. However, my later development was completely normal, except for the peculiarity that I used to repeat my own words softly." Even so, considering that little Albert was to become none other than Einstein, his start was hardly auspicious.

2

The Child and
the Young Man

The house in Ulm where Einstein was born no longer stands. World War II reduced it to rubble. A street in Ulm had been named Einsteinstrasse. But the Nazis could not bear to see a Jew thus honored, especially one so great and one who by his whole life-style shone forth as a symbol of all that they sought to destroy. In Ulm the new Nazi mayor, on his first day in office, hastened to change the name Einsteinstrasse to Fichtestrasse, in honor of the eighteenth-century German philosopher and nationalist orator. Only with the defeat of the Nazis was the name Einsteinstrasse restored.

In letters written in 1946 Einstein said:

> I had heard the droll story of the street names at the time and it caused me no little amusement. Whether anything has been changed since then I do not know, and I know even less when the next change will take place; but I do know how to restrain my curiosity. . . . I think that a neutral name such as "Windfahnenstrasse" [Weather Vane Street] would be better suited to the political mentality of the Germans and would make further rechristenings in the course of time unnecessary.

Actually, Einstein had spent little time in Ulm. A year after his birth the family moved to a much larger city, and there his father, Hermann, and Hermann's brother—Albert's uncle Jakob—went

The house in Ulm where Einstein was born: Bahnhofstrasse 20.

All that was left of the house in Ulm after World War II.

into business together, setting up a small electrotechnical factory. What is ironic is that they set it up in Munich, which was later to become the cradle of Nazism, and that the Einsteins retained in their way of life little trace of their Jewish ancestry.

Indeed, they sent Albert and his sister, Maja, two and a half years his junior, to the nearby Catholic elementary school, where the two children learned the traditions and tenets of the Catholic faith. Their education in Judaism was not, however, neglected. Young Albert quickly became intensely religious, both spiritually and ritualistically. For years he refused to eat pork, for example, and he took it amiss that his parents were lax in their Jewish observances.

Maja and Albert Einstein, about three and five years old.

Perhaps in a brief biography it seems almost irrelevant to dwell on the religious evolution of one who was to become famous as a scientist. But Einstein's scientific motivation was basically religious, though not in the formal, ritualistic sense. We have already seen the magnetic compass needle pointing the way for the enchanted child. The man never lost this early childlike sense of awe and wonder. "The most incomprehensible thing about the world," he said, "is that it is comprehensible." When judging a scientific theory, his own or another's, he asked himself whether he would have made the universe in that way had he been God. This criterion may at first seem closer to mysticism than to what is usually thought of as science, yet it reveals Einstein's faith in an ultimate simplicity and beauty in the universe. Only a man with a profound religious and artistic conviction that beauty was there, waiting to be discovered, could have constructed theories whose most striking attribute, quite overtopping their spectacular successes, was their beauty.

Albert's parents, Hermann and Pauline Einstein, were by all accounts a devoted couple—he the good-natured, free-thinking optimistic businessman, and she the housewife, quieter and artistically inclined, eagerly playing the piano when household duties were done. In Munich they and the Jakob Einsteins were close neighbors, living near their factory in a pair of attached houses that shared a large garden. Thus in those early days Albert saw much of his uncle Jakob, the engineer in the partnership.

Young Albert was by instinct a loner. When children of relatives came to play in the garden, he took little part in their livelier games. In a document written much later his sister, Maja, recalled that he preferred games that required patience and perseverance, building complicated structures with building blocks and erecting houses of cards as high as fourteen stories. Even as a child, Albert recoiled instinctively from coercion. He shuddered at the sight and sound of military parades. While other children looked forward eagerly to the time when they too could don uniforms, he loathed the very thought of marching in mindless unison to the empty beat of a drum.

In 1886, when he was seven years old, his mother, Pauline, wrote to her mother saying, "Yesterday Albert got his school marks. Again he is at the top of his class and got a brilliant rec-

School class photograph, Munich, 1889. Einstein is third from the right in the front row.

ord." And a year later his maternal grandfather wrote, "Dear Albert has been back in school a week. I just love that boy, because you cannot imagine how good and intelligent he has become."

From these excerpts one might be tempted to conclude that Albert had quickly overcome the handicap of his slow start and had developed into a brilliant pupil, happy at school, and loved by relatives and teachers alike. But Einstein in later life spoke bitterly of his schooling. He disliked particularly the harsh, drill-sergeant methods of rote instruction that then prevailed. This dislike was heightened when, at the age of ten, he left the elementary school to enter the Luitpold Gymnasium.° To an inquirer he wrote in 1955, "As a pupil I was neither particularly good nor bad. My principal weakness was a poor memory and especially

° The German word *Gymnasium* is not to be confused with its athletic English counterpart. It is pronounced with a hard *G* and a broad *a*, as Ghymnahsium, and it means a secondary school or high school at which students receive a classical education, studying intensively the Latin and Greek classics in the original languages.

a poor memory for words and texts." Indeed, his teacher of Greek
had said to him, "You will never amount to anything." This hardly
makes him seem a dazzling student. But note Einstein's next
words: "Only in mathematics and physics was I, through self
study, far beyond the school curriculum, and also with regard to
philosophy so far as it had to do with the school curriculum."

Here at last we have a clearer picture of how the young Einstein
was developing. The key phrase is "self study," which was crucially linked with his passionate curiosity and his sense of wonder.

His violin playing gives further insight into the manner of his
development. He wrote:

> I took violin lessons from age 6 to 14, but had no luck with my
> teachers for whom music did not transcend mechanical practicing.
> I really began to learn only when I was about 13 years old, mainly
> after I had fallen in love with Mozart's sonatas. The attempt to
> reproduce, to some extent, their artistic content and their singular
> grace compelled me to improve my technique, which improvement
> I obtained from these sonatas without practicing systematically. I
> believe, on the whole, that love is a better teacher than sense of
> duty—with me, at least, it certainly was.

From his uncle Jakob, young Einstein undoubtedly received
important encouragement. Apparently before Albert had studied
geometry, Uncle Jakob told him of the Pythagorean theorem: that
the sum of the squares on the sides of a right-angled triangle is
equal to the square on the hypotenuse; or, put differently, if in the

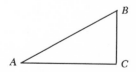

triangle ABC angle C is a right angle, then $AB^2 = AC^2 + BC^2$.
Albert was fascinated. After strenuous effort he found a way to
prove the theorem—an extraordinary feat under the circumstances
and one that must have given both him and his uncle intense
pleasure. Yet, strangely, this pleasure seems to have been negli-

Maja and Albert
Einstein, about
twelve and fourteen
years old.

Albert Einstein, about fourteen years old.

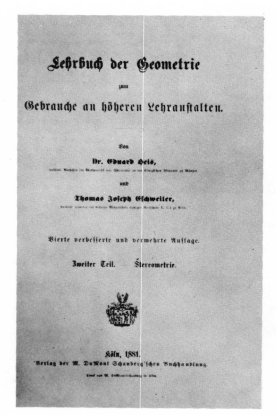

Title page of the "holy geometry book."

gible compared with the emotion later aroused in him by a small textbook on Euclidean geometry in which he became utterly absorbed. He was twelve at the time, and the book had as powerful an effect on him as the magnetic compass had had some seven years earlier. In his "Autobiographical Notes" he speaks rapturously of "the holy geometry booklet" and says:

> Here were assertions, as for example the intersection of the three altitudes of a triangle in one point, which—though by no means evident—could nevertheless be proved with such certainty that any doubt appeared to be out of the question. This lucidity and certainty made an indescribable impression on me.

To people who instinctively abhor mathematics, this passion for geometry must seem incredible—something akin to the herpe-

liegt. Man ziehe deshalb durch die Punkte A und B zwei Seitenlinien AC und BD bis zur Curve MNO, längs welcher die beschreibende Linie der Cylinderfläche sich fortbewegt hat, und verbinde die Punkte C und D. Daraus, daß die geraden Linie oder Sehne CD keinen Punkt mit dem Bogen CND gemein hat und $AC \parallel BD$ ist, läßt sich, mit Hülfe zu ziehender Parallelen, nachweisen, daß auch die Gerade AB keinen Punkt mit der Cylinderfläche gemein hat.

3. Satz. Die Cylinderfläche ist eine Fläche, die sich zur Ebene aus= strecken oder entrollen läßt (surface développable).

Denkt man sich durch jede von mehreren Seitenlinien der Cylinderfläche a) eine Ebene gelegt, welche diese und die folgende Seitenlinie in sich enthält, b) eine Ebene, welche die Fläche berührt, so entstehen zwei prismatische Räume, von welchen der eine der Cylinderfläche eingeschrieben, der andere ihr umgeschrieben ist. Die Seitenfläche eines jeden dieser prismatischen Räume läßt sich in eine Ebene ausbreiten, indem man sich vorstellen kann, jede der Ebenen, woraus sie besteht, drehe sich um eine der sie begrenzenden Kanten so lange, bis sie in die Erweiterung der benachbarten Ebene fällt und dann mit dieser nur eine Ebene ausmacht. Da nun die Cylinderfläche zwischen den Seitenflächen der prismatischen Räume liegt und die Grenze bildet, welcher jene Seitenflächen sich durch Vermehrung der Anzahl von Ebenen, aus denen sie bestehen, beliebig nähern können, so wird dasselbe von der Cylinderfläche gelten.

Fig. 89.

4. Satz. Die Durchschnitte der Cylinderfläche mit zweien unter sich parallelen Ebenen sind jeder= zeit congruente Figuren. (Fig. 89.)

Beweis. Diese Durchschnittsfiguren seien DEF und MNP, AB aber irgend eine den Seitenlinien parallele Gerade, welche die Ebenen jener in A und B trifft. Zieht man nun in einer dieser Ebenen z. B. in DEF von A aus zwei beliebige Gerade AD und AE bis zum Umfang der Figur und legt durch jede derselben und durch AB eine Ebene, deren Durch= schnitte mit der andern Figur und der Cylinderfläche für die eine BM und DM, für die andere BN und EN seien, so ergibt sich gleich, daß $ADMB$ und $AENB$ Parallelogramme sind, daß also $AD = BM$, $AE = BN$ sei. Auch

Page 76 of the "holy geometry book," with young Einstein's marginal note about the proof of Theorem 3. Einstein says: "The proof makes no sense, because if we can assume that these prismatic spaces are capable of being flattened out, we could just as well say it of the cylinder."

tologist's love of snakes. Since Einstein took the easy, if honest, path of describing the impression as indescribable, let us borrow a description from Bertrand Russell, who had an experience that must have been strikingly similar, even as to age. Russell wrote, "At the age of 11 I began Euclid. . . . This was one of the great events of my life, as dazzling as first love. I had not imagined there was anything so delicious in the world." And let us not forget the words of the poet Edna St. Vincent Millay: "Euclid alone has looked on Beauty bare."

As a child, Albert read popular science books with what he later described as "breathless attention." These books had not come to him by accident. They had been deliberately put into his hands by Max Talmey, a perceptive medical student who for a while was a weekly visitor of the Einsteins. Talmey had long discussions with young Albert, guiding him and widening his intellectual horizons at a crucial formative age. When Albert began teaching himself higher mathematics, Talmey, in self-defense, had to turn their discussions to philosophy, where he could still hold his own. Recalling those days, Talmey wrote, "I recommended to him the reading of Kant. At that time he was still a child, only thirteen years old, yet Kant's works, incomprehensible to ordinary mortals, seemed clear to him."

One striking effect of the science books on the impressionable Albert was to make him suddenly antireligious. He could not fail to see that the scientific story conflicted with the biblical. Hitherto he had found the solace of certainty in religion as it had been taught him. Now he felt he had to give it up, at least in part, and this he could not do without an intense emotional struggle. For a while he became not just a nonbeliever but a fanatical skeptic, profoundly suspicious of authority. Some forty years later he could bring himself to say with wry amusement, "To punish me for my contempt for authority, Fate made me an authority myself." His early suspicion of authority, which never wholly left him, was to prove of decisive importance. For without it he would not have been able to develop the powerful independence of mind that gave him the courage to challenge established scientific beliefs and thereby revolutionize physics.

But as a boy who had temporarily lost religion, he yearned for an alternative sense of certainty—a firm foundation on which to build an inner life and an external universe. It was at this stage that the geometry booklet came to him, and surely there is significance in the fact that a half-century later he spoke of it as the holy booklet.

After a few prosperous years, the factory of Hermann and Jakob Einstein in Munich encountered hard times. In 1894 it was given up and the two Einstein families moved to Italy to seek better fortune with a factory in Pavia, near Milan. They decided, though, that Albert should be left behind in lodgings to finish his school year at the Gymnasium.

Now, suddenly, at the age of fifteen, Albert was alone and lonely. He found little consolation at the Gymnasium. Not for nothing had his childhood schoolmates earlier given him the possibly taunting nickname *Biedermeier*, which means, more or less, Honest John. With his transparent simplicity he could not sufficiently conceal his dislike of the Gymnasium teachers and their Draconian methods. Naturally, this did not endear him to the teachers. Nor did he ingratiate himself with them when he asked questions that they found difficult to answer. Here is how Einstein described the situation in a letter written in 1940:

> When I was in the seventh grade at the Luitpold Gymnasium [and thus about fifteen] I was summoned by my home-room teacher* who expressed the wish that I leave the school. To my remark that I had done nothing amiss he replied only "your mere presence spoils the respect of the class for me."
>
> I myself, to be sure, wanted to leave school and follow my parents to Italy. But the main reason for me was the dull, mechanized method of teaching. Because of my poor memory for words, this presented me with great difficulties that it seemed senseless for me to overcome. I preferred, therefore, to endure all sorts of punishments rather than learn to gabble by rote.

Despite this mutual desire for severance, rules and prudence alike dictated that Albert endure till the final examinations and earn his diploma. But there are things more compelling than rules and prudence. Italy beckoned. In their letters, Albert's family

* This was the teacher of Greek who had prophesied that Einstein would never amount to anything.

had painted it in rosy hues. Fifteen years old, rebuffed and alone, Albert decided to leave the Gymnasium. This desperate decision gives vivid indication of the depth of his misery in Munich. It is not the only such indication. Before his parents had left, he had already decided to change his citizenship. This he could not accomplish on his own. The law would not permit it: he was a minor. Nevertheless his resolve was firm and his motives ran deep. As he wrote in 1933, "The over-emphasized military mentality in the German State was alien to me even as a boy. When my father moved to Italy he took steps, at my request, to have me released from German citizenship because I wanted to become a Swiss citizen."

Leaving the Gymnasium entailed risks, and Albert took such precautions against them as he could. He managed to obtain from the family doctor a convenient medical certificate saying that for reasons of health it was necessary for him to rest and recuperate with his family in Italy. And from his mathematics teacher he obtained a letter attesting that his mathematical knowledge and powers were already of university caliber.

Armed with these documents, Albert threw further caution to the winds. The future would have to take care of itself. After all, he could prepare himself by self study for entrance to a university. Although the medical certificate troubled his conscience, it saved him from being branded a truant, but, to put it bluntly, he became a school dropout. Fleeing his bleak Munich existence, he rejoined his family in Milan, and what followed was one of the most joyous periods of his life. He allowed no ties of school or state to mar his new-found liberty. For better or worse, he roamed far and wide in mind and body, forsaking all cares—an independent spirit wedded to freedom, studying only the subjects he loved. With his friend Otto Neustätter he hiked fancy-free through the Apennine mountains to Genoa, where he had relatives. Museums, art treasures, churches, concerts, books and more books, family, friends, the warm Italian sun, the free, warmhearted people—all merged into a heady adventure of escape and wonderful self-discovery.

But the idyll could not last. Worldly cares, too long held at bay, came crowding in. Hermann Einstein's business began to fail, and Hermann had to urge his son to look to the future.

In Zurich, in the German-speaking part of Switzerland, stood the famous Federal Institute of Technology, familiarly known as the Polytechnic or the Poly. Here, in 1895, after his glorious year —his fleeting, carefree moment away from school—Albert Einstein took the entrance examinations of the Department of Engineering.

And he failed.

It was a painful blow, even though half expected. Besides, he was only sixteen and a half, and the prescribed entrance age was eighteen. Fortunately his failure was not catastrophic. Rote subjects like languages and botany had been his undoing. As for subjects like mathematics and physics, let actions speak louder than words: Professor Heinrich Weber took an unusual step. He went out of his way to have Albert told that if he stayed in Zurich he could sit in on Weber's physics lectures. While this was encouraging, it could not solve Albert's problem. But there was more. Albin Herzog, the Director of the Zurich Polytechnic, urged Albert not to give up hope but to seek a diploma at the progressive Swiss Cantonal School of Aargau in the town of Aarau.

In Aarau, to Albert's surprise and delight, he found an atmosphere far different from that of the Munich Gymnasium. A refreshing spirit of freedom pervaded the cantonal school. Albert was lucky to find lodging in the house of one of the teachers, Jost Winteler, for the Wintelers treated him almost as one of the family. His close ties with the Wintelers were to grow even closer, since one of the Winteler sons was to marry Albert's sister, Maja, and one of the daughters to marry Michele Besso, of whom we shall be hearing further. Einstein recalled "Papa Winteler" fondly.

At the age of sixteen Albert had already taught himself calculus and acquired an extraordinary scientific insight. As evidence of the latter we might offer this excerpt from a letter greeting Einstein on his fiftieth birthday. It came from Otto Neustätter, his hiking companion of the memorable, fancy-free year in Italy. The excerpt tells of an incident involving uncle Jakob when Albert was only fifteen:

> Your uncle . . . had told me that he had great difficulty with some calculations for the construction of some machine. Some days later . . . he said, "You know, it is really fabulous with my nephew.

After I and my assistant-engineer had been racking our brains for days, that young sprig had got the whole thing in scarcely 15 minutes. You will hear of him yet."

Such precosity is certainly impressive, but hardly unique. Clever children often solve technical problems that baffle their elders. Here is something more remarkable. At the age of sixteen, while in Aarau, Albert asked himself what a light wave would look like to someone keeping pace with it.

Compared with the other incident, this one seems inconsequential. It appears to be no achievement at all but merely an unanswered question. But this question that Albert asked himself at the age of sixteen haunted him for years. It strikingly reveals his ability to go to the heart of a problem. For the question contains the germ of the theory of relativity, and at the time no one in the world could have given a satisfactory answer. Einstein found an answer himself, but it took him ten years.

Meanwhile, after an unexpectedly pleasant year in Aarau, Einstein obtained his diploma. With the age requirement waived, it made him eligible for admission to the Zurich Polytechnic. He entered in the fall of 1896, though no longer intending to become an engineer. With Jost Winteler as a shining example, Einstein now looked on teaching as a preferable way of earning a living. Accordingly, he enrolled in the course for training specialist teachers of mathematics and science. Uncles in Genoa resolved his immediate financial problems by giving him an allowance of a hundred francs a month, and at last his career seemed safely on its way.

But freedom once tasted is rarely forgotten. And a youth whom playmates had once called *Biedermeier* does not readily acquire tact. At the Zurich Polytechnic, Einstein could not easily bring himself to study what did not interest him. Most of his time he spent on his own in joyful exploration of the wonderland of science, performing experiments and studying at first hand the works of great pioneers in science and philosophy. Some of these works he read with his Serbian classmate Mileva Maric, whom he later married.

As for the lectures, they were for him an intrusion. He attended them only fitfully, and for the most part with little enthusiasm.

The graduating class of the cantonal school, Aarau, 1896. (Einstein seated at left.)

Reunion in Zurich in May 1933 of members of the Aarau graduating class of 1896.

Einstein in his student days at the Zurich Polytechnic Institute.

By now he knew that his true interests lay not in mathematics but in physics; yet even the physics lectures did not attract him. Unfortunately, in the four-year course two major examinations had to be passed. Again disaster threatened, and again it was narrowly averted. His classmate Marcel Grossmann, a brilliant mathematician, had quickly recognized Einstein's quality. The two became friends. Grossmann was meticulous in attending the lectures, and meticulous, too, in taking notes that were models of detail and clarity. He gladly let Einstein study these notes, and without them to cram from, Einstein might well have failed the examinations. He graduated in 1900.

Grossmann's notes had given Einstein freedom to pursue his own studies. Among the fields he mastered was what is known as Maxwell's theory of electromagnetism, an important theory that, to Einstein's disappointment, had not been taken up in the lectures of Heinrich Weber. Keep the name Maxwell in mind. We shall be hearing it again.

In Zurich, Einstein lived frugally. Not that his allowance was inadequate. From the start he had deliberately set aside a fifth of it, saving up to be able later to pay the fees for acquiring Swiss

II. Jahreskurs.

834. Biefeld, Paul, von Watertown (V. St. A.).
835. Du Pasquier, Gustav, von Neuenburg.
836. Ehrat, Jakob, von Lohn (Schaffhausen).
837. Einstein, Albert, von Ulm (Deutschland).
838. Grossmann, Marcel, von Höngg (Zürich).
839. Kollros, Louis, von Chaux-de-Fonds (Neuchâtel).
840. Leich, Walther, von Evansville (V. St. A.).
841. Marić, Mileva, von Titel (Ungarn).

Official list of the eight students in Einstein's second-year class at
the Zurich Polytechnic Institute in 1898.

citizenship. With his father's help he applied for it in October of
1899, and after the majestic unrolling of red tape he became in
February of 1901 a citizen of the city of Zurich and thereby of
the canton of Zurich and of Switzerland itself. He retained his
Swiss citizenship through all vicissitudes for the rest of his life.

The four years at the Poly had not been altogether pleasant. As
he wrote in his "Autobiographical Notes":

> One had to cram all this stuff into one's mind for the examinations,
> whether one liked it or not. This coercion had such a deterring
> effect on me that, after I passed the final examination, I found the
> consideration of any scientific problems distasteful to me for an
> entire year.

With graduation came bitter times for Einstein. Everything
went wrong. His beloved science had lost its appeal. By his forth-
rightness and his distrust of authority he had alienated his professors, among them Heinrich Weber, who apparently conceived
a particular dislike of him. This was the same Heinrich Weber
who, five years before, had generously gone out of his way to
encourage the youth who had failed the entrance examinations.
The relationship had since deteriorated, Weber on one occasion

saying to Einstein with probably justified exasperation, "You're a clever fellow! But you have one fault. You won't let anyone tell you a thing. You won't let anyone tell you a thing."

With the end of the course Einstein's allowance had stopped and he had to look desperately for a job. He was now twenty-one. When he sought university positions, he was rebuffed. Writing in 1901, he said, "From what people tell me, I am not in the good graces of any of my former teachers," and, "I would long ago have found [a position as assistant in a university] had not Weber intrigued against me."

Einstein managed to keep body and soul together by finding temporary jobs—performing calculations, teaching in school, and tutoring. Yet even here his independence and unworldliness caused difficulties.

However, his love of science gradually returned, and, while tutoring in Zurich, he wrote a research article on capillarity that was published in 1901 in the important scientific journal *Annalen der Physik*. Later in life Einstein dismissed this article as "worthless," but by then he was judging it by unusual standards.

Actually, young Einstein pinned high hopes on this paper on capillarity. In Germany, especially in those days, a Professor was an Exalted Personage, almost unapproachable by lesser men. And the Professors, well aware of their prestige and power, tended to be autocrats. It took the courage of desperation for Einstein, a struggling nobody, to write the following letter to the great physical chemist at the University of Leipzig, Professor Wilhelm Ostwald, who later won the Nobel Prize:

> Since I was inspired by your book on general chemistry to write the enclosed article [on capillarity], I am taking the liberty of sending you a copy. On this occasion I venture also to ask you whether perhaps you might have use for a mathematical physicist who is familiar with absolute measurements. I am taking the liberty of making such a request only because I am without means and only such a position would give me the possibility of further education.

The letter was sent on 19 March 1901. As the days passed and the postman brought no response. Einstein's high hopes began to fade. On 3 April he followed up his letter with a postcard saying how important the decision would be for him and—perhaps as a pretext for writing the postcard—wondering whether he had given his Milan address in the letter, which in fact he had.

Still there was no response. On 17 April Einstein tried elsewhere, writing a brief note to Professor Heike Kamerlingh-Onnes in Leiden, Netherlands, again enclosing a reprint of his paper on capillarity. In those days it was his main tangible asset. Nothing came of this application. Meanwhile there had occurred a beautiful event in Einstein's life of which he knew nothing. It reveals his father's love for him and reveals too the aspirations and heartbreaks of Albert Einstein at this bitter time. On 13 April 1901 Hermann Einstein, the unsuccessful merchant, in ill health and a stranger to the academic community, took it upon himself to write to Professor Ostwald. Here is his letter:

I beg you to excuse a father who dares to approach you, dear Professor, in the interests of his son.

I wish to mention first that my son Albert Einstein is 22 years old, has studied for four years at the Zurich Polytechnic and last summer brilliantly passed his diploma examinations in mathematics and physics. Since then he has tried unsuccessfully to find a position as assistant, which would enable him to continue his education in theoretical and experimental physics. Everybody who is able to judge praises his talent, and in any case I can assure you that he is exceedingly assiduous and industrious and is attached to his science with a great love.

My son is profoundly unhappy about his present joblessness, and every day the idea becomes more firmly implanted in him that he is a failure in his career and will not be able to find the way back again. And on top of this he is depressed by the thought that he is a burden on us since we are not very well-to-do people.

Because, dear Professor, my son honors and reveres you the most among all the great physicists of our time, I permit myself to apply to you with the plea that you will read his article published in the *Annalen der Physik* and, hopefully, that you will write him a few lines of encouragement so that he may regain his joy in his life and his work.

If, in addition, it should be possible for you to obtain for him a position as assistant, now or in the fall, my gratitude would be boundless.

I beg again your forgiveness for my audacity in sending you this letter and I want to add that my son has no idea of this extraordinary step of mine.

Whether as a result of this letter Professor Ostwald wrote to Albert Einstein is not known. What is known is that Einstein did not receive an assistantship, and that the seeds of a great irony were thus planted.

Throughout the black days of 1901 Einstein could still find consolation and escape in his music. And, more important, exciting scientific ideas and speculations once more came crowding into his mind. Yet even as his mind soared, he felt himself sinking helplessly in the quagmire of a world that had no place for him. Rescue, however, was on its way. It came just in time—and once more from his friend Marcel Grossmann, whose meticulous lecture notes had proved invaluable at the Poly. Grossmann could not offer Einstein an assistantship. He was still only an assistant himself. But early in 1901 he had spoken earnestly to his father about Einstein's troubles, and the father had strongly recommended Einstein to his friend Friedrich Haller, the Director of the Swiss Patent Office in Bern.

Haller called Einstein for an interview, which quickly revealed Einstein's lack of relevant technical qualifications. But as it continued its grueling two-hour course, Haller began to realize that there was something about the young man that transcended technicalities. There are strong reasons to believe that it was Einstein's rare mastery of Maxwell's electromagnetic theory that ultimately prompted Haller to offer Einstein a provisional job in the Patent Office. Since there was no immediate opening, and since the law required that all openings be advertised, this meant delay.

While waiting, Einstein supported himself precariously by teaching and private tutoring. From May to July 1901 he had a temporary job as a substitute teacher of mathematics in the Technical School in Winterthur, and while there he completed a research article on thermodynamics. This he submitted in November to the University of Zurich in order to obtain a doctoral degree. Einstein's article was ultimately accepted for publication by *Anna-*

len der Physik. But this was after Professor Kleiner had rejected it as a Ph.D. thesis.

The outcome of his doctoral attempt was still in doubt when, on 11 December 1901, a vacancy at the Patent Office was advertised in the federal gazette. Einstein immediately applied for the position: Engineer, Second Class.

In February 1902 he went to live in Bern, supporting himself there as best he could by private tutoring. On 14 March he became twenty-three, and a week later, according to the official calendar, winter gave way to spring. The tutoring continued.

April came, and May, and June. And at long last, on 23 June 1902, almost simultaneously with the advent of summer, Einstein started work at the Swiss Patent Office: a probationary Technical Expert, Third Class, with a modest salary of 3500 francs a year.

At last Einstein had a steady job. He quickly became adept at the work. He was well content to be free of the hostile academic world that had brought him repeated heartache. Through his friend Marcel Grossmann he had found a haven in which, in his spare time, he could work serenely, with growing excitement, on his burgeoning ideas. And in this unlikely conservatory his genius matured.

In the last year of his life he wrote of the recommendation to

	Eidg. Amt für geistiges Eigentum.
Vakante Stelle:	**Ingenieur II. Klasse.**
Erfordernisse:	Gründliche Hochschulbildung in mechanisch-technischer oder speciell physikalischer Richtung, Beherrschung der deutschen und Kenntnis der französischen Sprache oder Beherrschung der französischen und Kenntnis der deutschen Sprache, eventuell auch Kenntnis der italienischen Sprache.
Besoldung:	Fr. 3500 bis 4500.
Anmeldungstermin:	28. Dezember 1901.
Anmeldung an:	Eidg. Amt für geistiges Eigentum, Bern.

The advertisement in the *Schweizerisches Bundesblatt*, 11 December 1901, of the vacancy at the Patent Office for an Engineer, Second Class. The requirements for the position are primarily "Thorough university training in mechanics and technology, or specifically in physics."

Haller at the Patent Office as "the greatest thing Marcel Grossmann did for me as a friend." Not that Grossmann now vanishes from our story. On the contrary, the destinies of the two men were intertwined in a way that strains credulity, and we shall see Grossmann do yet more for Einstein. When, in 1936, after a long, crippling illness, Grossmann died of multiple sclerosis, Einstein wrote a heartfelt letter of condolence to Grossmann's widow. Trying to convey to her how much Grossmann had meant to him, he wrote:

> . . . our student days together [at the Polytechnic] come back to me. He a model student; I untidy and a daydreamer. He on excellent terms with the teachers and grasping everything easily; I aloof and discontented, not very popular. But we were good friends and our conversations over iced coffee at the Metropol every few weeks belong among my nicest memories. Then the end of the studies . . . I suddenly abandoned by everyone, facing life not knowing which way to turn. But he stood by me and through him and his father I came to Haller in the Patent Office a few years later. In a way, this saved my life; not that I would have died without it, but I would have been intellectually stunted.

3

Prelude

With Einstein ensconced in the Patent Office, there would seem little point in returning to his waiting period in Bern. Why dwell further on the past when the future has so much to offer?

But Einstein's tutoring interlude in Bern was not as bleak and empty as we may be imagining. Around Easter of 1902, a week after the advent of spring, a Rumanian, Maurice Solovine, saw an advertisement in a Bern newspaper saying that an Albert Einstein offered tutoring in physics for three francs an hour. Solovine, a philosophy student at the University of Bern, had wide-ranging interests. Going to the address given, he explained to Einstein that, being dissatisfied with the intangibles of philosophy, he wanted to learn more about a solid subject like physics. This struck a responsive chord in Einstein and a spirited discussion ensued. Some two hours later, when Solovine took his leave, Einstein accompanied him to continue the discussion for a further half hour in the street. Next day they met for the first tutoring session, but the discussion continued instead, and on the third day Einstein said that discussions with Solovine would be far more interesting than needlessly tutoring him in physics. Thereafter the two met regularly. Soon they were joined by Konrad Habicht, a mathematician friend of Einstein's, and thus there came into being what the three men fondly called their "Olympia Academy." Much as other men meet to play cards, Einstein and his friends met to dis-

The Olympia Academy: Konrad Habicht, Maurice Solovine, and Einstein.

cuss philosophy and physics and, on occasion, literature and whatever else caught their fancy—intensively, and often boisterously. Einstein was the leading spirit. The meetings usually took place in his apartment, beginning with a frugal dinner and often continuing in lively debate far into the night to the annoyance of the neighbors. The friends read together and dissected together major works of philosophy and science that powerfully influenced the development of Einstein's ideas, and as these ideas developed Einstein tried them out on his friends. Though still fundamentally a loner, he was here in his element. The Olympia Academy was in earnest, and above all it was fun.

Habicht ultimately became a schoolteacher in his home town of Schaffhausen, where Einstein had once briefly tutored. Solovine, who settled in Paris as an editor and writer, became the authorized translator of Einstein's books into French. Since Habicht left Bern in 1904 and Solovine left it a year later, the Olympia Academy had only a brief formal existence. But the three friends kept in touch, and the Academy lived on in their memories.

On 10 October 1902 death came to Einstein's father. He died too soon to know what manner of man he had begotten. Dazed and uncomprehending, Einstein was overwhelmed by a feeling of desolation, asking himself repeatedly why his father should have died rather than he. Many years later he still recalled vividly his shattering sense of loss. Indeed, on one occasion he wrote that his father's death was the deepest shock he had ever experienced.

But in his science Einstein had an antidote for his sorrow. His mind was now teeming with scientific ideas that he worked on at every possible moment. At the Patent Office, for example, he soon learned to do his chores efficiently and this let him snatch precious morsels of time for his own surreptitious calculations, which he guiltily hid in a drawer when footsteps approached. Years later, long after he had become world-famous, the recollection still gave him twinges of conscience.

When, in 1903, he married Mileva Maric, who was of the Greek Orthodox faith, Solovine and Habicht were the witnesses. The Einsteins' first son, Hans Albert, was born in 1904, and their second, Eduard, in 1910, but the marriage was not a happy one. Nevertheless, after the divorce Mileva and Einstein remained friends.

In 1902 Einstein had already completed his third scientific paper, which, like his earlier ones, was published in *Annalen der Physik*. In January 1903 he wrote a letter that we shall find doubly interesting. It was written to his friend of Zurich days, Michele Besso, whom we have already mentioned as marrying Jost Winteler's daughter. In telling of a fourth research paper, the letter gives a glimpse of the painstakingly high standards that Einstein had set for himself: "On Monday I finally sent off my work, after many changes and corrections. Now it is perfectly clear and simple, so that I am quite satisfied with it." The letter also reveals both Einstein's academic aspirations at the time and his lingering hurt: "Recently I have decided to become a *Privatdozent**—that is, provided I can go through with it. On the other hand, I shall

---

* Becoming a *Privatdozent,* or private lecturer attached to a university, was a prime prerequisite for an academic career.

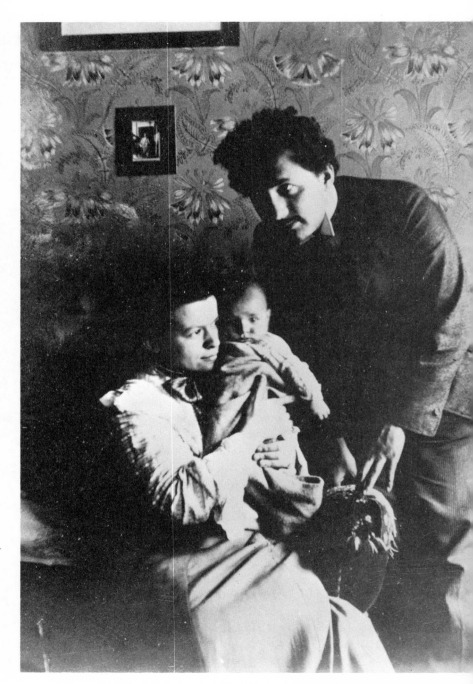

Einstein with his wife Mileva and his son Hans Albert, Bern, 1904.

not become a Ph.D., which, after all, does not help me much, and the whole comedy has become a bore to me."

The fourth research paper was duly accepted by *Annalen der Physik,* and in 1904 so was a fifth. The chances are that some of the patent applications that Einstein had to examine contained models of perpetual-motion devices. If so, even though their particular fallacies may have been hard to find, Einstein well knew that in principle they could not possibly work. For his third, fourth, and fifth papers dealt with thermodynamics, a powerful science built on two laws that essentially assert the impossibility of making perpetual-motion machines. When expressed more technically, the second law of thermodynamics involves a key concept, *entropy,* whose meaning fortunately need not concern us. We remark only that the Austrian scientist Ludwig Boltzmann gave it an interpretation in terms of probability, for Einstein was to make masterly use of this concept. How did he acquire his mastery of the statistical aspects of thermodynamics? In the best possible way for deep understanding. He took off from the pioneering work of Boltzmann and developed the ideas in detail for himself. They were the main topic of his third, fourth, and fifth papers. He did not know at the time that, albeit with novel aspects, he was covering ground already explored by Boltzmann, and ground to some extent explored almost simultaneously with Einstein by the American scientist Willard Gibbs. But this gives us an indication of what the largely self-taught Einstein had already made of himself, for Boltzmann and Gibbs were among the scientific giants of their times. Moreover, in developing certain statistical ideas that he was later to put to major use, he had already gone well beyond Gibbs and Boltzmann.

These early papers of Einstein's were still just a prelude—a laying of a foundation. They were not written under the easiest of circumstances. The scientific libraries at Einstein's disposal were wretchedly inadequate. And while he was working on these papers he was meeting exacting standards at the Patent Office. Indeed, on the basis of a civil service examination, his status there was changed in September 1904 from probationary to permanent.

It was at this time that Michele Besso, at Einstein's urging, took a job at the Patent Office. Besso, an Italian, was an engineer. But even more important than his talent and breadth of knowl-

Michele Besso and his
bride, Anna, the daughter
of Jost Winteler, 1898.

edge was his gentle generosity. For Einstein's ideas were approaching a spectacular multiple climax, and Einstein and Besso used to discuss them not only at the Patent Office but also on the way home from work. By being deliberately critical, Besso helped Einstein sharpen his concepts. Yet, throughout, Besso remained not merely encouraging but enthusiastic. He was the ideal mental whetstone for Einstein at the time, and Einstein, exiled by academe, was fortunate indeed in having had Besso, as well as Habicht and Solovine, as friends in Bern.

In 1905 Einstein's genius burst into dazzling flower. It was a fabulous year. In the annals of physics it ranks with the years 1665–66, when the plague that ravaged England forced Cambridge University to close and caused young Newton to leave Cambridge for his home in the quiet village of Woolsthorpe, where— all in secret—he developed the calculus, made major discoveries about light and color, and started on the path that was to lead him years later to his law of universal gravitation.

In the spring of 1905 Einstein, in high spirits, wrote to Habicht chiding him humorously for not having kept in touch. "You wretch," he said, after calling Habicht outrageous names, "why have you still not sent me your thesis? Don't you know that I would be one of the one or two fellows who would read it with interest and pleasure? I promise you four papers in exchange. . . . the first . . . is very revolutionary. . . ."

4

Dawn of a
New Light

The first was indeed revolutionary. Was it the theory of relativity? No. We have to wait a little for that. What we tell here is part of what Einstein later spoke of as his *Gelegenheitsarbeit,* and we begin with something seemingly trivial:

If we heat a lump of iron it gets warm. If we heat it further it gets warmer, and after a while it begins to glow dull red. As we continue heating it, the glow becomes brighter and changes color, turning to orange, then yellow, and soon to a dazzling bluish white. This sounds commonplace enough. Yet within it there proved to be something profoundly puzzling.

How might scientists set about trying to find a mathematical formula to describe the glow of the iron at various temperatures? One possibility would be for the experimenters to measure the glow and its color, graph the results, and hope that a neat mathematical relationship would then leap to the eye. But even if it did, the theorists would not be satisfied. They would want to deduce the mathematical formula from what they already knew about the behavior of heat and light and matter.

What *did* they already know? That depends on the era. By the latter part of the nineteenth century they knew quite a number of beautifully interlocking rules and concepts that in many ways worked amazingly well. These had not come easily, but there is so much to tell that we can here only skim a few of the highlights of their development.

Take light, for example. In the seventeenth century Newton produced a theory of light and color that accounted for all the experimental optical data known in his day. Roughly speaking, he conceived of light as a stream of particles, each with a sort of pulsation whose rate determined its color. His contemporary, the Dutch physicist Christiaan Huygens, had proposed a quite different theory. For him light was propagated not as a stream of particles but as a rudimentary sort of wave. Since Newton's particle theory could account for more phenomena, it prevailed.

But the new century brought a major upheaval. Starting in 1799, the English physician, physicist, and later Egyptologist Thomas Young found striking evidence that powerfully favored a wave theory of light. Although we need not understand the details, the general idea has a claim on our attention. Essentially, Young showed that light falling on light can produce darkness. For example, if light from a tiny source passes through two slits in a screen, it produces bands of light and darkness on a farther screen. How could light superposed on light produce dark bands? In terms of particles there was no adequate explanation. But in terms of waves the dark places presented no problem. They were places where the superposed waves canceled by being continually out of step, one at crest whenever the other was at trough and vice versa. Young called this wave phenomenon *interference;* the light and dark bands are called *interference fringes.*

It is noteworthy that Young advocated a wave theory of light without waiting to find wave explanations of all known optical effects. As is customary when established ideas are seriously challenged, his work was bitterly attacked. But a dozen years later Young found a brilliant ally in the French physicist Augustin Fresnel, who hit on the idea of interference independently and found further devastating evidence against the particle theory. And now the evidence mounted so rapidly that within a decade or so the particle theory was already as good as dead. Indeed, there was little need to administer the *coup de grâce,* but scientists like to make sure. So the decisive experiment was performed of measuring the speed of light in water. According to Newton the speed should be greater than in air; according to the wave theory less. The experiment showed it to be less.

This was not all. Further confirmation of the wave theory of light came from an unexpected quarter. In 1819 the Danish physicist Hans Christian Orsted discovered a specific connection between electricity and magnetism. He showed that an electric current in a wire affects a magnetic compass needle. Thereupon the French physicist André Marie Ampère analyzed the effect mathematically and experimentally with such detailed brilliance that he was hailed as the Newton of electromagnetism.

Meanwhile, however, the English experimenter Michael Faraday was making outstanding experimental discoveries in electricity and magnetism. Being largely self-taught and lacking mathematical facility, he could not interpret his results in the manner of Ampère. And this was fortunate, since it led to a revolution in science. Ampère and others had concentrated their attention on the visible hardware—magnets, current-carrying wires, and the like—and on the numbers of centimeters separating the pieces of hardware. In so doing they were following the action-at-a-distance tradition that had developed from the enormous success of Newton's system of mechanics and law of gravitation. But Faraday regarded the hardware as secondary. For him the important physical events took place in the surrounding space—the *field*. This, in his mind, he filled with tentacles that by their pulls and thrusts and motions gave rise to the electromagnetic effects observed. Although he could thus interpret his electromagnetic experiments with excellent precision and surprising simplicity, most physicists adept at mathematics thought his concepts mathematically naive.

Among the few who did not was the Scottish physicist James Clerk Maxwell, of whom we have already heard briefly in connection with Einstein and the Patent Office. Maxwell realized that Faraday's seemingly primitive field concepts had powerful mathematical content, and he trusted Faraday's intuition implicitly. His own intuition was equally remarkable. It led him to envisage for the electromagnetic field a pseudomechanical model of vortices and ball bearings that was intended more as a temporary intellectual prop than a serious physical concept—a model so

Three portraits of scientists graced the walls of Einstein's study. The portrait of Newton has been lost. The other two portraits, of Faraday and Maxwell, are here shown in their frames.

bizarre that Maxwell himself thought it hardly credible. At least it avoided action at a distance. And such was the power of Maxwell's intuition that hidden within this unbelievable model were the essentials of electromagnetism. By its aid, and using a smoothed-out concept of the electromagnetic field, Maxwell constructed a highly successful set of electromagnetic field equations possessing a beautiful symmetry. As a mathematical consequence of this symmetry he deduced that there should be electromagnetic waves, that these waves would travel with the speed of light, and that they would possess, among other properties, all those with which Young and Fresnel had endowed their waves of light to account for experiment. He declared, therefore, that light waves and electromagnetic waves must, in essence, be one and the same.

This was in the years 1861–64. But because aspects of the symmetry strained physical credulity, Maxwell's theory, though admired, failed to gain general acceptance during his lifetime. He died in 1879, the year in which Einstein was born. Not till 1888 was Maxwell's theory confirmed. In that year the German physicist Heinrich Hertz electromagnetically generated and detected what we now call radio waves, and he showed in incontrovertible detail that they behave as Maxwell had predicted they would. As a result Maxwell's equations at last came into their own, and a year or two later Hertz himself said, "The wave theory of light is from the point of view of human beings a certainty."

Light waves are electromagnetic waves whose frequencies, or rates of oscillation, lie within a quite narrow range, the colors depending on the frequencies. Outside this narrow range of frequencies electromagnetic radiation is not directly visible. At higher frequencies it is what we call ultraviolet radiation; and at yet higher, X-radiation and gamma radiation. At lower frequencies it is infrared and heat radiation; and at yet lower, radio waves. This is a notable unification. Diverse radiations, here linked together, are seen as members of a large family of electromagnetic phenomena, cousins of the magnetism of the compass needle that attracted the five-year-old Einstein.

So much for light and electromagnetism, for the time being. Next, what about heat? You will say that we have just told about it. But that was heat in the form of radiation. The glowing iron has an inner heat too, which is nowadays regarded as a microscopic internal vibration and, along with radiation, as one of the many forms of energy.

The story of heat and the development of the science of thermodynamics is long and confused, and we shall leave it largely untold. This is unfair to the daring innovators who laid the foundations of thermodynamics against strong opposition from physicists, but this is a book about Einstein and he stands in the wings of this chapter awaiting his entrance cue, which cannot come yet. Let us mention briefly that the theorists, notably Maxwell and Boltzmann, had developed a theory of gases as consisting of colliding particles in chaotic motion, and that the energy of this motion, like the energy of the inner vibrations of solids, counted as heat. And having said this, let us hasten to the year 1900 to tell of what prompted the first of Einstein's famous papers of 1905.

In Berlin in October 1900 the eminent German physicist Max Planck heard disturbing news. Like others, he had been trying to account for the details of the glow of a hot "black body"—an idealization of the hot iron. In previous years he had helped in the deduction from physical principles of a formula telling how much of each color there was in the glow, or to put it more technically, how much of the total energy of the radiation belonged to each frequency. This formula for black-body radiation had first been deduced by the German physicist Wilhelm Wien, who was to receive the Nobel Prize in 1911. It had seemed to agree well with experiment, but now experimenters had just told Planck that although it worked for the higher frequencies it failed for the lower. What was to be done? By a deft mathematical maneuver, Planck created a new formula for black-body radiation, and his formula has withstood the test of experiment to this day.

Having obtained the formula by a mathematical artifice, Planck found himself faced with the task of deducing it from physical principles. The ensuing weeks, as he said in his Nobel Prize acceptance speech eighteen years later, were the most strenuous of his life. By December he had a solution, but judge for yourself whether it was credible. Suppose Planck had said in all seriousness that a swing can swing *only* in arcs of three feet, six feet, nine feet, and so on, and not four feet, half a foot, or any other such prohibited value. Surely you would say he was talking nonsense.

Max Planck, ca. 1900.

Yet this, on a microscopic scale, was part of what Planck had had to assume in order to deduce his formula. Put differently, he had had to assume that these microscopic oscillations did not change energy smoothly but in jumps of discrete amounts that he called *quanta.* He had also had to assume that the fraction *energy/oscillatory frequency* must have the same value for every such quantum jump. This value, which he denoted by h, is now called Planck's constant, and his quantum hypothesis towers as a transcendent landmark in the history of science. It transformed physics.

But we must not let hindsight becloud our vision. To Planck in 1900 the quantum hypothesis was highly distasteful. He had introduced it, he said much later, as "an act of desperation."

Despite his misgivings, he presented his work before the German Physical Society on 14 December 1900 in a lecture that was duly printed in the Proceedings, and he sent an amplified version to *Annalen der Physik*, where it appeared in 1901, only to be greeted, shall we say, by polite silence. Planck himself spent many subsequent years trying unsuccessfully to deduce his radiation formula by nonradical means. Not that he tried to be rid of h, for that, as part of the radiation formula, was certainly here to stay. Indeed it was already implicitly present in the defective formula of Wien.

From late 1900 to 1905 the quantum concept remained in limbo. In all the world there seems to have been in those years only one man to dare take it seriously. That man was Einstein. He had

Einstein in the Patent Office, Bern.

quickly sensed the importance of Planck's work, and on 17 March 1905, three days after his twenty-sixth birthday, he sent to *Annalen der Physik* the first of the four papers that he had mentioned to Habicht—the one that was "very revolutionary."

Einstein's paper began with a profoundly simple remark that went to the heart of the problem.

There was, he pointed out, a fundamental conflict between the way in which theoretical physicists regarded matter and the way in which they regarded radiation. Matter was treated as made up of particles. But Maxwell's equations, being field equations, treated radiation as something smooth and continuous, with no trace of atomicity. Thus when one treated matter and radiation together, the traditional theories would clash. One could not expect them to mesh harmoniously. Einstein then went on to show mathematically that the clash was inevitable.

What was the remedy? Einstein was fully aware of the tremendous triumphs of the electromagnetic wave theory of light. Yet he knew, too, that there were situations in which it failed, and he daringly proposed as a working hypothesis that light be thought of as consisting of particles.

This was no amateur stab in the dark. Einstein would not have dared to put forward so outrageous an idea without strong reasons. Let us sketch them, if only to show his instinctive feeling for what was essential. He had to proceed boldly yet cautiously, using such stepping stones as he could trust amid the morass. He built on the defective black-body formula of Wien, which he saw would suffice for his purposes: for where it was good it was very very good. In this way he avoided committing himself to any particular mechanism such as the one proposed by Planck. It was safer that way.

From Wien he quoted a formula for the entropy of radiation. Confronting it with Wien's own black-body formula, Einstein showed that the entropy of radiation then took a mathematical form typical of that of a gas, *and thus of particles.* Then by confronting this in a novel way with Boltzmann's probabilistic formula for entropy, Einstein showed that these particles of light would have to be such that the ratio *energy/frequency* had precisely the value that Planck had used for his quantum jumps.

Imagine the intimate knowledge of physics that Einstein must have had, and the sure-footed intuition, to be able to pick just those fundamentals that would yield these remarkable results. He was well aware of the many objections that physicists could bring against his proposal. Yet, as if Planck's hypothesis were not trouble enough, Einstein was spreading the quantum infection to light itself. He could explain the Maxwellian smoothness as a blurring due to the passage of time, much as a photo of a runner becomes blurred when the shutter speed is too slow. But he knew full well that he could not explain away the Maxwellian waves that had been overwhelmingly authenticated by Hertz; or the decisive experiment of the speed of light in water; or, to get down to fundamentals, the powerful "interference" evidence against Newton's particle theory produced by Young and Fresnel, starting almost exactly a century before the advent of Planck's key idea.

There is here a striking parallelism between Young and Einstein. When Young first used interference arguments—light canceling light—against the dominant particle theory, he knew that he did not know how to meet all the difficulties facing a wave theory. Yet this did not deter him, for he could see that Newton's particle theory was vulnerable. And subsequent developments fully justified his boldness. A century later, in the face of a dominant wave theory, Einstein too remained unintimidated. For with the advent of new evidence he knew that Maxwell too was vulnerable.

Temporarily putting aside the staggering problems surrounding quanta of light, Einstein concentrated on the possible advantages of his idea. These, as he demonstrated, were not inconsiderable, especially since they appeared at places where light interacted with matter and where Maxwell was in trouble. Einstein showed that his light quanta could account for a known effect connected with fluorescence. He showed that they could also account for an effect already observed when ultraviolet light passed through gases. And above all he applied his idea to the ejection of electrons from metals by light, a phenomenon called the *photoelectric effect*.

This last is particularly important. Three years before, pioneering experiments on the photoelectric effect had been made by the German physicist Philipp Lenard. He stressed that his experimental results were in sharp conflict with what was expected on the basis of Maxwell's theory. For example, raising the frequency of the light increased the energy of the ejected electrons, a fact that made no Maxwellian sense at all. Einstein showed that the idea of quanta of light could account with the utmost ease for the puzzling results found by Lenard. Take the effect of changing the frequency, for example. To shine light on the metal was to hurl light quanta at it. Since the ratio *energy/frequency* had a fixed value, the higher the frequency the greater the energy, and thus the bigger the clout that a light quantum would give to any electron it happened to hit. No wonder, then, that the electrons came off with greater energies when the frequency of the light was increased. The other puzzling effects were dealt with just as easily, and Einstein was able to deduce an utterly simple photoelectric formula while the powerful theory of Maxwell stood powerless. His photoelectric results went far beyond what was known experimentally at the time.

Such, in brief, was the content of Einstein's paper. Let us round out this chapter by looking beyond 1905.

Physicists did not greet Einstein's idea with open arms. Quite the contrary. Planck and other important scientists easily found devastating objections to the concept of light quanta. Fortunately Einstein had further quantum ideas. The theory of inner heat as motional energy of both the colliding particles of gases and the inner vibrations of solids had had notable successes. But even before 1900 it had encountered severe difficulties that threatened its survival. In 1907 Einstein saved it. He argued that if, as he firmly believed, Planck's idea had to be taken seriously, it ought to apply to all types of inner vibrations without exception. He showed how the quantum would resolve the main difficulties, and in particular he removed experimental discrepancies connected with the inner vibratory heats of solids, and deduced unexpected interrelationships that were later verified experimentally.

As a result of these quantum investigations of Einstein, and because the quantum did not seem as dangerous when confined within matter as it did when let loose, other physicists began to take Planck's idea seriously and, along with Einstein, to apply it with considerable success. But still Einstein's quanta of light failed to excite their enthusiasm. Experimenters did try to test his photoelectric formula, but the experiments were difficult, and even as late as 1913 the results were inconclusive. In that year Planck and a distinguished group of scientists had occasion to write an important recommendation of Einstein. Though they spoke of his achievements in glowing terms, they were apologetic about his idea of light quanta, pleading delicately that a daring innovator should not be taken to task if his speculations occasionally overshot the mark.

The American experimenter Robert Millikan, having accurately measured the electric charge of the electron, looked for fresh fields to conquer. Being the man he was, he deliberately sought a particularly difficult problem and decided to investigate the photoelectric effect. He spent ten years on the task, intending to show once and for all that Einstein's unbelievable theory was not in accord with experiment. To his surprise he found a most beautiful concordance. Yet when he published his final results in 1916, he still could not bring himself to accept the revolutionary idea of light quanta. Nevertheless, it was becoming clear that, despite the extraordinary problems they raised, light quanta must be taken seriously; and that Einstein, in the Patent Office back in 1905, had seen more clearly than all his contemporaries. So vividly did the light quantum—the particle of light—come to be regarded that it was given the substantiality of having a name of its own, being called the *photon*. But that was some twenty years after its conception. Millikan received the Nobel Prize in 1928. And when Einstein won it in 1921, the only work of his that was specifically mentioned in the citation was his discovery of the law of the photoelectric effect.

A closing irony: the photoelectric effect was discovered by Heinrich Hertz—in the course of the very experiments that confirmed Maxwell's prediction and led Hertz to proclaim the wave theory of light a certainty.

5

Atomic Agitation

"I shall not become a Ph.D. . . . the whole comedy has become a bore to me." Einstein's words to Besso in 1903 reverberate as we return to 1905.

Of the four papers that Einstein mentioned in his letter to Habicht, the second is the least important. Einstein apparently completed it barely a month after the first. And he sent it to the University of Zurich as a possible doctoral thesis. Professor Kleiner, who in 1901 had rejected Einstein's first proffered thesis, rejected this one as being too short. Einstein promptly resubmitted it with a single sentence added, and it was accepted. Thus in 1905 he became a Ph.D. under circumstances that conspired to let him remain true to the spirit even though not the letter of his bitter words to Besso. There is reason to believe that he even considered borrowing from Besso to pay for the special printing of the thesis. Next to the formal title page of the printed thesis appear the words "Dedicated to my friend Dr. Marcel Grossmann." Unfortunately this token of gratitude had to be deleted when the paper was published in *Annalen der Physik* in 1906.

The idea for the paper may well have come to Einstein as he was having tea. We all know that if we drop a lump of sugar into water it dissolves and diffuses through the water making the liquid somewhat more viscous. But we are not likely to guess what Einstein deduced from this. Let us see what his ingenuity could extract from sweetened water.

As usual, he went to the bare essentials, thinking of the water as a structureless fluid and the sugar molecules as small hard spheres. This simple model let him make calculations that had hitherto been impossible, and after much work he derived equations telling how the spheres would diffuse and how their obstructive presence would increase the viscosity.

Now comes the surprise. Having worked out the theory, Einstein looked up diffusion rates and viscosities of solutions of actual sugar in actual water, put these numbers into his equations, and found—what? For one thing, what he had promised in the title of his paper, namely "A New Determination of the Sizes of Molecules"—in the case of sugar it came to about a twentieth of a millionth of an inch across, which, under the circumstances, was reasonably close.

But this was not all. He found, too, a value—some hundred thousand billion billion—for what is called *Avogadro's number,* which is the number of molecules of any gas in a certain standard volume under specified standard conditions.

We must not imagine that Einstein was the first to find values for these fundamental quantities. There had already been ingenious estimates based, for example, on the properties of gases, but none hitherto on the properties of solutions in liquids.

Avogadro's number was of particular importance. Knowing its value, one could immediately deduce such things as the mass of any atom. Who, then, was the first to find a reliable value for this key number? Planck was the man. And he found it in what will seem an unlikely place: in the measurements of black-body radiation. Indeed, he deduced it in 1900 in his paper on the quantum hypothesis, a feat that both Planck and Einstein had instinctively recognized as fundamental.

But how could Avogadro's number possibly be found from the glow of a black body? The two seem totally unrelated.

It is hard to convey how tightly interlocking and broadly applicable were the principles on which physicists relied. Take Boltzmann's probabilistic formula for entropy as an example. Having been based on the molecular theory of gases, it contained a key number, the so-called *gas constant,* that intruded whenever one calculated entropy probabilistically, whether for gases or not.

This inadequate remark will have to suffice, for if we are to keep up with the headlong pace of Einstein's discoveries we must hasten on. Within a month of submitting the sugar paper, he sent to *Annalen der Physik* the third of the four papers that he had mentioned to Habicht. This one is justly famous.

Einstein's sister, Maja, writing of earlier days, told of young Einstein's pleasure in smoking a yard-long pipe his father had given him as a present. In her recollections she wrote that "he loved to observe the smoke clouds' wonderful shapes, and to study the motions of the individual particles of smoke and the relationships among them."

Perhaps it was from this that there grew the inspiration for Einstein's paper. As before, let us look at his general line of argument and its surprising denouement. Again he considered the idea of small hard spheres in a liquid, but this time he let the liquid have a molecular structure and the spheres be relatively enormous—the size of a tiny particle of smoke or some such speck visible in a microscope. According to the theory that inner heat is motional energy, the molecules of the liquid would have to be in violent jostling agitation. In his earlier researches Einstein had rediscovered a result of Boltzmann's: that in a mixture of substances this jostling would cause the agitational energy, on the average, to be shared equally by the molecules, no matter what their masses.

But why confine oneself to molecules? So far as the sharing of energy was concerned, Einstein saw that molecules and specks were on an equal footing. Of course, there would be a difference. We all know, for example, that a billiard ball does not have to move as fast as a ping-pong ball to match its energy. The specks would have speeds sharply lower than those of the molecules of the liquid. Indeed, the speed of a speck could be comparable to that of a pen point during the act of writing. But the motion of the specks would be far from simple. Take a single speck at rest, for example, buffeted on all sides by the molecules. Since, on the whole, the blows on opposite sides will more or less balance, we may expect the speck to remain more or less at rest. But if we do we are forgetting the laws of probability. Einstein showed that statistical fluctuations—analogous to runs of luck when throwing dice—would cause imbalances large enough to give the speck a lively, erratic, zigzag motion that should be visible in a microscope.

Lacking numerical data, Einstein could not be sure that the motion he predicted was the so-called *Brownian motion,* first observed by the Scottish botanist Robert Brown in 1828. But Einstein was sure that if the molecular theory of inner heat was valid some such motion must occur. He did not know at the time that in 1888 the French physicist M. Gouy had already concluded that the Brownian motion was a form of heat, nor that in 1906, independently of Einstein, the Polish physicist Marian von Smoluchowski was to take a similar view.

The rapid zigzagging of the specks hampered direct measurements of their speeds. Was it possible, then, to put the theory to a sharp quantitative test? Einstein found a novel method. He showed that if one waited, the random zigzags would give rise to migrations of various amounts. He pointed out that this migratory process was essentially a process of diffusion, such as he had studied in the case of sugar and water. By calculating it both ways —as random zigzag migration and as diffusion—and comparing the results, he found the formula he wanted. By means of it a sort of average migration, which could be measured, was linked to numbers connected with diffusion rates and with the theory of gases.

But enough of such details. Let us come to the climactic point. If the theory was correct, the agitational motion of the specks would count as heat, and the specks would thus have to obey the heat laws governing the chaotic motions of molecules: the specks would display the molecular theory of heat on a scale that, in effect, would give visible evidence of the molecular hypothesis itself. Subsequent experiments not only confirmed the validity of Einstein's equation but in so doing showed that a key quantity governing the Brownian motion had the same numerical value as its counterpart did in the molecular theory of gases.

This was of outstanding importance. Let Einstein tell us why. In his "Autobiographical Notes" he said:

> My main aim . . . was to find facts that would guarantee as far as possible the existence of atoms of definite finite size. . . . The

[experimental verification of the] statistical law . . . of the Brownian motion . . . coupled with Planck's determination of the true molecular size from the law of radiation . . . convinced the skeptics, who were quite numerous at the time (Ostwald, Mach) of the reality of atoms.

This, then, is the climax. And with the atom at last accepted, our chapter ends.

What follows here is postscript. Ernst Mach, whom Einstein mentions parenthetically, was an Austrian physicist whose penetrating views—on other scientific matters—had a profound effect on Einstein. What of the even more formidable skeptic, Wilhelm Ostwald? Does the name not sound familiar? He was the German physical chemist to whom, in 1901, Einstein and Einstein's father had written in vain. It is pleasant to record that Ostwald and Einstein became good friends, each holding the other in the highest esteem.

6

Better Times

" "On the Electrodynamics of Moving Bodies." In the annals of science the title is famous. It is that of the last of the four papers mentioned by Einstein in his letter to Habicht, and with it we come at last to relativity. In his letter Einstein had said that the paper was only in draft form. Let us not be too harsh with him on that account. He did complete the manuscript without inordinate delay. Indeed, the timing is staggering. The paper reached *Annalen der Physik* on 30 June 1905, a mere fifteen weeks after the "very revolutionary" paper on light quanta; and in between Einstein had completed the doctoral thesis and the paper on the Brownian motion—all while earning his living full-time at the Patent Office. No wonder he felt exhausted when the relativity paper was done.

Where am I? How am I moving? These powerful questions lie at the root of relativity, and they hold many surprises. Imagine what emotions the questions might conjure up in primitive man, even in his dreams: nightmares of being lost in the jungle fleeing in zigzag panic from unseen dangers; and relief on waking to find himself safe in his cave—at home and at rest, with the questions answered.

But answered too easily. What of more civilized men—ecclesiastics safe in their cloisters, who believed in a fixed Earth, about which all else, both physical and spiritual, revolved? They too, for a time, had easy answers. But Copernicus, followed by Kepler and Galileo, preached the heresy of a moving Earth, and ecclesiastics were terrified into acts of repression. For a moving Earth dethroned Man from his central place in their conceptual scheme. Later the heresy deepened. And with Mother Earth just an itinerant speck lost in the reaches of a vast universe, where was the cloister? Where the cave? And how were they moving?

Men had long believed, with Plato and Aristotle, that the heavens were subject to rules quite different from those prevailing on earth; and with good reason, for even as the moon circles, does not the apple fall?

But in 1687 Newton completed his *Principia*, the greatest scientific book of all time. In it he linked heaven and earth in a mighty synthesis: apple and moon and all other objects in the material universe obeyed the same simple laws, moving inexorably in their appointed paths as parts of a vast machine.

Newton's laws were brief and surprisingly few: three laws of motion and an action-at-a-distance law of gravitation. In stating them, Newton had to speak of rest and motion. But rest and motion relative to *what*? Certainly not to a hurtling earth. Newton was setting down cosmic, not earthbound laws, and with his genius he realized that the laws of the cosmos must be given a cosmic setting.

As the "what" he daringly conceived a limitless, featureless *absolute space*, which he declared immovable and later spoke of as arising from the omnipresence of God. He introduced, too, the idea of an *absolute time*, which he said flowed uniformly and which he later spoke of as arising from the enduring existence of God. With unmoving absolute space he could speak cosmically of absolute rest and absolute motion. With unwavering absolute time he could speak of the motion as uniform or not. With both he could face the cosmic questions: Where am I? How am I moving?

If we pause to think, we can easily see that there is a sort of nonsense in all this. Does an absolute space devoid of features strike us as a likely standard against which to determine position and motion? And does not a clock, however erratic, keep exact time with itself? How then could the flow of absolute time be other than uniform if there is only itself as a standard against which to compare its flow?

Never mind. The foundations of science are always a morass.

PHILOSOPHIÆ

NATURALIS

PRINCIPIA

MATHEMATICA.

Autore *JS. NEWTON*, *Trin. Coll. Cantab. Soc.* Mathefeos
Profeffore *Lucafiano*, & Societatis Regalis Sodali.

IMPRIMATUR·
S. PEPYS, *Reg. Soc.* PRÆSES.
Julii 5. 1686.

LONDINI,

Juffu *Societatis Regiae* ac Typis *Josephi Streater*. Proftat apud
plures Bibliopolas. *Anno* MDCLXXXVII.

The title page of Newton's *Principia*. (S. Pepys, the President of
the Royal Society, is the noted diarist.) In the third volume of the
Principia Newton lays down four rules of scientific reasoning. The
first says: *"We are to admit no more causes of natural things than
such as are both true and sufficient to explain their appearances."*
Newton adds the following commentary: "To this purpose the
philosophers say that Nature does nothing in vain, and more is in
vain when less will serve; for Nature is pleased with simplicity,
and affects not the pomp of superfluous causes."

Newton was no simpleton. He knew full well what he was doing. He had to start somewhere, and his introduction of absolute space and time was an act of consummate genius. True, his ideas were at once attacked by such powerful critics as the Irish philosopher and bishop George Berkeley and the German philosopher, mathematician, and diplomat Gottfried Leibniz. But since nothing succeeds like success, initial objections were largely forgotten. Absolute space and absolute time survived and acquired the status of scientific dogma. In the nineteenth century, two hundred years after their introduction, Ernst Mach criticized them anew. But still they survived. For Newton was a master builder and his system of mechanics had been built to endure.

Before we proceed let us agree, for convenience, that from now on whenever we speak of motion being "uniform" we shall mean uniform in a straight line and without rotation.

Of the many deductions from his laws that Newton made in his *Principia*, here (with the above agreement) is the fifth:

> *The motions of bodies included in a given [vehicle] are the same among themselves whether that [vehicle] is at rest or in uniform motion.* ·

What this says—and it agrees with our experience—is that inside a vehicle in *uniform* motion there is no effect of that motion.

Do you object that in an open vehicle the passing scenery and the rush of air would reveal the vehicle's motion even if the motion was uniform? We could lull you into silence by saying that the vehicle has to be windowless and airtight. But why be dishonest to no purpose? The passing scenery and the rushing air tell us only how we are moving relative to *them.* Newton was talking cosmically of absolute rest and absolute uniform motion relative to featureless absolute space. Let us, then, imagine ourselves in a scientifically equipped vehicle in uniform absolute motion, somewhere in absolute space. Our task is to answer in an absolute sense the question: How am I moving?

Our first thought is to observe landmarks such as the moon and Jupiter and the stars. But what use would they be to us? Like the rushing air and the passing scenery on Earth they can tell us only relative motions. Our next idea is to set up mechanical experiments within the vehicle to detect its absolute motion. But now the import of Newton's fifth deduction begins to dawn on us. For it tells us that we are wasting our time. The experiments are bound to fail. Mind you, if we were looking for *deviations* from uniform absolute motion, we could easily succeed. But our uniform absolute motion is physically undetectable.

Thus in Newton's theory, practice and principle did not quite mesh. In practice neither rest nor *uniform* motion could be absolute: Newton's laws themselves declared it. Yet Newton had set his laws in absolute space and time, which in principle denied it.

Let us not pause to tell how Newton went outside his laws to ease this awkwardness. When Young and Fresnel overthrew his particle theory of light the situation changed. For if light is propagated as a wave, the whole visible universe should be filled with something—call it an *ether*—to carry the waves. This by itself would not be significant here. But, as Young pointed out, optical experiment implied that this ether should pass freely through matter. Except for the rippling light waves, it could therefore be considered at absolute rest. Thus despite Newton's fifth deduction —which applied to mechanical devices—optical experiments could well succeed in detecting a vehicle's uniform motion through the ether, and this motion could count as absolute.

The point was not lost on the experimenters. Starting as early as 1818, they made ingenious optical experiments to measure the absolute motion of the earth—its motion relative to the quiescent ether. But the results were by no means what they expected.* The early experiments revealed no sign of such motion; no sign of an ether wind.

Fresnel was able to account for all such negative results by a brilliant assumption. He said that some of the ether was trapped within matter even as the rest flowed freely through. But his assumption contained a glaring contradiction: each different color of light would require a different amount of trapped ether, which is absurd. This does not diminish the brilliance of Fresnel's idea. On the contrary, it enhances it, for, as became clear much later, he was intuitively groping toward something that belonged in the theory of relativity and was out of place in the Newtonian picture.

We now introduce the outstanding Dutch theorist Hendrik

* If you have read about relativity before, do not jump to conclusions. At this point we are not talking about what you probably have in mind.

H. A. Lorentz.

Antoon Lorentz, who was to be awarded the Nobel Prize in 1902. Towards the end of the nineteenth century he made a major refinement of Maxwell's electromagnetic theory in the course of which he obtained the formula of Fresnel—without its self-contradiction, and with the ether absolutely stationary, except for the light waves coursing through it.

All would now have seemed well had not Maxwell, in the last

year of his life, already proposed a new optical method of measuring the motion of the earth through the ether. It required such extraordinary sensitivity that he was sure it could not be performed. Yet in theory it would overtop Fresnel's formula, according to which all less sensitive optical methods would fail.

But Maxwell had been too pessimistic. He had not foreseen the experimental ingenuity of the German-American physicist Albert Michelson, who was to receive the Nobel Prize in 1907. In a preliminary attempt in 1881, making exquisite use of interference fringes, Michelson demonstrated that the experiment was feasible. And in 1887, with his colleague, the chemist E. W. Morley, he performed it with enhanced precision.

The Michelson-Morley experiment is too well known to need detailed description here. It looked for an effect of the earth's motion on the speed of light as measured on the earth. If the earth is moving through the stationary ether, a sort of ether wind will flow through the laboratory. Send light in the direction of flow to a mirror and let the light return. Calculation shows that the time for the journey will be slightly greater than that for a similar journey transverse to the flow. And by measuring the differences in the times light takes for there-and-back journeys in different directions, one can measure the velocity of the ether wind and thus the velocity of the earth through the ether. The apparatus had ample precision for its task, but to Michelson's disappointment no differences of times were detected. He therefore regarded the experiment as a failure, and as late as 1902 spoke of it apologetically.

Viewed as an attempt to measure the absolute motion of the earth, it was indeed a failure. But in this very failure lay its triumph. The negative result of the Michelson-Morley experiment was disconcerting to the few people able to recognize some of its implications. Michelson had assumed that the null result meant that the earth carries local ether bodily along with it. But since there were overwhelming experimental and theoretical reasons against this, the theorists were faced with a problem. The ether flow *had* to be there. Why, then, did it not show up?

The Irish physicist G. F. FitzGerald, and later Lorentz, independently offered an explanation: that objects contract in the direction of their motion through the ether, this contraction being of just the amount needed to nullify the effect of the ether wind in the Michelson-Morley experiment. The greater the speed through the ether, the greater the needed contraction. For the orbital speed of the earth, which is some eighteen miles per second, lengths would be shortened by only about one part in a hundred million. But at the speed of light, which is some 186,300 miles per second, lengths would need to shrink to zero.

For the most part, this *ad hoc* assumption aroused no great enthusiasm. The great French mathematician, theorist, philosopher of science, and popularizer Henri Poincaré found the situation by no means satisfactory. He objected to the patchwork approach: first Fresnel with his trapped ether explaining away the null results of the earlier, cruder experiments, and now FitzGerald and Lorentz with their contraction explaining away the null results of the more probing ones. What if the experimenters became even more precise and found further unexpected results? Would one then rush to add yet other assumptions specially tailored to fit the facts? Spurred by Poincaré's strictures and promptings, Lorentz made a systematic attempt to reconcile Maxwell's equations with the null results of the Michelson-Morley experiment and of further experiments already performed or not yet conceived. By 1904, after great effort, he had essentially solved the mathematical problem. Since the details need not concern us, let the following suffice, even if it seems like mumbo jumbo. The problem was to keep Maxwell's equations unchanged in form when making a transition from a vehicle at rest in the ether to one moving uniformly relative to it. To achieve this, Lorentz used, among other things, contracted lengths. But he did not quite succeed in preserving the form of Maxwell's equations. A small blemish crept in.

Meanwhile Poincaré had been making penetrating remarks. For example, in 1895—just about when the sixteen-year-old Einstein was asking himself what a light wave would look like if one kept abreast of it—Poincaré spoke tentatively, and, from 1899 on, more confidently, of what, in 1904, he called the *principle of relativity*. Essentially it said what Newton's fifth deduction had said: that we cannot determine absolute rest or uniform motion. But Poincaré, thinking of it in terms of Maxwell's theory, realized with startling prophetic precision that Newton's theory would have to be drastically changed. Indeed, scattered through Poincaré's writings one finds astonishing anticipations of ideas and results of the theory of relativity.

In June 1905, almost simultaneously with Einstein, Poincaré sent two papers to scientific journals, both entitled "On the Dynamics of the Electron." They leaned heavily on Lorentz's 1904 paper. The first, a short note removing the blemish in the Lorentz paper, alluded briefly to what Poincaré set forth in great mathematical detail in his second paper.

Einstein, of course, did not know of Poincaré's two not-yet-published papers when he wrote his own. Nor did he know of the 1904 paper of Lorentz. Indeed Einstein's method is quite different. Moreover, he accomplished the transfer of Maxwell's equations without blemish.

Practically all of the basic mathematical formulas of Einstein's 1905 paper on relativity are to be found in the 1904 paper of Lorentz and the two papers of Poincaré, both of which latter warrant the date 1905 even though the major one did not appear until early 1906. The presence of often-identical formulas was almost inevitable, since relativity is intimately linked mathematically to Maxwell's equations and the mathematics of wave propagation. Indeed the mathematical transformation that is fundamental in relativity—a formula to which Poincaré in 1905 gave the name *Lorentz transformation*—had already been found by the Irish-born physicist Joseph Larmor in 1898 on the basis of Maxwell's equations; and an almost identical transformation had been found by the German physicist Woldemar Voigt in a study of wave motion as early as 1887, the year of the Michelson-Morley experiment.

These things, unfortunately, need to be said because the mathematical similarities have misled some people into the belief that Einstein's contribution was marginal, which it certainly was not. Yet in fairness we must add that among the writings of Poincaré one finds so many of the relevant ideas that, with hindsight, one is surprised that he failed to take the crucial step that would have given him the theory of relativity, so close did he come to it.

After these long preliminaries, we are ready for Einstein's 1905 paper on the electrodynamics of moving bodies. It will repay our close attention—and, alas, require it too.

Impressed by the primordial power of the laws of thermodynamics that assert the impossibility of perpetual-motion machines,
Einstein looked for a comparable principle of impossibility. But
the real key to the theory of relativity came to him unexpectedly,
after years of bafflement, as he awoke one morning and sat up
in bed. Suddenly the pieces of a majestic jigsaw puzzle fell into
place with an ease and naturalness that gave him immediate confidence. Yet he also had confidence in his more speculative work
on light quanta with its unexpected pieces of what seemed an
alien and conflicting jigsaw puzzle.

He must have realized that he was writing for the ages. But,
as the illustrations (pages 70-71) indicate, he probably did his
calculations on odd slips of paper, and although in submitting his
now-famous works of 1905 to *Annalen der Physik* he presumably
wrote them out reasonably neatly, once they were in print he discarded the manuscripts, perhaps after using them as scraps of
paper on the backs of which to perform other calculations. Thus
the originals no longer exist. But that was the way Einstein was.

Let us now look at the content of his paper of 1905 on what
came to be called the special theory of relativity. First we remark
that Einstein makes no specific mention of the Michelson-Morley
experiment. He seems hardly to have needed it in his argument.
Moreover he here ignores the proposal in his paper of only a few
weeks earlier that light must somehow consist of quanta.

As in that paper, he begins by noting a conflict that goes to the
heart of the matter: Maxwell's theory makes unwarranted distinc-
tions between rest and motion. Einstein gives an example. When
a magnet and a loop of wire move past one another, an electric
current appears in the wire. Suppose we think of the magnet as
moving and the loop as at rest. Then Maxwell's theory gives an
excellent explanation. Suppose we now switch and think of the
coil as moving and the magnet at rest. Then Maxwell's theory
again gives an excellent explanation; but it is a quite different
one physically, and this even though the calculated currents are
equal.

Having thus aroused our suspicions about Maxwellian rest and
motion, Einstein bolsters them by adducing "the unsuccessful attempts to discover any motion of the earth relative to the [ether]."
He therefore makes the impossibility-type postulate that no ex-

Holograph page of Einstein's lecture "Geometry and Experience," given in 1921.

periment of any sort can detect absolute rest or uniform motion: that Newton's fifth deduction holds for all physics. In view of the evidence, this postulate, which he calls the *principle of relativity*, is certainly plausible. Einstein now quickly adds a second principle that seems, if anything, even more plausible; and with these deft strokes he sets the stage for revolution.

His second principle says that in empty space light travels with

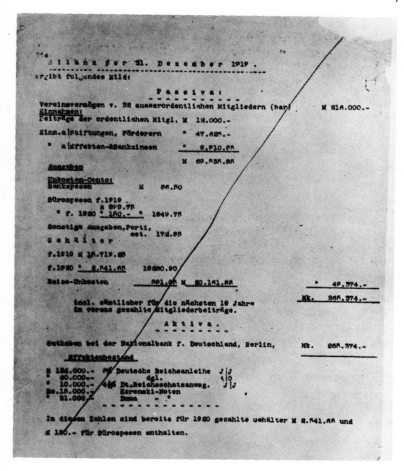

The other side of the page.

a definite speed c that does not depend on the motion of its source. Perhaps this startles us. If, for example, we think of light as consisting of particles, we would naturally say that their speeds depend on the way their sources move. But from the point of view of the wave theory of light, Einstein's second principle takes on the aspect of an utter triviality. For, no matter how a light wave is started, once it is on its way it is carried by the ether at the standard speed with which waves are transmitted therein. If this is so obvious, why does Einstein state it as a principle? Because early in his paper he says that the introduction of an ether will prove "superfluous." His second principle extracts from the ether the essential that he needs. Note his audacity. Fresh from his quantum proposal that light must somehow consist of particles, he takes as the second principle of his theory of relativity something inherent in the wave theory of light, even as he declares the idea of an ether superfluous. There is in this a striking indication of the sureness of his physical intuition.

Here, then, we have two simple principles, each plausible, each seemingly innocent, each bordering on the obvious. Where is the harm in them? Where the threat of revolution?

In his paper, Einstein speaks of them as "only apparently irreconcilable." *Irreconcilable?* Where is the conflict? Only *apparently* irreconcilable? What can he possibly have in mind?

Watch closely. It will be worth the effort. But be forewarned. As we follow the gist of Einstein's argument we shall find ourselves nodding in agreement, and later almost nodding in sleep, so obvious and unimportant will it seem. There will come a stage at which we shall barely be able to stifle a yawn. Beware. We shall by then have committed ourselves and it will be too late to avoid the jolt; for the beauty of Einstein's argument lies precisely in its seeming innocence.

Consider, then, two similar, well-equipped vehicles in uniform motion, as shown in the accompanying diagram, and imagine them far out in space so that they are unaffected by external influences. The vehicles, named *A* and *B* after their captains, have a uniform relative motion of, shall we say, 10,000 miles per second, as indicated. At the center of each vehicle is a lamp. When

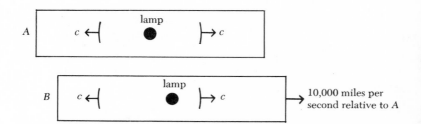

A and B come abreast, they flash their lamps on for an instant, thus sending out pulses of light to left and right. The diagram shows these pulses and the vehicles a moment later. For convenience, we have drawn it as though A were "at rest."

We now set the stage for a question. By Einstein's second principle the speeds of the pulses of light do not depend on the motions of their sources. Therefore—and this is important—the pulses keep abreast as shown. In his vehicle, A measures their speeds to the right and the left and finds the value c for both. B makes corresponding measurements within his own vehicle. He is moving at 10,000 miles per second relative to A, while his light pulses keep abreast of A's. Agreed? Then here is the question: What values of the speeds of the pulses relative to himself does B obtain?

Because of his motion relative to A, we would expect B to find his leftward-moving light pulse traveling relative to him with a speed of $c + 10,000$, and the other with the vastly different speed of $c - 10,000$.

But if this were the case, we should run afoul of Einstein's first postulate. How so? Because A and B are performing identical internal experiments within their respective vehicles, and since they are in uniform motion they must obtain identical results. Therefore B, like A, must find that the speeds are both c. Indeed, no matter how fast B may travel relative to A in an attempt to overtake the receding light, it will always recede from him with the same speed c. He cannot catch up with the receding light any more than one can reach the horizon on earth. No material object can travel as fast as light. Here in this startling result we see an unexpected answer to the sixteen-year-old Einstein's question about keeping abreast of light waves.

Since the result is so startling, let us look at it differently, if only to convince ourselves that it necessarily follows from Einstein's two principles. Suppose A found the speed in both directions to be c while B found it to be $c + 10,000$ in one direction and $c - 10,000$ in the other. Then A could legitimately conclude that he was at absolute rest and B could legitimately conclude that he was traveling at an absolute speed of 10,000 miles per second. And this would belie the principle of relativity.

A lesser man finding this calamitous consequence of two seemingly innocent postulates would immediately have abandoned one or the other. But Einstein had chosen his two principles precisely because they went to the heart of the matter, and he boldly retained both. Their very plausibility—taken separately—gave his theory a firm foundation. In such treacherous regions of thought he could not afford to build on quicksands.

We have now seen why Einstein used the word "irreconcilable." Yet he had said that his two principles were only "apparently" irreconcilable, and this meant that he was going to reconcile them nevertheless. But how?

Here we enter the crucial stage of the argument. The remedy obviously had to be something drastic. What flashed on Einstein as he sat up in bed that momentous morning was that he would have to give up one of our most cherished notions about time.

To understand Einstein's revolutionary idea about time, we return to the vehicles A and B and give their captains a new task. Four superlatively accurate clocks a_1, a_2, b_1, b_2 are fastened down in the two vehicles as indicated. For convenience let us pretend that the vehicles are millions of miles long so that we can talk of minutes rather than billionths of a second.

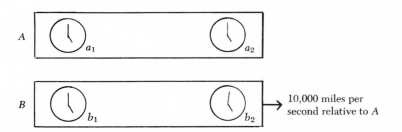

A sends a flash of light from a_1 to a_2, where it is immediately deflected back to a_1. The light leaves a_1 when the hands of a_1 read noon, and reaches a_2 when *its* hands read 3 minutes past noon. We can not be sure from this that the light took 3 minutes to travel from a_1 to a_2: for example, the workmen who installed the clocks may inadvertently have moved the hands. How can we synchronize clock a_2 with clock a_1? Let us consider the double journey. Suppose the light leaves a_1 when the hands of a_1 read noon, reaches a_2 when *its* hands read 3 minutes after noon, and returns to a_1 when a_1's hands read 4 minutes after noon. We immediately suspect that something is wrong. The clocks are alleging that the light took 3 minutes to travel from a_1 to a_2 but only 1 minute to return from a_2 to a_1. We do the obvious thing. We move the minute hand of a_2 back 1 minute. Now, when we perform the experiment, the clocks will indicate that the light took 2 minutes to travel from a_1 to a_2 and 2 minutes to travel back from a_2 to a_1. Since, as we have seen, we want the speed of the light to be c in both directions, we would agree with Einstein that the hands of the clocks a_1 and a_2 are now so set that the clocks are synchronized. And if, a little later, something happens at a_1 when the hands of a_1 read 4:30, and something else happens at a_2 when the hands of a_2 also read 4:30, we would agree with Einstein that the two separated events had occurred simultaneously.

Perhaps all this seems rather pointless—so obvious that we can barely stifle the yawn we spoke about. But, as we have mentioned before, the beauty of Einstein's argument is that it is based on concepts of beguiling acceptability. While politely stifling our yawn, we have unknowingly committed ourselves to a staggering consequence.

As A synchronizes his clocks a_1 and a_2 in the above manner prescribed by Einstein, B observes him in utter amazement. For, relative to B, A is moving to the left at 10,000 miles per second. Thus although A claims that his light is traveling equal distances forward and back like this

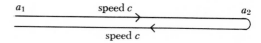

B sees the distances as manifestly unequal, like this

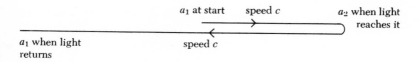

What is B to think? What is he driven to conclude? That since the forward and backward distances are *unequal*, the very fact that the forward and backward journeys of the light take equal times according to a_1 and a_2 is proof to B that clocks a_1 and a_2 are *not* synchronized.

Naturally, when B tells A about this, A is upset. So he asks B to synchronize clocks b_1 and b_2 according to the agreed-upon Einsteinian procedure. B does so, and at once A has his revenge. For, relative to A, B is moving to the right at 10,000 miles per second, and although B claims that his light is traveling equal distances forward and back like this

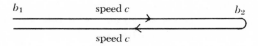

A sees the distances as manifestly unequal, like this

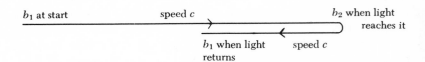

Thus A says that clocks a_1 and a_2 are synchronized, but B says they are not. And B says that clocks b_1 and b_2 are synchronized, but A says they are not. So if A says that events occurring at a_1 and a_2 are simultaneous, B will deny it. And vice versa.

Do we side with A or do we side with B? Einstein's first postulate, the principle of relativity, puts A and B on an equal footing. We must therefore conclude with Einstein that both are right.

Now comes the supreme stroke of genius. Einstein looks on this divergence of views not as a minor squabble but as a characteristic of Time itself. Our common-sense, Newtonian concept of a universal time providing a universal simultaneity has been shattered before our eyes. Time, according to Einstein, is of such a nature that the simultaneity of separated events is relative. Events simultaneous for A are, in general, not simultaneous for B; and events simultaneous for B are, in general, not simultaneous for A. Though this may be shocking, we have to learn to live with it. And to live with further shocks. For time is fundamental, and a drastic change in our conception of it brings the whole structure of theoretical physics tumbling down like a house of cards. Hardly anything remains untouched.

Take length, for instance, that other mainstay of theoretical physics. Imagine a rod moving past A and B. To measure its length as it rushes by, A notes the positions of its ends at a particular instant—which is to say simultaneously. So does B. But since A and B disagree about simultaneity, A will say that B noted the positions of the two ends at different moments and thus did not measure the true length. B will say the same about A. And in general A and B will find different values for the length thus measured.

We see from this that because simultaneity is relative, so too is distance. And there is obviously no stopping the epidemic. Speed, acceleration, force, energy—all these and more depend on time and distance: the very fabric of physics is changed.

What of the relationship between the measurements of time and space made by A and those made by B? Or by any two observers in vehicles in uniform relative motion? Einstein typically looked for the simplest mathematical relationship deducible from his two principles. In this way he derived from them none other than the Lorentz transformation—a transformation with which, almost certainly, he had not been previously acquainted.

Armed with this transformation, he made further deductions. His two principles may at first have seemed innocent, but their logical consequences are often such as to outrage common sense. For example, as Einstein showed, A finds B's clocks going at a slower rate than his own. After recovering from our surprise— for, were not the clocks all equally reliable?—we expect that B finds A's clocks going at a faster rate than his own. But no. Each finds that the other's clocks go the more slowly.

Again, we recall the proposal of FitzGerald and Lorentz that objects contract in the directions of their motion through the ether. Einstein obtained precisely the same formula for the amount of the contraction. But in Einstein's theory this is a mutual, relative effect: A finds that B's longitudinal yardsticks are contracted compared with his own, while B finds that A's are the shorter. Nothing could reveal more strikingly the revolutionary boldness of Einstein's ideas compared with those of his elders Lorentz and Poincaré. All three had the Lorentz transformation, in which the startling consequences were implicit. But, when interpreting it, neither Lorentz nor Poincaré dared to give the principle of relativity full trust. If *A* was at rest, as they put it, then *B*'s yardsticks would be contracted. But nothing was said about *B* finding *A*'s contracted. It was tacitly assumed that *B* would find *A*'s the longer. As for the rates of actual clocks, no such discussion as Einstein's was given.

Poincaré, one of the greatest mathematicians of his time, was a man of subtle philosophical insight. In his major paper of 1905 he had extraordinary command of the detailed mathematical apparatus of the theory of relativity. For years he had preached the purely conventional nature of physical concepts. He had early sensed the probable validity of a principle of relativity. Yet when he came to the decisive step, his nerve failed him and he clung to old habits of thought and familiar ideas of space and time. If this seems surprising, it is because we underestimate the boldness of Einstein in stating the principle of relativity as an axiom and, by keeping faith with it, changing our notions of time and space.

In making this revolutionary change Einstein was greatly influenced by the ideas of Mach, whose critical book on Newtonian mechanics Besso had brought to Einstein's attention in his student days. Mach will enter our story further, even though Einstein's early enthusiasm for his philosophical ideas did not last. Mach had been profoundly skeptical of concepts like absolute space and absolute time—and atoms. Roughly speaking, he looked on science as a sort of neat cataloguing of data, and he wanted all concepts to be clearly definable in terms of specific procedures. Einstein's treatment of simultaneity in terms of specific synchronizing procedures clearly shows Mach's influence. But others, Poincaré among them, also knew Mach's ideas, yet it was Einstein who made the crucial advance.

The mutual contractions of lengths, like the mutual slowings of clocks, are not self-contradictory. They are closely analogous to effects of perspective. For example, if two people of equal height walk away from one another, stop, and look back, each appears to the other diminished in size; and the reason this particular mutual contraction does not strike us adults as a contradiction is simply that we have grown used to it.

We have told barely enough to give a hint of the revolutionary nature of Einstein's paper of 1905 on relativity. Once the foundations are laid, the paper becomes highly mathematical. Einstein shows how, with the new ideas of time and space, Maxwell's equations conform to the principle of relativity, even as these ideas require a revision of Newtonian mechanics. For example, the faster an object moves relative to an experimenter, the greater will be its mass relative to him. Characteristically, Einstein leads up to a prediction that can be put to experimental test. He gives formulas for the motion of electrons in an electromagnetic field, taking account of the relativistic increases in their masses as their speeds increase relative to the observer. By a different route, Lorentz had made essentially the same prediction in 1904, and had compared it favorably with results already found by an experimenter. The equivalence of the formulas need not surprise us, since, as we have said, Lorentz and Einstein had a common Maxwellian heritage. But there is a difference between the men that is worthy of note. In 1906 the same experimenter, publishing new measurements, categorically declared them incompatible with the prediction of Lorentz and Einstein but compatible with certain rival theories. Lorentz was distinctly disheartened. But Einstein was unperturbed. Looking at the rival theories with aesthetic disapproval, he confidently suggested that the experimenter could be in error. And subsequent measurements by others showed that Einstein was correct.

It would be wrong to close this account of Einstein's 1905 paper on relativity without quoting its final words:

> In conclusion, I wish to say that in working at the problem here dealt with I have had the loyal assistance of my friend and colleague M. Besso, and that I am indebted to him for several valuable suggestions.

We have now looked at the four papers that Einstein offered Habicht in return for Habicht's thesis. Copies of the famous volume 17 of *Annalen der Physik,* containing the three major papers of the four, are now precious, sometimes kept under lock

Einstein and Besso at a reunion in Zurich.

and key by librarians fortunate enough to have custody of them. Such an outpouring of genius in so short a period of time—three different topics, each touched by magic—make the year 1905 memorable.

But our chapter cannot stop here. Einstein was not yet done with 1905. In late September, three months after the relativity paper, he sent to *Annalen der Physik* a further paper that was published in November. It occupies three printed pages. Using electromagnetic equations taken from his previous paper, Einstein here shows by calculation that if a body gives off an amount E of energy *in the form of light,*° its mass diminishes by an amount E/c^2.

With his instinctive sense of cosmic unity he now tosses off a penetrating and crucially important remark: that the fact that the energy is in the form of light "evidently makes no difference." He therefore announces a general law to the effect that if a body gives off or takes in an amount E of energy *of any sort,* it loses or gains an amount of mass E/c^2.

According to this, because c is so large, if a light bulb emitted 100 watts of light for a hundred years it would give off in that time energy whose total mass was less than a millionth of an ounce. But radium, through its radioactivity, gives off relatively enormous amounts of energy, and Einstein suggested that the theory could thus be tested.

In this paper of 1905 Einstein said that all energy of whatever sort has mass. It took even him two years more to come to the stupendous realization that the reverse must also hold: that all mass, of whatever sort, must have energy. He was led to this by aesthetic reasons. Why should one make a distinction in kind between the mass that an object already has and the mass that it loses in giving off energy? To do so would be to imagine two types of mass for no good reason when one would suffice. The distinction would be inartistic and logically indefensible. Therefore all mass must have energy.

With mass and energy thus wholly equivalent, Einstein was able in 1907, in a long and mainly expository paper published in the *Jahrbuch der Radioaktivität,* to write his famous equation $E = mc^2$. Imagine the audacity of this step: every clod of earth, every feather, every speck of dust becoming a prodigious reservoir of entrapped energy. There was no way of verifying this at the time. Yet in presenting his equation in 1907 Einstein spoke of it as the most important consequence of his theory of relativity. His extraordinary ability to see far ahead is shown by the fact that his equation was not verified quantitatively till some twenty-five

---

° He uses the letter L for this energy in the form of light. And, as in his previous paper, he uses V, not c, for the speed of light. The symbols in the text will be more familiar to the reader.

years later, and then only in difficult laboratory experiments. He could not foresee the tragic events that were to grow from his artistically motivated $E = mc^2$.

In the past three chapters we have told of the flowering of Einstein's genius in the fabulous year 1905. On the first of April 1906, at the Patent Office in Bern, Einstein was promoted to Technical Expert Second Class.

7

From Bern to Berlin

S ometimes a revolution gains quick adherents. Einstein's paper on relativity, received by *Annalen der Physik* at the end of June 1905 was already in print by 26 September. And as early as November 1905 an outstanding scientist had reported favorably on it. Indeed, in his autobiography he wrote that Einstein's paper had at once aroused his enthusiastic attention.

Who was this scientist? Poincaré? No. Then, of course, it must have been Lorentz.

But again no. Planck was the man—Planck who shared the general dislike of the idea of light quanta. He gave his favorable report to the Berlin Physical Colloquium. But that was not all. He immediately began to develop the theory, publishing in 1906 and 1907 papers on relativity in which he made approving reference to Einstein. Moreover, he used his great influence to persuade other scientists to study the new ideas. And he wrote warmly to Einstein in a lively scientific correspondence treating him as an equal. Here, for example, are excerpts from a long letter that Planck wrote to Einstein on 6 July 1907:

> Mr. Bucherer [whose experiments strongly supported relativity] has already written to me about his sharp opposition to my last research [on relativity]. . . . All the more gratifying is it to me therefore . . . that for the present you are not of Mr. B's opinion. So long as the enthusiasts for the principle of relativity form as tiny a group as they do at present, it is doubly important that they

agree among themselves. . . . I shall probably be going to the Bernese Oberland next year. Admittedly, this is rather far in the future, but I am happy to think that perhaps I shall then have the pleasure of making your personal acquaintance.

Lorentz was not wholly comfortable with Einstein's revolutionary ideas of time and space: when praising them in later years he could not always hide his regrets for a lost fixed ether. As for Poincaré, it is hard to tell whether he ever fully appreciated the revolutionary nature of Einstein's relativistic concepts. So far as printed references to relativity are concerned, Poincaré rarely if ever mentioned Einstein, and Einstein, on his part, rarely if ever mentioned Poincaré—although each had ample opportunity.

Planck's assistant Max von Laue wrote to Einstein asking to meet him in Bern in the summer of 1906. It seems—though the evidence is unclear—that Laue automatically assumed that Einstein was at Bern University. Certainly Laue was surprised to discover that the man who had conceived the ideas of time and space that had so impressed Planck was the unimposing, shirt-sleeved employee whom Laue at first gave scarcely a glance when he sought out Einstein at the Patent Office. Their meeting was the beginning of a lifelong friendship, and Laue, who later won the Nobel Prize, was to be the first to write a major technical book on relativity. It appeared in 1911.

Meanwhile, without waiting for general acceptance of his work, Einstein continued to produce research papers, extending his ideas on quanta, the Brownian motion, and relativity. Indeed, we have actually slighted the fabulous year 1905, for in December of that year Einstein sent to *Annalen der Physik* a second paper on the Brownian motion; it appeared in 1906. In 1907, as we already know, he completed the formulation of the equivalence of mass and energy epitomized in the fateful equation $E = mc^2$. What we have not yet mentioned is that in the same paper he took the first step on the path that was to lead him after many years from the special to the general theory of relativity, one of the supreme masterpieces of science. This alone would make 1907 memorable. But there was more. For example, Einstein unexpectedly acquired a major new ally in the Russo-German mathematician Hermann Minkowski, professor at the illustrious Göttingen

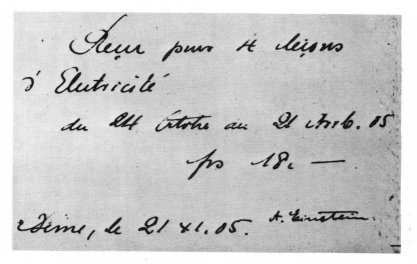

Signed receipt for eighteen francs in payment for four private
lessons given by Einstein to Lucien Chavan. These lessons were
given from 24 October to 21 November in the fabulous year 1905.

University in Germany. In December of 1907 Minkowski presented there an outstanding contribution to relativity.

Of the details of these advances by Einstein and Minkowski in
1907 we shall tell later in their logical rather than their chrono-
logical places. Meanwhile we mention that Minkowski had been
Professor of Mathematics at the Zurich Polytechnic when Einstein
was a student there, that Einstein had irregularly attended his lectures, and that in those days Minkowski had considered Einstein
a "lazy dog."

Not everyone was enthusiastic about relativity. Even physicists
favorably inclined towards it found the new ideas of time and
space hard to grasp. And as word spread of what Einstein had
proposed, many people—physicists, philosophers, and laymen alike
—denounced his ideas bitterly. What was important, however,
was that outstanding scientists were more and more coming to
accept them.

But although he was beginning to achieve a measure of fame
among scientists, Einstein was still in Bern, and he had long been

feeling the strain of his intense research activity coupled with his eight hours a day at the Patent Office. Toward the end of 1907 favorable circumstances led him to think again of becoming a *Privatdozent* so that he would someday be eligible for a professorship. Since the first step was to submit an inaugural thesis, he sent in to Bern University his 1905 paper on relativity.

It was rejected, one of the reasons given being that it was incomprehensible.

Understandably bitter, Einstein gave up his attempt to build a university career. On 3 January 1908 he wrote as follows to his friend Marcel Grossmann, who, at a remarkably early age, was already Professor of Mathematics at the Zurich Polytechnic Institute:

> At the risk of your thinking me ridiculous, I must ask your advice on a practical matter. I want very much to launch an attack on a teaching position at the Technical School in Winterthur (Mathematics and Physics). A friend who is a teacher there has told me in strictest confidence that the position will probably become vacant pretty soon.
>
> Do not imagine that I am driven to such careerist ways by megalomania or some other questionable passion; rather, I came to this hankering only because of an ardent desire to be able to continue my private scientific work under less unfavorable conditions, as you will certainly understand.
>
> "But why does he want to grab at just this job?" you will say to yourself. The reason is only that I believe I have the best chance there because
>
> (1) I once taught there for a few months as a substitute teacher.
>
> (2) I am rather friendly with one of the teachers there.
>
> I now ask you: How does one go about it? Should I perhaps pay someone a visit so as to demonstrate to him face to face the high value of my worthy self as teacher and citizen? Who would be the man to see? Would I not be likely to make a bad impression on him (not speaking Swiss German, Semitic features, etc.)? Furthermore, would it make sense if, at this interview, I were to extol my scientific work?

Einstein did not put all his eggs into this one basket. In the same January he applied for a position as teacher of mathematics at the Zurich Canton Gymnasium, where there was a vacancy. But by now the grim comedy was nearing its end. On 28 January Professor Alfred Kleiner—he who had been involved in both the rejection and acceptance of doctoral theses submitted by Einstein to Zurich University—sent Einstein a cryptic postcard expressing a desire to get in touch with him about a matter of mutual importance.

Seeking to bring Einstein to Zurich University as a professor, Kleiner urged him not only to try once more to become a *Privatdozent* at Bern University but also to report any developments, so that, if things went badly, Kleiner could try to think of less orthodox ways in which Einstein might meet the prerequisites for a professorship.

So Einstein tried once more. This time matters went better, and in 1908 he became a *Privatdozent* at Bern University. Not that he was immediately benefited thereby. He still had to work the same hours as before at the Patent Office, and in addition he now had to give university lectures. There was no salary attached to the position of *Privatdozent* either in Bern or elsewhere. The students who attended lectures paid fees that went to the lecturers. And since the professors, who did have salaries, increased their incomes by giving the well-attended required courses, a *Privatdozent* usually gave specialized lectures that attracted few students and thus brought in a pittance. Einstein's income from his lectures at Bern University was minuscule: Besso and one or two others were the only auditors to attend them regularly.

In those days Einstein was none too good a lecturer. He had more important things on his mind. But if he was ever to obtain a professorship he had to go through with the tribal initiation rites of academe. Naturally he did so reluctantly and even rebelliously. He made no attempt to improve his appearance or alter his manner to accord with academic custom. Among the students in Bern in those days were many Russian Jews, poor, ill-clad, and unkempt, and therefore frowned upon. Einstein's sister, Maja, tells of an incident that suggests what sort of outward impression Einstein made on the authorities. She was a student at Bern University at the time. Wishing to hear one of Einstein's lectures, she asked the doorman which room her brother, Dr. Einstein, was lecturing in. Looking at the neat young lady before him, the doorman blurted out in utter astonishment, "What? That . . . Russ is your brother?" And when Kleiner, after a surprise visit to the class of his protégé, criticized his lecturing ability, Einstein said, "I certainly don't demand to be made a university professor at Zurich."

In the spring of 1909 the expected authorization came through to create at Zurich University a new position of Associate Professor (*Professor Extraordinarius*) of Theoretical Physics for the fall. Councilor Ernst urged the nomination of Friedrich Adler, a friend of Einstein's, for the post. Adler was indeed a strong contender since his father, as founder of the Austrian Social Democratic Party, wielded considerable political power. But young Adler, a man of the highest ideals, insisted on withdrawing in favor of Einstein, begging the politically minded Board of Education to realize that Einstein's scientific powers were extraordinary, far overshadowing his own. So eloquent was his plea that Ernst found himself in a position in which he was unable to advocate Adler's appointment, and as a result of Adler's selfless act Einstein was elected to the professorship on 7 May 1909 at the age of thirty.

There is in this something reminiscent of an event in the life of Newton when he was twenty-seven. For in 1669 his Cambridge mentor, Isaac Barrow, resigned his professorship so that it could be given to Newton. The fates of Adler and Barrow were vastly different, however. Barrow immersed himself contentedly in theology. Adler involved himself more and more passionately in politics, and in 1916 his very idealism, perverted by the horrors of World War I, led him to assassinate the Austrian Prime Minister, an act for which he received a light sentence.

In 1909 Einstein was far too engrossed in his researches to let his attention stray more than momentarily to politics. On 6 July he submitted his resignation to the Patent Office to take effect on 15 October 1909. Writing to Besso in 1919, he spoke nostalgically of the Patent Office as "that secular cloister where I hatched my most beautiful ideas and where we had such good times together." Einstein had remained there a magical seven years.

We have already mentioned the 1907 lecture of Minkowski in Göttingen. In Cologne on 21 September 1908 he presented a less technical account at the week-long Eightieth Congress of German Scientists and Physicians. His lecture is famous—in part for these sensational introductory words: "From now on space by itself, and time by itself, are destined to sink completely into shadows, and only a kind of union of both to retain an independent existence." If these words pique our curiosity, they will have served Minkowski's purpose. Behind them lay a beautiful unification.

Newton had pictured the world as—how shall we put it?—fitted neatly together within absolute space and absolute time. Einstein broke away from this picture by saying that different observers in uniform motion set up different systems of simultaneity. Since their measurements of lengths are also affected,* we may say that the different observers have different private systems of time and different private systems of space.

Yet despite their disagreements, the observers have much in common. For example, they find for the speed of light the same constant value c. But above all they inhabit the same universe.

This last may sound disappointingly obvious. But it brings us to the heart of the matter. For the private times and spaces of the different observers do not exist in isolation. In the theory of relativity, Minkowski showed, they all belong to a single, universal, public domain that is a conglomerate of space and time. It is called *space-time*. How do the different observers come by their private times and spaces? By separating this conglomerate space-time into space and time in different ways. It is a little as if in finding their private spaces different observers were conceptually slicing a communal lump of cheese in different directions.

But a four-dimensional lump of cheese. Space-time has four dimensions. Time enters as a dimension more or less on a par with the three dimensions of space.

Having said this, let us dispel the feeling of bafflement and mystery that it may have engendered. First, do not try to visualize four-dimensional space-time. It is quite impossible. Not even Einstein and Minkowski could do it. The professionals deal with it by mathematical analogy, and although this lets them discuss it with extraordinary virtuosity, it still does not enable them to visualize it.

---

* Strictly speaking, this is not the best reason, but it will suffice.

On a piece of graph paper two numbers specify the position of a point. We therefore say that the surface of the graph paper is two-dimensional. In a room, three numbers are needed—for example, the distances from the ground and two walls—and we say that space has three dimensions. If we are talking not about points but about points at particular instants, we need four numbers, three for the spatial position and one for the time. In this sense the world is four-dimensional.

Well, then, you will say with relief, if that is all there is to it, Newton's universe was four-dimensional. And in a sense it was. But because absolute time stood aloof from absolute space—except that absolute space existed for all time—one thinks of the Newtonian universe as having $3 + 1$ rather than 4 dimensions. Not so with the space-time of relativity, for space and time are there intermingled so intimately that the term "four-dimensional" is almost unavoidable.

This is worth looking into a little further. Let us return to our space vehicles and their captains A and B, and imagine that B is typing a report of his mission. He hits the key t and then the key h. These events, these hittings, are about an inch apart and the time between them is, let us say, exactly half a second—that is, according to B not A. In half a second B travels 5000 miles relative to A. Thus A finds the distance between the two events spectacularly greater than the inch or so that separates them according to B. Under the circumstances, it seems as if there is no hope of A and B finding something numerical in common when discussing the two events. Indeed, because of the slowing of clocks, A finds that for him the two events occur slightly more than half a second apart, so that A and B disagree not only about the distance but also about the time between the events.

However, let each now do the following. First convert the time interval he finds into a distance. How? In the obvious way. By calculating the distance that light, with its agreed-upon speed c, would travel during the time in question. For convenience, call this the *time-distance* between the events, and call the spatial distance between them the *space-distance*.

Remember: A and B disagree sharply about both the space-distance and the time-distance separating the two events. But now let A and B each calculate the quantity

$$(space\text{-}distance)^2 - (time\text{-}distance)^2$$

and, according to the equations of relativity, they will obtain the same result. So too will any other observer in uniform motion.

In Newton's system the space-distances by themselves would all be equal, and the time-distances would also all be equal. But relativistically only the above mixture of the two has the same value for all the observers. This is already remarkable enough. But now let us recall the Pythagorean theorem, which had engrossed Einstein as a child. Imagine two people, C and D, separately covering this page with superposed graph-paper lines. C's as indicated on the left and D's as on the right in the diagram. Consider

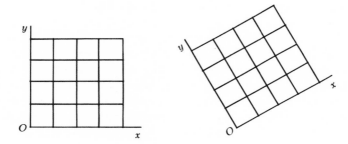

the x- and y-coordinate distances between two points O and P. With C's graph-paper lines these distances will be OQ_1 and Q_1P; with D's they will be OQ_2 and Q_2P. Obviously there is no agreement between C and D as to the coordinate distances. But, since

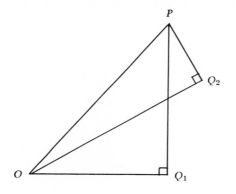

the angles at Q_1 and Q_2 are both right angles, we see from the Pythagorean theorem that the sum of their squares is the same, being equal to OP^2 Thus, despite their disagreements, C and D obtain the same value for the quantity

$$(x\text{-}coordinate\ distance)^2 + (y\text{-}coordinate\ distance)^2$$

and we note that, except for the plus sign here and the minus sign previously, this is precisely the same sort of formula as the relativistic one involving space-distance and time-distance. Indeed, by using the so-called "imaginary" quantity $\sqrt{-1}$ (the square root of minus one) we can even change the relativistic minus to a plus, if we so desire. ·

Minkowski was aware that this striking mathematical similarity, though not its Einsteinian implications, had already been noted and used by Poincaré in the major paper that he wrote in 1905. Because of the similarity, we are tempted to regard time as a fourth dimension which, when expressed as a length, mixes on more or less equal terms with the three dimensions of space to form a single, conglomerate, four-dimensional space-time. Indeed, with hindsight, the temptation is mathematically irresistible— even though four-dimensional space-time remains unvisualizable.

Imagine that the period at the end of this sentence represents a point. We are apt to think of it as just a point. But it is an enduring point. It persists in time. It is not here and gone in a flash. Thus in space-time it stretches out as a filament or, as it is called, a *world line*. For the sake of visualization let us imagine the time dimension of space-time to be represented in the downward direction on this page. Then, for example, two world lines like those shown here would represent two points approaching one another,

as we can see by thinking of our attention—our "now"—as a horizontal line moving steadily down the page. But the world lines themselves do not move. For in space-time past, present, and future are all spread out before us, motionless like the words of a book.

Minkowski did not stop with these ideas. He went on to show, for example, that, when embedded in space-time, Maxwell's equations take on an extraordinarily simple and unified form, as if they and space-time were made for each other.

Such is the gist of what Minkowski had in mind when he said dramatically at the 1908 Congress that space and time by themselves were destined to sink completely into shadows and only a kind of union of both to retain an independent existence. He would have been well justified in adding that the same could now be said more cogently than ever before of electricity and magnetism.

The next Congress, the Eighty-first, was held in Salzburg, and in view of such mind-stirring utterances by a man of Minkowski's eminence it is not surprising that this time Einstein himself was invited. He gave his lecture there on 21 September 1909, exactly a year after Minkowski's, and he spoke on "The Development of Our View of the Nature and Constitution of Radiation," a topic that embraced both relativity and quanta.

Among those who attended Einstein's lecture were some of the world's foremost physicists. In Einstein's austere opinion his lecture, regarded strictly as a work of science, was of little importance since, as he wrote to a co-worker, it contained nothing new. This was not wholly true. Einstein was being overmodest. Besides, to many in Einstein's audience the lecture came as a revelation. Not that his auditors necessarily accepted, or even understood, all that he presented, but they had come to see and assess the man of whom they had already heard, and it took them little time to recognize that he was a master. The occasion was important for Einstein too. He had been working for years in a sort of scientific exile, and his curiosity as to what great scientists were like in face-to-face discussion was at least as great as their curiosity about him. His confidence in himself was certainly not harmed when he found that he was able to hold his own easily in their company. Moreover, at this congress he first met Planck. In addition he made new lasting friendships leading to a voluminous scientific correspondence.

Thus when, next month, he took up his professorial duties at Zurich University, his career had already taken an enormous stride. It was now to progress at a headlong pace, making handsome amends for its heartbreakingly slow start. Einstein was glad to be back among old friends in Zurich, a town that held many memories of his student days. But his stay was not long. In 1911, despite difficulties caused by his being both a Jew and a foreigner, he was offered the position of full professor at the German University in Prague, where Mach had once been Rector. As was Einstein's custom when officially asked his religion, he had declared himself unaffiliated. But, having done so in this case, he learned that the Austro-Hungarian Emperor Franz Josef, through whose hands the Prague appointment had to pass, had long insisted that professors have a recognized religious affiliation—for if they did not believe in an officially recognized God, how could they adequately take the necessary oath of allegiance?

Accordingly, Einstein asked the official in charge of the records to change the entry about his religious affiliation, but was told that this was impossible in the absence of further proof. Thus Einstein was faced with a problem. His sister tells how he solved it. He asked on the basis of what declaration the official had listed him as unaffiliated. Naturally, the official replied that it was on the basis of Einstein's own declaration. In the official's eyes that must have seemed unanswerable. But Einstein responded by saying that he now solemnly declared himself a Jew. The official, having no ready response, was thus persuaded to change "unaffiliated" to "Mosaic," that being the official term for the Jewish faith.

In retrospect, as we shall see, this identification with Judaism takes on prophetic symbolic significance. It would be wrong to think of Einstein as a ritualistic Jew. He was one of the most religious of men, but his religious beliefs, too deep for adequate delineation in words, were close to those of the seventeenth-century Jewish philosopher Spinoza, whom Jews had excommunicated. Einstein, with his feeling of humility, awe, and wonder and his sense of oneness with the universe, belongs with the great religious mystics. In a letter in 1929 he spoke of himself as a "disciple" of Spinoza, who looked upon all nature as God. Shortly before, when asked via transatlantic cable if he believed in God, he cabled in reply: "I believe in Spinoza's God who reveals himself in the orderly harmony of what exists, not in a God who concerns himself with the fates and actions of human beings." His attitude toward Spinoza was one of profound reverence. In 1932 he declined an invitation to write a brief study of the philosopher, saying that nobody could do it since it required not only expertise but also "exceptional purity, imagination—and modesty." In that same letter is this passage, whose relevance to our story will become apparent in a later chapter: "Spinoza was the first to apply with true consistency to human thought, feeling, and action, the idea of the deterministic constraint of all that occurs." In a letter in 1946 Einstein spoke of Spinoza as "one of the deepest and purest souls our Jewish people has produced." And the next year, when asked to sum up his views on belief in a Supreme Being, he wrote in English:

> It seems to me that the idea of a personal God is an anthropological concept which I cannot take seriously. I feel also not able to imagine some will or goal outside the human sphere. My views are near those of Spinoza: admiration for the beauty of and belief in the logical simplicity of the order and harmony which we can grasp humbly and only imperfectly. I believe that we have to content ourselves with our imperfect knowledge and understanding and treat values and moral obligations as a purely human problem—the most important of all human problems.

These excerpts may seem explicit enough. Yet they are too bare. Much of Spinoza and Einstein escapes them. And Einstein often used the word "God" as a metaphor for something that may well have transcended them.

Prague offers further prophetic symbolism. From Einstein's biographer Philipp Frank, who succeeded Einstein in the professorship there, we learn that protocol required not only that a professor take the oath of allegiance but also that when doing so he wear a gaudy, gold-braided uniform resembling that of a naval officer. Einstein the antimilitarist donned this ludicrous uniform. And part of the uniform was a sword.

It was in Prague that the then-struggling Viennese physicist Paul Ehrenfest, a pupil of Boltzmann's, first met Einstein. Ehrenfest, visiting Prague, had been invited to be the Einsteins' house guest, and the Einsteins met him at the station. Soon the two scientists were embarked on an excited discussion that continued with hardly a letup for two days, by which time Einstein the violinist and Ehrenfest the pianist were playing duets together. In his diary Ehrenfest wrote: "Yes, we will be friends. Was awfully happy." And Einstein, in 1934, recalling the visit, wrote: "Within a few hours we were true friends—as though our dreams and aspirations were meant for each other." These words were written by Einstein in an obituary of his friend.

Einstein remained in Prague a year and a half. There, as in Zurich, he was a most untypical professor. He felt no puffed-up pride of office. He put on no airs, and he did not stand on ceremony. Nor did he become involved in the usual professorial bickering over status.

He proposed Ehrenfest as his successor at Prague. But Ehrenfest balked at declaring that he was of the Jewish faith. For previously, in order to circumvent the Austro-Hungarian law against Jew marrying Christian, Ehrenfest and his physicist wife Tatyana had officially declared themselves to be without religious affiliation, and Ehrenfest, despite the urgings of Einstein, would not now declare otherwise even as a formality.

In 1911, in Prague, Einstein made further progress toward his slowly maturing general theory of relativity, and in 1912 he propounded a fundamental quantum law of photochemical processes that was quickly confirmed experimentally by Emil Warburg in Berlin. Meanwhile, in June 1911, he received an invitation to attend in Brussels in the fall the first of a series of scientific conferences that will forever be associated with the name of the Belgian industrialist Ernest Solvay, who sponsored and financed them. The conference was organized by Planck's Berlin colleague the German physicist Walther Nernst, who after strong initial skepticism had enthusiastically accepted Einstein's quantum ideas concerning internal heat. Only a select few were invited. The invitation pointed out that the quantum work of Planck and Einstein —it did not mention the still highly suspect idea of light quanta— had created a crisis in physical theory. The essential purpose of the Solvay Congress was to bring European leaders of physics together in the hope that five uninterrupted days of intense discus-

The 1911 Solvay Congress. Seated, from the left: Nernst, Brillouin, Solvay, Lorentz, Warburg, Perrin, Wien (behind), Mme. Curie, Poincaré. Standing: Goldschmidt, Planck, Rubens, Sommerfeld, Lindemann, de Broglie, Knudsen, Hasenöhrl, Hostelet, Herzen, Jeans, Rutherford, Kamerlingh-Onnes, Einstein, Langevin.

sion in luxurious quarters would enable them to heal the quantum-caused dislocation of theoretical physics. Twenty-one scientists took part, the sessions being presided over by the incomparable Lorentz. That Einstein should have been invited to the Congress, though virtually inevitable, is a vivid indication of the high esteem in which he was now held. He was already counted as one of the elite.

Although the discussions were learned and lively and long, the problems did not yield their secrets. They bided their time, and the Solvay Congress seemed to have solved nothing. Nevertheless it was to have resounding repercussions in theoretical physics, for, among other things, it gave to the enigmatic quantum a status such as it had never had before. That it convinced the enormously influential Poincaré that the quantum was important is only the beginning of what grew out of it.

To his intimate friend Professor Heinrich Zangger, Director of the Institute of Forensic Medicine at Zurich University, Einstein wrote two letters in November 1911 containing some impressions of the Congress. Here are excerpts. In reading them one must remember that they were not meant for publication.

> Lorentz presided with incomparable tact and unbelievable virtuosity. He speaks all three languages equally well and has a unique scientific acuity. I was able to persuade Planck to accept many of my concepts, after he had resisted them for years. He is an utterly honest man who thinks of others rather than himself. . . . It was extremely interesting in Brussels. In addition to the French participants Curie, Langevin, Perrin, and Poincaré, and the Germans Nernst, Rubens, Warburg, and Sommerfeld, there were Rutherford and Jeans. Also, of course, H. A. Lorentz and Kamerlingh-Onnes. Lorentz is a marvel of intelligence and exquisite tact. A living work of art! . . . Poincaré was in general simply antagonistic [*ablehnend*] (against the theory of relativity) and, for all his acuity, showed little understanding of the situation. Planck is blocked by some undoubtedly false preconceptions . . . but nobody knows anything. The whole affair would have been sheer delight to diabolical Jesuits.

Hardly had Einstein become a professor in Prague when Grossmann, and a little later Zangger and others, began seeking a way to bring him back to Zurich, this time to the Polytechnic. Requests were sent to key people for their opinions of Einstein.

Shortly after the Solvay Conference, Marie Curie responded with a glowing testimonial:

> I have greatly admired the works that were published by M. Einstein on questions concerning modern theoretical physics. Moreover, I believe that the mathematical physicists all agree in considering these works as being of the highest order. In Brussels, where I attended a scientific conference in which M. Einstein took part, I was able to appreciate the clarity of his mind, the breadth of his documentation, and the profundity of his knowledge. If one

considers that M. Einstein is still very young, one has every right to build the greatest hopes on him and to see in him one of the leading theoreticians of the future. I think that a scientific institution that would give M. Einstein the opportunity to work that he desires by appointing him to a professorship in the conditions he merits, could only be greatly honored by such a decision and would certainly render a great service to science.

Among others who wrote in support of Einstein was Poincaré, whose letter is of particular interest. He wrote:

M. Einstein is one of the most original thinkers I have ever met. Despite his youth he has already achieved a most honorable place among the leading scientists of his time. What we must particularly admire in him is the facility with which he adapts himself to new concepts and knows how to draw from them every conclusion. He does not remain attached to classical principles, and when presented with a problem in physics he quickly envisages all its possibilities. This leads immediately in his mind to the prediction of new phenomena which may one day be verified by experiment. I do not mean to say that all these predictions will meet the test of experiment when such tests become possible. Since he seeks in all directions, one must, on the contrary, expect the majority of the paths on which he embarks to be blind alleys. But one must hope at the same time that one of these directions he has indicated may be the right one, and that is enough. This is exactly how one should proceed. The role of mathematical physics is to ask questions and only experiment can answer them.

In January 1912 Einstein was offered a ten-year appointment as professor at the Zurich Polytechnic. He was in these days much sought after. While in Prague he received offers of professorships in Utrecht and Leiden—the latter as successor to Lorentz, who was about to retire—and one from Vienna carrying a princely salary. But Einstein's heart was in Zurich and he had already committed himself there. Writing to Zangger in the summer of 1912, he said of this offer from Vienna, "I refused. . . . It would have been most ignoble of me to 'sell' myself in this way behind people's backs."

So in October 1912 Einstein returned as professor to the Zurich Polytechnic, where years before he had failed the entrance examination and where, on graduating, he had sought a position in vain. Of his important work there as professor we shall tell in the following chapter. As for the professorship at Leiden, with Einstein unobtainable the discerning Lorentz chose Ehrenfest.

Einstein's stay in Zurich was destined to be brief. Planck and Nernst hatched plans to bring him to Berlin. In the summer of 1913 they journeyed in person to Zurich to make him an offer: he would be elected—at the early age of thirty-four—to the illustrious Royal Prussian Academy of Science; his membership would carry a special stipend; he would hold the rank of professor; he would be Director of the about-to-be-founded scientific research branch of the Kaiser Wilhelm Institute; he would be closely associated with some of the greatest scientists of Germany; above all, he would be free to teach or not, as he pleased; and, if he wished, he could devote all his time and energy to his research.

Such was the offer. There was every likelihood that it would be officially approved. If so, would he accept it? After careful consideration Einstein found that he could not reject it.

Remember that when Planck and Nernst were thus wooing Einstein to Berlin, they did not yet accept his theory of light quanta, and he had not yet fully formulated his monumental general theory of relativity. Even without counting these two mighty works, they were looking on him as the greatest scientist of his time.

With the help of Nernst, Rubens, and Warburg—all leading Berlin scientists, all members of the Prussian Academy of Science, all mentioned by Einstein when writing to Zangger about the Solvay Congress—Planck drafted for submission to the Ministry of Education a long handwritten document, signed by all four. It extolled Einstein as a scientist and persuaded the authorities that Einstein was indeed worthy of what they wished the State, in the name of the Kaiser, to bestow on him—despite his being a Swiss citizen and a Jew, and despite his absolute insistence that he not be required to become a German citizen. It was in this persuasive document that Planck made the apologetic remarks already mentioned, in chapter 4, about Einstein's idea of light quanta.

Einstein had misgivings, likening himself to a hen that is expected to lay eggs, and wondering whether he would be able to produce further ideas on demand; as he put it years later in a different connection: "ideas come from God." Moreover he still mistrusted German militarism. But the offer was irresistible, and in April 1914 he and his family left traditionally neutral Switzerland for Berlin. He had now reached the top of his profession, and was known to scientists throughout the world. But he was still little known to the public.

Mileva Einstein with sons, Hans Albert and Eduard, 1914.

8

From *Principia* to Principe

In the summer of 1914, while Einstein stayed behind in Berlin, Mileva took the children to Zurich. In effect it was the end of the marriage.

With August came World War I. Aiming for speedy victory, the Germans in a quick flanking movement deliberately violated the neutrality of Belgium, an act that in those far-off days was widely considered the height of barbarism. But the gamble proved unsuccessful. The fighting was to drag on till November 1918, taking millions of lives. Patriotic fervor swept both sides of the conflict. Scientist went to war against scientist, intellectual against intellectual, with an unscholarly bloodthirstiness that astonished men like Bertrand Russell in England and Einstein in Germany. Attempting to mitigate the adverse psychological effect of the invasion of Belgium, the Germans drew up a "Manifesto to the Civilized World" that denied all guilt and pictured German militarism as the blameless defender of German culture. The manifesto was signed by ninety-three German intellectuals, Planck among them, and their action caused great resentment abroad.

Einstein said later that, as a Swiss citizen, he was not asked to sign it. He would not have done so anyway. He at once supported his colleague Professor Georg Nicolai who, with great courage, was preparing an opposing "Manifesto to Europeans." This document, which, according to Nicolai, Einstein helped draft, took sharp issue with the previous manifesto. It called for cooperation among scholars of warring nations for the sake of the future of Europe, and proposed the establishment of a League of Europeans. Only four people dared to sign it: Nicolai, Einstein, and two others.

Einstein took no part in the war. He did what little he could to aid the cause of peace, and with anguished intensity he immersed himself in his researches. At the Patent Office he had guiltily snatched time for his calculations. Now, as he worked in Berlin while Europe bled, he again could not escape a feeling of guilt.

We pause at this point to tell of his work on the general theory of relativity since, for all its cosmic remoteness, it became linked in a curious way with the war. In the telling, let us not hasten. The theory was not built in a day.

We ask first: what about Newton's theory of gravitation? It obviously could not survive relativity intact. It was not a field theory such as Maxwell's in which a field transmits electromagnetic effects with the speed of light. In Newton's theory there was no comparable transmission. Gravitation was an instantaneous action-at-a-distance force. Lift a finger, and the gravitational effect would at once—in absolutely no time—be present throughout the universe. Yet according to relativity no signals should travel faster than light. Besides, with a multitude of differing simultaneities how could the gravitational effect be suddenly everywhere at a common simultaneous instant? Newton's own views are not without relevance here. He wrote in a letter:

> That gravity should be innate, inherent and essential to matter, so that one body may act upon another at a distance through a *vacuum*, without the mediation of any thing else, by and through which their action and force may be conveyed from one to another, is to me so great an absurdity, that I believe no man who has in philosophical matters a competent faculty of thinking, can ever fall into it.

Various scientists, Einstein among them, looked for relativistic ways of modifying Newton's theory of gravitation. Almost from the start, however, Einstein was concerned about a deeper problem. Why, he asked, should uniform motion be something special?

How much more satisfying it would be if all motion, uniform or not, were relative.

But the facts were clearly against him. Acceleration is obviously absolute. We all know this. We do not need to study Newton's *Principia* to be convinced of it. In a smoothly-moving vehicle we feel no motion. But if the vehicle gives a lurch we feel it at once, as every straphanger will testify.

With facts of this sort staring him in the face, Einstein obviously could not have acceleration relative. But he was not one to be daunted by hostile facts that went counter to his intuition. Besides, previous criticisms of absolute space and absolute motion, particularly by Mach, played a major role in pointing the way for Einstein and bolstering his confidence, even though the path he took was typically his own. Indeed, Mach was to say harsh things about Einstein's special theory of relativity.

In the paper of 1907 in which Einstein enunciated $E = mc^2$ he had already begun his attack on the problem of acceleration, and he returned to it in his Prague paper of 1911. His argument, particularly in its 1911 form, must rank as one of the most remarkable in the history of science, not only because of what grew out of it, but also because Einstein went, so to speak, into the enemy camp and found, long embedded there, armaments that he—and only he—could turn against the very concepts that they appeared to be defending. Here is the essence of his argument.

Acceleration is absolute? All right. Let us take it to be so and see what we can make of the fact. Imagine a vehicle—a small laboratory—adrift in space, far from other gravitational bodies, so that people inside it feel no weight. Now let it be uniformly accelerated in a direction that the people in the laboratory would call "upwards," and let its acceleration be such that in each second its speed increases by 32 ft/sec.

Accelerated relative to what?

Why ask? Are we not agreeing that acceleration is absolute?

Yes. But if uniform velocity is relative, what does 32 ft/sec mean? It cannot be detected inside the laboratory.

Don't be fussy. Although the speed cannot be detected there, the acceleration, the *increase* of 32 ft/sec every second, can. For example, it gives the people within the laboratory the sensation of weight.

If these brusque answers seem to hide a certain awkwardness, so much the better. They show us the unnaturalness of having a partial relativity: a relativity of uniform motion but not of acceleration. Nevertheless we know from our own experience that acceleration is absolute. Besides, Newton has said it is so, and Newton is a formidable man. And Einstein himself has concurred in a way, since acceleration is absolute in the special theory of relativity.

So back to our laboratory accelerated "upwards" with an absolute acceleration of 32 ft/sec per second. All free objects within it move uniformly in straight lines. Newton's first law of motion tells us this. But relative to the accelerated laboratory, these unaccelerated objects will seem to be accelerated "downwards" at 32 ft/sec per second; and by measuring, for example, this "downward" acceleration, we can determine that our laboratory indeed has an absolute "upward" acceleration of 32 ft/sec per second.

But wait. Whatever their masses and whatever their composition, the thrown objects will all have the *same* "downward" acceleration. Have we not heard of such behavior before? Why, of course: in the familiar, if apocryphal, story of Galileo dropping objects from the Leaning Tower of Pisa. All local objects, dropped or thrown, fall under gravity with the same acceleration (if we ignore, for example, air resistance). Thus, at least so far as thrown objects are concerned, effects in the small accelerated laboratory in space mimic effects in a small unaccelerated laboratory on earth. But we can go further. It is an elementary exercise in physics to show that, according to Newton's laws, *all* mechanical effects in the small accelerated laboratory in space will be duplicated in the small laboratory on the gravitational earth.

What, then, of mechanical experiments within our laboratory? We thought they would tell us that it had an absolute "upward" acceleration of 32 ft/sec per second. But we now see that they could just as well be telling us that we were in a laboratory on earth, under the influence of gravity. Or in a laboratory having, in appropriate amounts, a mixture of acceleration and gravity. In this mechanical sense, then, acceleration is not absolute after all.

Note the audacity of the argument. We start by agreeing to accept acceleration as absolute. We argue in terms of absolute acceleration. We use Newton's laws with a straight face. And suddenly we show that, *so far as mechanical effects are concerned,* acceleration is relative.

This momentous conclusion was just a preliminary based on simple concepts known to scientists for centuries—concepts whose implications no one else in all those years had had the wit to see. Now came the aesthetic stroke of genius. Having gone this far, Einstein boldly removed the italicized words above, thereby saying without qualification that acceleration is relative. How did he do this? By proposing in 1907 what he later called the *principle of equivalence.* It is justly famous. It says in effect that *no* internal experiment, whether mechanical or not, can reveal any difference between the small accelerated laboratory in space and its companion laboratory on the gravitational earth.

Why is this of staggering importance? For the present let us be content with a major yet relatively minor answer: since Einstein could make simple approximate calculations in terms of an "accelerated" laboratory, he could carry his results over to a laboratory on a gravitational planet and thus make testable predictions about gravitation.

This we shall see for ourselves in a moment. But before we proceed, we must fill in a major gap by telling of the crucial flash of insight that set Einstein's mind in this particular direction. Fortunately he later gave his own account of the development of these ideas. He had changed the Newtonian theory of gravitation to make it fit the special theory of relativity. But calculation convinced him that, in his new theory, objects with different energies would fall with different accelerations; and this was contrary to Galileo's law that all local bodies fall with the same acceleration. "This law," said Einstein, "which may also be formulated as the law of the equality of gravitational and inertial mass, was now brought home to me in all its significance. I was in the highest degree amazed at its existence and guessed that in it must lie the key to a deeper understanding of inertia and gravitation." What had dawned on Einstein was that there was something suspect in the way Newton's theory accounted for Galileo's law. Newton used the concept of mass in two senses: first as a measure of an object's inertia, its degree of resistance to being accelerated by a force, and second as a measure of the object's gravitational effect. Double the mass of a body and the earth will pull it with doubled gravitational force. True. But since the inertial resistance to being accelerated will also be doubled, the acceleration will be the same as before. Thus Newton accounted for Galileo's law by tacitly taking gravitational and inertial mass to be equal. But this belies their intrinsically different roles in Newton's theory and, as Einstein suddenly realized, it introduces what amounts to an accidental numerical concurrence. By his principle of equivalence, Einstein was making Galileo's law a cornerstone of his general theory of relativity. He was treating it as fundamental rather than the result of a numerical accident. He was attesting to the primal power of simplicity.

This said, let us see some of the conclusions that Einstein drew from his principle of equivalence in 1907 and 1911. For simplicity we shall slightly change the order; for vividness we shall continue to speak of the earth where Einstein spoke somewhat more carefully; and for convenience, we shall refer to the accelerated laboratory in space as *Aclab,* and the laboratory on the gravitational earth as *Gravlab.*

First imagine a lump of matter hung from the ceiling by a spring in Aclab, and an identical lump hung by an identical spring in Gravlab. Both springs will be stretched. In Aclab the stretching occurs because the inertia of the lump resists acceleration, while in Gravlab the stretching comes from the pull of gravitation. The two springs will be stretched by equal amounts. Therefore the inertial and gravitational masses of the lumps are the same. Since

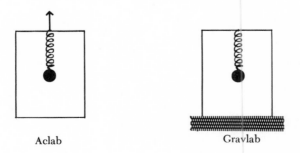

Aclab   Gravlab

this lay at the basis of the principle of equivalence, its emergence should not surprise us. But now suppose that the lumps absorb equal amounts of energy, say from radiation. Then, by $E = mc^2$, each lump will acquire extra mass, and the springs will be stretched by equal additional amounts. Why by *equal* amounts? Because the principle of equivalence insists that what occurs in Aclab must, under like circumstances, occur in Gravlab too. But in Aclab the additional stretching measures inertial mass, while in Gravlab it measures gravitational mass. Therefore energy too has equal inertial and gravitational mass, and we see a neat Einsteinian unity growing before our eyes—with barely a hint of mathematics. Indeed a remarkable feature of this work of 1907 and 1911 is that Einstein reached his major conclusions using, for the most part, only the most elementary mathematics. Rarely has there been so dazzling a display of sheer intuition.

Let us follow Einstein further. Imagine light sent in a ray across Aclab. It travels in a straight line (in absolute space—we are still

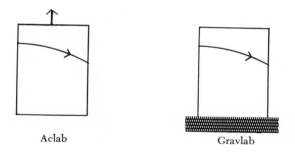

Aclab   Gravlab

keeping up the pretense). But because of Aclab's "upward" acceleration, the ray will seem to curve "downwards" relative to Aclab.* Therefore, as Einstein deduced in 1907, light sent in a ray across Gravlab will also have to curve downwards: *gravitation will bend light rays.*

This in itself is a major deduction. But it carries a further implication. Think of light as waves. Then, as the top diagram on page 110 shows, for a downward change of direction the lower part of the wave must lag: And this means—what? That *the speed of light is not constant.* That gravitation slows it down. Heresy! And by Einstein himself.

* In the diagram the amount of curvature is highly exaggerated.

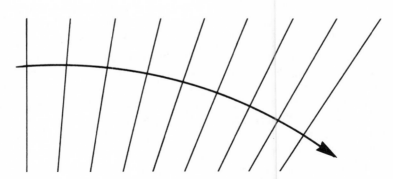

But we are still not done with the principle of equivalence. Place experimenters A. Low and A. High in Aclab and G. Low and G. High in Gravlab as shown, and let each have an accurate

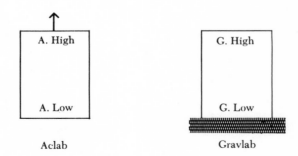

Aclab   Gravlab

clock. Einstein showed—we need not go into the details—that because of the acceleration, A. High sees A. Low's clock going more slowly than his own while—surprise—A. Low sees A. High's clock as the faster. (Who would have thought that we would come to regard such agreement as a surprise.)* By the principle

* For those who are interested, here is the essence of the reasoning. Think of A. Low's clock as emitting electromagnetic waves whose oscillations keep time with its ticking. Because of the ever-increasing speed of Aclab, successive wave crests have to travel steadily increasing distances to overtake the receding A. High. They will thus reach him at instants more widely separated in time than the ticks of his own clock. (This is called a Doppler effect.) When A. High sends out corresponding waves they travel to an approaching, not a receding A. Low, and the Doppler effect works to increase instead of decrease the rate of arrival of the wave crests.

of equivalence, when G. Low and G. High in Gravlab compare clocks by looking at them they must agree that G. Low's appears to go more slowly than G. High's. Thus gravitation warps time, and does so in an unexpected way.

Einstein was not just exploring ideas. He was also seeking experimentally verifiable effects. Take the rates of the clocks, for example. Replace them by the rates of oscillation—the frequencies —of the light given off by atoms. Then, as Einstein pointed out in 1907, if we compare the frequencies of light reaching us from atoms on the sun with the frequencies of the light from similar atoms on the earth, the former frequencies will be lower than the latter by one part in half a million. Since this famous effect would show up as a small shift of the spectral lines of the solar light toward the red end of the spectrum, it is referred to as a *gravitational red shift*.

As for the gravitational bending of light rays, in 1907 Einstein could think of no feasible way of testing it experimentally. By 1911 he had found a possible method. He calculated that a ray of starlight grazing the sun ought to be deflected by 0.83° seconds of arc—the angular width of a quarter viewed from a distance of about four miles. This deflection, Einstein suggested, could be detected during a total eclipse of the sun.

The German astronomer Erwin Finlay-Freundlich, seeking evidence of the deflection, examined existing photos of eclipses without success, and since an eclipse would occur in Russia in 1914, he went there to test Einstein's theory. That the outbreak of war prevented him from making the test may well seem unfortunate, but as we shall see it has its brighter side.

Eager to know whether light rays are in fact bent by the sun, Einstein had written from Zurich on 14 October 1913 to the famous American astronomer George Hale asking if the matter could be put to the test without having to wait for an eclipse. After consulting other astronomers, Hale replied that it could not; and this too was to have its brighter side. Einstein's letter to Hale is not without interest as a personal document, especially since it was written after Einstein had been invited to Berlin but before

---

° It should have been 0.87, but arithmetic was never one of Einstein's strong points.

Letter of Einstein to George Hale, 1913, asking if the gravitational bending of light rays could be detected when the sun is not eclipsed. The "Ans" at the top left is in Hale's handwriting and is Hale's way of indicating to himself that the letter has been answered.

he had left Zurich. In the letter Einstein says that he is writing on the advice of his colleague Professor Maurer; and, as we see in the photograph, Einstein had Maurer write a note (in somewhat continental English) saying, "Many, many thanks for a favorable reply to Mr. Professor Dr. Einstein, my honorable Collègue of the Polytechnicalschool," with Maurer's signature given added weight by the official stamp of the Polytechnic. From this we see that Einstein was eager to have his request taken seriously, and that, with his innate modesty, he felt by no means sure that his own name standing alone would carry sufficient weight. Such was Einstein. Under the circumstances one might have expected Einstein to have taken special care in writing the letter. Yet, as we see, it has words scratched out and replaced by others, and is in general concerned with essentials rather than externals. Here too we glimpse something of Einstein the man.

Even without observational confirmation, Einstein had faith in his principle of equivalence. He was well aware that it was only a rough, approximate sketch, an initial groping toward something vaguely sensed but not yet formulated. But he knew in his bones that it contained powerful aesthetic and physical concepts that must be his guides. First of all, it had artistic unity: for why should he needlessly assume one type of relativity for mechanical effects and a different one for the rest of physics? Besides, it was for him the decisive indication that he was not pursuing a will-o'-the-wisp in wishing to have all motion relative. Moreover, it showed him that the fulfillment of his wish must lead to a theory of gravitation that could not be contained within the bounds of the special theory of relativity. And as if this were not already enough, we shall see for ourselves the extraordinary precision with which the principle of equivalence guided him to the general theory of relativity. All this from a sudden astonished insight concerning the equality of inertial and gravitational mass in Newton's theory. Not that Einstein made no mistakes on the way. But always his intuition brought him back to the path from which he had strayed.

A scientific masterpiece is not built easily. Einstein still had far to go. Where should he look next? At gravitation affecting the speed of light, since this already transcended the special theory of relativity in which the speed of light was constant and the same for all observers. Besides, for well over a century physicists had known that Newton's action-at-a-distance law of gravitation could be expressed by a single "field" equation governing a single variable mathematical quantity called the *gravitational potential*. Why not let the variable speed of light play the relativistic role of this Newtonian gravitational potential? It was a neat, unifying idea that had a natural appeal for Einstein. But after working on it he convinced himself that an acceptable theory of gravitation was not to be won thus easily. This skirmish was the necessary prelude to a major advance. For if the variable speed of light was not adequate for representing gravitation mathematically—then what was?

Let us refresh our memories of Aclab and Gravlab. If Aclab were unaccelerated, free particles would move within it in straight lines with constant speed, for this is the law of inertia, Newton's first law of motion. Switch on the acceleration and these same free particles, their motions unchanged, would seem in Aclab to be falling as if they were in Gravlab under the influence of gravity.

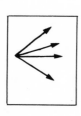
Paths of thrown
objects in unaccelerated
laboratory

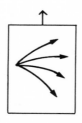
The same, as
seen in Aclab

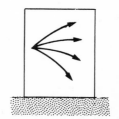
Paths of thrown
objects in Gravlab

Einstein had conceived a plan of campaign. Here it is in simplified form. First express the law of inertia in its relativistic form, which says that in space-time the unmoving world lines of free particles are straight. Then by a mathematical transformation represent the situation in Aclab. Automatically, this would have to represent the physical situation in Gravlab, and in this way one could find a hint as to how to treat gravitation mathematically.

Why just a hint? Why not a full-fledged theory? Because the results could tell only about local effects of gravitation. If Aclab and Gravlab were large they would no longer be adequately equivalent, as we easily see by a glance at the diagram on the opposite page, comparing a large Aclab in space with a large Gravlab on the curved surface of the earth.

Nevertheless a hint is a hint, and every hint is precious when the way is unclear. Indeed, it seemed to be rapidly growing more so, for Einstein was faced with a host of interrelated troubles.

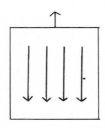

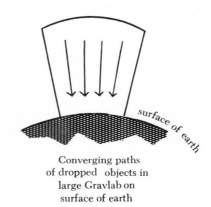

Parallel paths
of dropped
objects in
large Aclab

Converging paths
of dropped objects in
large Gravlab on
surface of earth

The warping of time by gravitation showed him that space, with its intimate relativistic linkage to time, must also be warped. Moreover the transition to the accelerated laboratory involved a distortion of the space-time coordinate system—the four-dimensional analogue of graph-paper lines—and such distortions implied that coordinates could no longer be directly linked to standardized clocks and yardsticks. Bereft of direct contact with physical measurements, Einstein felt utterly lost. It was a long time before he realized that here too was a hint, and a powerful one. He was forced to re-examine the whole problem of coordinates and measurement, and the task was far from easy.

What enabled him to proceed was a major insight that was long in coming. Let us approach it by means of an analogy. Two cars collide. The police list the "coordinates"—the place and time—of the accident. Suppose the place is the corner of 20th Street and 15th Avenue. Then we at once picture a city laid out in graph-paper style, with the coordinates 20 and 15 enabling us to tell precise driving distances to the site of the accident from, for example, police headquarters at 5th Street and 8th Avenue. But suppose the location of the accident is listed as the corner of King's Lane and Linden Crescent, with police headquarters at Highland Terrace and Bolton Place. From these coordinates we form a picture of a rambling city whose streets are neither straight nor regularly spaced; and without a map we have not the slightest idea of any of the distances involved.

Not the slightest idea? That is not quite true. We do know that the two cars were separated by zero distance and zero time when they collided. "Oh," you will say, "that is too utterly trivial to be worth mentioning." But it was precisely this that came to Einstein as a revelation. Space-time coordinates are mere labeling devices. Physics, of which the car collision is itself an instance, deals ultimately with coinciding events, and whatever the coordinates we use, coinciding events will show up as being indubitably coincident.

Once stated, this sounds obvious. But that is the beauty of it, as of many other of the profound insights that came to Einstein after long struggle. He was now able to continue along the road to his general theory of relativity. If all motion was to be relative, all sorts of distorted coordinate systems would apparently have to be tolerated, even if their relationship to direct measurement seemed next to impossible to specify. Einstein, for a mixture of reasons, concluded that he could play no favorites: the equations of physics would have to be expressed in a way that would place all space-time coordinate systems on an equal footing, a requirement that he later called *the principle of general covariance*.

In Prague he made little headway in applying this principle. He saw formidable mathematical problems ahead, and on his return to Zurich in 1912 he took what turned out to be precisely the right step to meet them: he sought expert help. In a letter of 29 October 1912 he wrote:

> . . . I occupy myself exclusively with the problem of gravitation and now believe that I will overcome all difficulties with the help of a friendly mathematician here. But this one thing is certain: that in all my life I have never before labored at all as hard, and that I have become imbued with a great respect for mathematics, the subtle parts of which, in my innocence, I had till now regarded as pure luxury. Compared with this problem, the original theory of relativity is child's play.

The mathematical helpmate referred to was none other than Einstein's staunch friend Marcel Grossmann, to whom once again in a time of need Einstein turned for help. As luck—or destiny —would have it, Grossmann's mathematical specialty precisely matched Einstein's needs, and without Grossmann's powerful mathematical aid Einstein would have been long delayed in bringing the general theory of relativity to fruition. Yet the collaboration must have been strange, since Grossmann, at heart a mathematician, had an outlook quite different from that of his physicist friend. This is nicely illustrated by an anecdote told by Einstein in "Reminiscences," written shortly before his death for a volume celebrating the hundredth anniversary of the founding of the Zurich Polytechnic. Speaking of student days, Einstein said:

> [Grossmann] once made a remark that is so charming and characteristic that I cannot resist quoting it here: "I concede [said Grossmann] that I did after all gain something rather important from the study of physics. Before, when I sat on a chair and felt the trace of heat left by my 'pre-sitter' I used to shudder a little. That is completely gone, for on this point physics has taught me that heat is something completely impersonal."

We recall that the mathematical problem confronting Einstein had been to write equations conforming to the principle of general covariance. Apparently a colleague in Prague told him that the appropriate mathematical tool already existed. But only in Zurich, with the lusty aid of Grossmann, does Einstein seem to have begun to wield it. For it was not a weapon easy to grasp. It is now called the *tensor calculus*, and it was mainly developed by the Italian mathematician Gregorio Ricci, who took the decisive step toward it in 1887—the year of the Michelson-Morley experiment and of the discovery of the photoelectric effect.

Since tensor equations play no favorites among coordinate systems, they were precisely what Einstein needed. With them, and with Grossmann's help, he was now able to carry out his plan of campaign for discovering the mathematical entity with which to represent gravitation. He started with the straight world lines in space-time. By noting the mathematical effect of transferring to Aclab, he had already concluded that the speed of light was not constant but was linked to gravitation. He now wrote the corresponding equations for free particles when c was not constant, thus incorporating a primitive form of the gravitational theory

Marcel Grossmann, 1920.

that he was seeking. And then, by going over to quite general distorted coordinates, he was led directly to a tensor of major geometrical importance. It is called the *metrical tensor*.

A two-dimensional example will indicate its role. On the two-dimensional surface of a smooth ocean we customarily specify location by means of coordinates that we call longitude and latitude. Let a boat make a small journey, and suppose that we know its initial and final latitudes and longitudes. If the boat took the shortest route, we can directly calculate by simple algebra the actual distance it traveled over the surface, even though neither the change in longitude nor the change in latitude is a distance. What enables us to convert these combined small changes of coordinates directly into the distance traveled is the metrical tensor belonging to the two-dimensional surface. In 1827, long before the advent of the idea of tensors, the great German mathematician Karl Gauss, in Göttingen, had shown that this metrical tensor contains deeper geometrical information. If we perform on it a rather complicated mathematical operation, it tells us, in this case, that we are on a surface curved like part of a sphere rather than, say, one curved like part of a saddle or flat like part of a plane. And, what is particularly important, it tells us this in an intrinsic way, without any reference at all to anything outside the surface.

If Einstein's intuition was not leading him astray, if his still-untested principle of equivalence was worthy of trust, then the metrical tensor of four-dimensional space-time, the tensor that links its coordinates with measurements, would have to be the entity that represents gravitation. From this there emerged the profound conclusion that gravitation must be something fundamentally geometrical.

Because of the metrical tensor's newly acquired gravitational role, Einstein and Grossmann denoted it by the letter g; and since the tensor calculus required that it have two subscripts, they wrote it $g_{\mu\nu}$. When Einstein decided to use $g_{\mu\nu}$ to represent gravitation, he took a gigantic step. For, as we recall, Newton's theory of gravitation could be expressed by a single field equation for a single gravitational potential. But the tensor notation is a compact one, and in four dimensions the innocent-looking symbol $g_{\mu\nu}$ stands for ten mathematical quantities. The dramatic jump from one gravitational potential to ten was daring in the extreme. And for his boldness Einstein was now faced with the task of finding ten corresponding gravitational field equations.

In 1913 he and Grossmann published a ground-breaking dual paper on their researches, the physical part being by Einstein and the mathematical part by Grossmann. In 1914 they jointly published a further paper. In retrospect it is heartbreaking to see how close the collaborators came to achieving their goal. Practically all the needed mathematical ingredients were there, and, as Einstein remarked later, he and Grossmann had considered the actual field equations only to discard them for what at the time seemed compelling reasons. Indeed, because the enormously complex problems of physical interpretation were not yet resolved in Einstein's mind, he believed he had proved that having all coordinate systems on an equal footing would conflict with the idea of causality. At a key place in their first paper the collaborators made a major aesthetic retreat: they did not even allow changes of coordinates that could be regarded as linked to acceleration.

This worried them, and in their second paper they made a partial recovery, but their equations still did not conform to the principle of general covariance. Later Einstein was to say that he had abandoned the principle of general covariance "only with a heavy heart."

When Einstein left Zurich for Berlin in 1914 the collaboration effectively came to an end, its mission unfulfilled. The importance of the collaboration was inestimable nevertheless, for Grossmann had provided Einstein with ample specialized mathematical equipment for his lonely continuing struggle in Berlin.

We cannot tell here of all the problems that Einstein overcame. It took him two years of misguided labor before he realized, among other things, that there was no physical objection to treating all coordinate systems on an equal footing—that the principle of general covariance did not, after all, conflict with causality. From then on, progress was swift. Everything fell beautifully into place, and by 1915 Einstein had found the gravitational field equations he sought. His theory, once found, was of majestic simplicity. Gravitation was not treated as a force but as an intrinsic curvature of space-time. Small bodies such as the planets moved in orbits around the sun not because the sun attracted them but because in the curved space-time around the sun there simply were no straight world lines. A straight line can be defined as the shortest distance between two points. In curved space-time the motions of the planets were represented by *geodesics*—the analogues of shortest distances.* Thus the planets, like free particles, obeyed Newton's first law, the law of inertia— to the extent that this was possible in a curved space-time. Two diagrams will be of help. The first indicates in terms of a two-dimensional surface the sort of three-dimensional gravitational curvature of the space around the sun; the curvature is highly exaggerated. Because of the curvature, a planet at P seeking to move laterally in a straight line will be unable to do so and will follow some such path as that indicated by PQ. From this we can see, in a way, how it could come about that a planet would orbit the sun.

---

* Because of a quirk of space-time, it would be mathematically more appropriate, but in other ways more confusing, to say "longest" rather than "shortest" here.

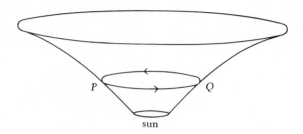

sun

The trouble with this diagram, though, is that it shows neither time nor the curvature of time. And although in one sense it is mathematically correct, in another it is quite false. For the principal contributor to the planetary motion is not the curvature of space but a curvature of time that, as it turns out, can be linked with the varying speed of light in a gravitational field. This striking throwback to Einstein's early idea of treating the speed of light as the gravitational potential is further testimony to the power of his intuition. The curvature of time cannot easily be illustrated diagrammatically. Without indicating it, let us nevertheless draw a second diagram (page 122) that includes time as a dimension pointing upward on the page. The double line represents the sun enduring in time—the sun's world line. The helical line represents the world line of a planet, a geodesic in the curved space-time associated with the sun. Imagine ourselves on a platform representing our "now." Since our "now" moves into the future, the platform will rise in the diagram— remember, we are representing time as an upward-pointing dimension. As the platform rises, the helix will cross it at successive points that will seem on the platform like a single point in orbit around the sun.

Each of these diagrams is admittedly imperfect. Yet each in its fashion gives an indication of what is going on, and if, in a loose way, we keep both in mind we obtain not too bad a picture of the Einsteinian state of affairs.

What of Einstein's gravitational field equations that govern the

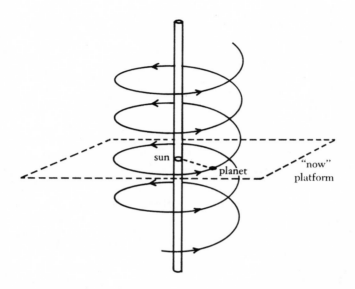

space-time curvature? There are ten of them, and they are enormously complicated. If written out in full instead of in the compact tensor notation, they would fill a huge book with intricate symbols. And there is something about them that is intensely beautiful and almost miraculous.

It may seem ridiculous to talk about beauty and near miracle after implying that the equations are ugly and cumbersome. Let us therefore ask a question. How did Einstein manage to find the equations? Could he have guessed the various terms—hundreds of thousands of them, or in one form millions, and all of them highly unpleasant? Impossible. Then how did he find them? That is where the beauty and near miracle come in. For the tensor calculus contained stringent rules. Einstein imposed, for physical reasons, a few almost trifling conditions that, for the most part, had the effect of a request for simplicity. And when, having done so, he sought ten tensor equations in which gravitation would be represented *solely* by the ten quantities $g_{\mu\nu}$, he found that his hands were tied. Because of his insistence on simplicity, the tensor calculus gave him no choice. The field equations were determined *uniquely*. In the tensor notation these equations are compact.

Einstein lecturing in Pasadena, ca. 1930. On the blackboard is
$R_{ik} = 0$, a tensor form of his ten field equations for pure gravitation.

Their power and their utter naturalness in both form and content
give them an indescribable beauty. Suppose someone had actually
written them out in full, term by term. A single misprint in the
bookful of terms, a ½ omitted or a 3 written instead of a 2, and the
equations would not satisfy the condition of general covariance.

We begin—but only begin—to see here the true stature of Einstein's intuition. What were the seeds that gave rise to this won-
derfully unique structure? Such things as Newton's theory and
the special theory of relativity of course, and Minkowski's idea of
a four-dimensional world, and Mach's powerful criticisms of New-

ton's theory. Also the mathematical framework already prepared, of which we shall tell more later. But after that what? The principle of equivalence, the principle of general covariance, and— why, essentially nothing else. By what magical clairvoyance did Einstein choose just these two principles to be his guide long before he knew where they would lead him? That they should have led him to unique equations of so complex yet simple a sort is in itself astounding. But once obtained, were the equations worth having? This could quickly be put to the test. The motion of the planet Mercury did not conform to the Newtonian prediction. Its *perihelion*, the point of its orbit nearest the sun, was observed to advance by just under 5600 seconds of arc per century, and, although most of this could be accounted for, one way or another, on Newtonian grounds, a residual increase of somewhere between 40 and 50° seconds of arc per century remained unexplained.

In 1915 Einstein showed that his new theory provided an additional perihelion advance for Mercury of approximately 43 seconds of arc per century. This dazzling result, announced to the Royal Prussian Academy of Sciences and published in its *Proceedings*, was a momentous climax to years of inspired, drudging labor concerning which Einstein said:

> In the light of knowledge attained, the happy achievement seems almost a matter of course, and any intelligent student can grasp it without too much trouble. But the years of anxious searching in the dark, with their intense longing, their alternations of confidence and exhaustion, and the final emergence into the light—only those who have themselves experienced it can understand that.

In the calculation of the motion of the perihelion of Mercury there was no room for fakery. There was nothing arbitrary that could be specially adjusted to fit the fact. There was no leeway for maneuver. If the result had not come out, of its own accord, to be close to 43—*and*, mark you, in the forward direction—the theory would have failed.

To his cherished friend Paul Ehrenfest in Holland Einstein wrote in January 1916: "Imagine my joy at the feasibility of the

* Recent, more refined estimates yield a probable range between about 41.5 and 43.5.

general covariance and at the result that the equations yield the
correct perihelion motion of Mercury. I was beside myself with
ecstasy for days."

We recall Einstein's remark that he had become imbued with
a great respect for mathematics. This was not just because of the
tensor calculus. The mathematicians, with their own special brand
of clairvoyance, had prepared the way for him even better than
he realized at the time. The general theory of relativity ran
counter to the beautiful Euclidean structure in the "holy geometry
booklet" that had enchanted Einstein in his youth; and central
to the theory was a denial of the strict validity of the Pythagorean
theorem, for which as a youth he had found a proof on his own.

Einstein, 1916.

Not the least of the coincidences linking Einstein and Grossmann is that Grossmann's doctoral thesis was on the topic of non-Euclidean geometry. This phrase alone is an indication that the mathematicians had not been idle. To most students of elementary geometry, a viable alternative to the Euclidean system would seem impossible. Indeed, the philosopher Kant had declared the Euclidean system inescapable and a necessity of human thought. But starting around the beginning of the nineteenth century, after an incubation period stretching back to Euclid, daring mathematicians actually produced non-Euclidean alternatives and, as Gauss realized, once Euclid had competitors, geometry necessarily became an experimental science.

Of particular interest for us is the work of the German mathematician Bernhard Riemann in Göttingen, starting in 1854. Building on the pioneering work of the Hungarian Wolfgang Bolyai, the Russian Nikolai Lobachevski, and Gauss, he conceived a quite general type of geometry that is to the geometry of Euclid what a mountainous terrain is to a plateau. While this difference can be visualized for surfaces, Riemann's daring extension of it to three and more dimensions defies visualization and can only be handled mathematically. It was this multidimensional, irregularly curved Riemannian geometry that Einstein found awaiting his needs.

Furthermore, as we recall, Gauss found a complicated mathematical procedure by which to extract from a two-dimensional metrical tensor information about the intrinsic curvature of the surface to which it belonged. Riemann, and independently Elwin Christoffel, extended this to the multidimensional case. In so doing they discovered, before the advent of the tensor calculus, a powerful mathematical quantity that is nowadays variously referred to as the Riemann-Christoffel or curvature tensor. It is built solely out of the metrical tensor, and within it are the key ingredients of Einstein's uniquely determined field equations of gravitation. Moreover, Riemann and later the English mathematician William Clifford were thought almost to have taken leave of their senses when they ventured to suggest that matter might be just curvature of space. As for Christoffel, it is not without interest that in the 1860s, when he independently found the curvature tensor, he was a professor at the Zurich Polytechnic.

What if Riemann had known of space-time? Would he have thought of matter as a curvature of a four-dimensional rather than a three-dimensional world? The answer is almost certainly yes. Would he, then, have constructed the Einsteinian theory of gravitation? It is tempting, after the event, to say yes. But the odds are enormously against it. For the path to Einstein's theory was not merely physical rather than mathematical, but in a highly characteristic way intuitive rather than physical. Unless we realize this, we cannot properly appreciate Einstein's achievement, for there was no logical path toward it. He built, as we know, on the principle of equivalence and the principle of general covariance. But he wavered so in his statements about the principle of equivalence that there are experts who, while recognizing its power, become positively angry in debate about what precisely he had in mind. And as for the principle of general covariance, Einstein's belief that it expressed the relativity of all motion was erroneous.° Worse, as was quickly pointed out, the principle of general covariance is, in a sense, devoid of content since practically *any* physical theory expressible mathematically can be put into tensor form—and this includes not only the special theory of relativity but also the Newtonian theory.

Conceding this, Einstein argued that the principle nevertheless had content if one asked for the simplest and most beautiful tensor equations to fit the occasion. And in fact Einstein's masterstroke of requiring that gravitation be represented *solely* by the ten $g_{\mu\nu}$ did indeed give the principle of general covariance powerful content—for an Einstein.

Yet when we see how shaky were the ostensible foundations on which Einstein built his theory, we can only marvel at the intuition that guided him to his masterpiece. Such intuition is the essence of genius. Were not the foundations of Newton's theory also shaky? And does that lessen his achievement? And did not Maxwell build on a wild mechanical model that he himself found unbelievable? By a sort of divination genius knows from the start in a nebulous way the goal toward which it must strive. In the

° This belief was based on a confusion between, among other things, coordinate systems and reference frames—a confusion that, in our narrative, we have deliberately done nothing to diminish. The problems with which Einstein had to contend were formidably subtle.

painful journey through uncharted country it bolsters its confidence by plausible arguments that serve a Freudian rather than a logical purpose. These arguments do not have to be sound so long as they serve the irrational, clairvoyant, subconscious drive that is really in command. Indeed, we should not expect them to be sound in the sterile logical sense, since a man creating a scientific revolution has to build on the very ideas that he is in the process of replacing. For example—and this will come as a shock—in the general theory of relativity it does not seem possible to give unequivocal definitions of mass and energy.

Einstein's theory came in the midst of a darkening war that either side could desperately win, or desperately lose. Yet almost at once it caused ripples of interest that spread beyond the small scientific circle to which it was addressed. In 1916 a German publisher asked Einstein to write a popular explanation of his theory. The book appeared in 1917. Using only elementary mathematics, Einstein succeeded in compressing the explanation into seventy lucid and charming pages; and if they were still none too easy for the layman, Einstein is not the one to blame—unless it be for having created so formidably difficult a theory in the first place. Because paper was scarce in wartime Germany, the edition was small. But the book evidently filled a need. By May 1918, with Germany hard-pressed, blockaded, and starving, the publisher was already contemplating a third printing. None too hopefully, he requested paper for as many as three thousand copies, and the German government made the paper available.

The inherent beauty of the general theory of relativity and the unforced emergence of Mercury's perihelion motion were proof enough for Einstein that his intuition had been sound. In telling of the perihelion result in his popular book on the theory, he said of the gravitational red shift and the bending of light, "I do not doubt that these deductions from the theory will be confirmed also"; and to friends he confided his confidence in the theory. He did not wait for further confirmation but went on at once to bold new developments. In 1916, and again in 1917, the year that saw the revolution in Russia and the later seizure of power by the Communists, he made two major scientific advances—the second one relativistic, the first one not. But rather than interrupt our story, let us hold them both in abeyance.

The Mercury result did not provide a *prediction:* the Newtonian discrepancy had already been known. There were, however, still two predictions of the general theory of relativity—the gravitational red shift and the deflection of light—whose verification would help to convince other scientists. It is remarkable that the red shift that Einstein had deduced from his primitive principle of equivalence had essentially the same value as the one that he now deduced from his full-blown general theory of relativity. More important is the fact that the deflection of light according to the new theory came to *double* its former value. For rays of starlight grazing the sun Einstein now predicted a deflection of 1.7 seconds of arc.

The war had distorted the international character of science. There was no longer free passage of scientific information between the warring countries. But Holland's neutrality had not been violated, and the Dutch astronomer Willem de Sitter in Leiden was in touch with his English confrère Arthur Eddington, who was a Quaker. In 1916 de Sitter sent Eddington in Cambridge a copy of a difficult paper of Einstein's explaining the general theory of relativity. Eddington was enchanted. In a detailed official report he said, "Whether the theory ultimately proves to be correct or not, it claims attention as being one of the most beautiful examples of the power of general mathematical reasoning."

In the midst of war Eddington and Frank Dyson, the British Astronomer Royal, made plans, with government support, for two expeditions, one to the village of Sobral in Brazil and the other to the tiny Portuguese island of Principe off the west coast of Africa. On 29 May 1919, as Dyson had pointed out, a particularly favorable total eclipse of the sun was to occur in those places, and the purpose of the expeditions was to test Einstein's theory, perfected in enemy Berlin.

Despite bad weather in Principe—in his official report Eddington wrote, "from [10 May] on no rain fell, except on the morning of the eclipse"—some of the photographs that Eddington and his assistant took through their telescope had stars showing amid the clouds. Eagerly Eddington made tentative micrometer measurements on the best of the photographs and to his delight found that they favored the new theory. Later he said that this was the greatest moment of his life.

Introductory paragraph of the original manuscript, now at the Hebrew University in Jerusalem, of Einstein's paper of 1915 *The Foundations of the General Theory of Relativity*. Einstein tells, among other things, of his indebtedness to the work of Minkowski, and thanks Grossmann for sparing him the task of unearthing the relevant mathematical literature and for helping in the search for the field equations of gravitation. (When key papers were reprinted in a source book, *The Principle of Relativity*, this paragraph was unfortunately omitted.)

Much work remained to be done in England before the eclipse data from Principe and Sobral could be fully evaluated. Although fighting had stopped, the war was still technically on. Direct communication between England and Germany was virtually impossible, and indirect communication was apt to be delayed. By early

September rumors had reached Einstein that the eclipse results were favorable, and on 22 September 1919 Lorentz sent him a telegram, evidently delayed in passage, confirming this, to which Einstein replied by telegram, "Heartfelt thanks to you and Eddington. Greetings." Thus on 27 September Einstein had the unique pleasure of sending his ailing mother in Switzerland a postcard saying, "Dear Mother, Good news today. H. A. Lorentz has wired me that the British expeditions have actually proved the light deflection near the sun. . . ."

But the news was still not official. On 6 November 1919 there was held in London a historic joint meeting of the Royal Society

Postcard from Einstein to his mother telling of the eclipse results, 1919.

and the Royal Astronomical Society. In 1703, more than two centuries earlier, Newton had been elected President of the Royal Society, and annually thereafter he had been re-elected till his death more than twenty years later. Now, in 1919, he was vividly present in the minds of the assembled scientists. His portrait, in its honored place on the wall, dominated the scene. Yet though he faced the audience, his eyes were turned sharply to the right in contemplation of far-off mysteries as Joseph John Thomson, discoverer of the electron, Nobel laureate, and President of the Royal Society, publicly hailed Einstein's work as "one of the greatest—perhaps the greatest—of achievements in the history of human thought," and the Astronomer Royal reported officially, for all the world to hear, that the results of the eclipse expeditions favored Einstein over Newton.

The drama of the occasion was undoubtedly heightened by the war that had just ended. Suppose the war had not come, and

Eddington and Einstein, 1930.

Finlay-Freundlich had been able to observe the 1914 eclipse, finding a deflection of 1.7 seconds of arc at a time when Einstein was predicting a deflection of only 0.83 seconds of arc. Or that in America Hale and his astronomer friends, without having to wait for an eclipse, had quickly been able to find that the deflection was double this predicted value. Imagine how tame Einstein's 1915 calculation of 1.7 would then have seemed. He would have been belatedly changing the value after the event, having first been shown to have been wrong. People would have felt that he had made an arbitrary *ad hoc* adjustment—which in fact he had not—and the deflection of light would have lost the tremendous impact that it had as a prediction.

But the war had occurred, and the predicted deflection had been confirmed under circumstances of high drama, at a time when nations were war-weary and heartsick. The bent rays of starlight had illumined a world in shadow, revealing a unity of man that transcended war. The English newspapers, while not straining themselves to link Einstein with Germany, enthusiastically carried the momentous news, which rapidly spread abroad. Writing to Einstein from England in December 1919, Eddington said:

> . . . all England has been talking about your theory. It has made a tremendous sensation. . . . It is the best possible thing that could have happened for scientific relations between England and Germany.

Fate had played its unexpected trick. The faintly deflected starlight had dazzled the public, and suddenly Einstein was world-famous. This essentially simple man, a cloistered seeker after cosmic beauty, was now a world symbol, a focus of widespread adoration—and of deep-rooted hatreds.

9

From Principe
to Princeton

The popular acclaim was as puzzling to Einstein as his theory was to the layman. Sales of his little book skyrocketed, and translations quickly appeared. In England the publisher begged the English translator to write a brief explanatory statement for use by the salesmen, who had found great ignorance in the public mind as to what relativity meant, many people seeming to think it had to do with the relations between the sexes.

On 11 February 1919 Einstein's marriage ended in amicable divorce, Mileva receiving custody of the children, and Einstein providing the support of all three. Einstein also agreed to give Mileva his Nobel Prize money. Admittedly, he had not yet been awarded the Prize, but both were sure he would someday receive it.

In Berlin, in the war years, he had often stayed with his father's cousin, Rudolf Einstein, whose wife was the sister of Einstein's mother. Their daughter Elsa was thus a double cousin, and she and Albert had played together as children in Munich. Widowed, she had lived in her father's house with her two daughters, Ilse and Margot. In 1917, when Einstein had a serious gastric illness, she nursed him back to health. There had always been a strong bond between them, and in June 1919 they were married. She looked after him as if he were an unworldly child, which indeed

in some respects he was, and she sheltered him from the irritating
minor intrusions of the world. But no one could shield him from
life's deeper sorrows. His mother was in the terminal stages of
cancer. Late in 1919 she came with a nurse to Berlin to spend
her last, pain-racked days with her son. She died there in February 1920, and Einstein was desolate. Early in March, in a letter
to Max Born, who had asked his advice about uprooting himself
to accept a professorship at Göttingen, Einstein wrote:

> . . . it is not so important where one settles. . . . Besides, as a man
> without roots anywhere, I do not feel qualified to offer advice. My
> father's ashes lie in Milan. I buried my mother here a few days
> ago. I myself have wandered continually hither and yon—a
> stranger everywhere. My children are in Switzerland under cir-
> cumstances that make it a troublesome undertaking for me when I
> want to see them. The ideal of a man such as I am is to be *at home*
> anywhere with his near and dear ones. He has no right to advise
> you in this matter.

There are echoes here of an earlier letter. In 1919, just before
the official announcement of the eclipse results, Einstein, on a
scientific visit to Holland, had spent happy days with Ehrenfest
and his family. Thanking him afterwards, Einstein wrote, "We
will keep in close personal contact with each other from now on.
I know that it is good for both of us, and that each of us feels
less of a stranger in this world because of the other."

Einstein's world fame brought obligations that his conscience
would not let him shirk. He was in a unique position to help heal
some of the rifts between nations. The war had been bitterly
fought, and when the fighting stopped passions still ran high—
among victor as well as vanquished. For example, in December
1919 the Royal Astronomical Society in England decided to award
Einstein its 1920 Gold Medal, but "patriotic" members mustered
enough votes to defeat ratification, with the result that no medal
was awarded that year. Not till 1926 was the Royal Astronomical
Society able to award its Gold Medal to Einstein.

In 1918 the Kaiser abdicated the throne and a republican government came into power in Germany. In Einstein's notes for his
weekly lectures on relativity for the winter term 1918–19, one

Page of Einstein's lecture notes, Berlin, 1918, containing for the date "9.XI" (9 November) the words *"fiel aus wegen Revolution"* ("canceled because of revolution").

finds no scientific topic listed for 9 November. Instead there appear for that date the words "canceled because of revolution." Behind this laconic remark were turbulent events in which, in a peripheral way, Einstein himself was directly involved. For during the week, student revolutionaries at Berlin University declared the Rector deposed and held him captive. Einstein, because of his stature and his socialistic leanings, was asked to intervene, and with two friends, Born and the psychologist Max Wertheimer, went before the rebel student leaders. He was asked his views. Not being one to put things fawningly when a matter of principle was at stake, he spoke sternly about the dangers to academic free-

This appropriate photomontage of Wertheimer, Einstein, and Born
was not intended as a memento of their intervention on behalf of
the Rector of Berlin University. Actually it was sent to Einstein
by the Borns as a postcard on 28 July 1918, months before
that event. (Responding to the card on 2 August 1918, Einstein
spoke of the picture as "the clover leaf"; some fifty years later,
Born—when telling, among other things, of the incident of the
Rector—did not recall the existence of the picture and could not
explain what "the clover leaf" referred to.)

dom, and his words were not at all to the rebels' liking. However,
they referred him and his friends to the new President of Germany, and even amid the revolutionary chaos the name Einstein
opened all doors. The President himself interrupted urgent matters of state long enough to write a brief memo, and the matter
was then quickly settled.

The revolution meant much more to Einstein than would appear
from the minor ripple in the even tenor of his lecture notes. He
rejoiced at the downfall of the Prussian militarists. Although defeated Germany was stunned and disheartened, and starving
because of the continuing Allied blockade, Einstein now held
high hopes for Germany's future. He felt that the situation called
for a gesture of sympathy and encouragement to the new German
Republic. So, while retaining his precious Swiss citizenship, he
became a German citizen, though not without misgivings. And
when Zangger and others tried to bring him back to Zurich University, and Ehrenfest, Kamerlingh-Onnes, and Lorentz to bring

Einstein, Ehrenfest, Langevin, Kamerlingh-Onnes, and Weiss in Leiden, ca. 1920.

him to Leiden with a most attractive offer, he gently declined. For he knew that he was now a symbol. In September 1919 he wrote to Ehrenfest, saying:

> . . . I promised [Planck] not to turn my back on Berlin unless conditions were such that he would regard such a step as natural and proper. . . . It would be doubly base of me if, just when my political hopes are being realized, I were to walk out unnecessarily, and perhaps *in part* for my material advantage, on the very people who have surrounded me with love and friendship, and to whom my departure would be doubly painful at this time of supposed

humiliation. . . . (I feel like some relic in an old cathedral—one doesn't quite know what to do with the old bones. . . .)

Einstein did however accept a visiting professorship at Leiden for a few weeks each year while remaining in his permanent position in Berlin.

At the request of *The Times* of London, he wrote an article about relativity that was published on 28 November 1919. It contained these healing words:

> After the lamentable breakdown of the old active intercourse between men of learning, I welcome this opportunity of expressing my feelings of joy and gratitude towards the astronomers and physicists of England. It is thoroughly in keeping with the great and proud traditions of scientific work in your country that eminent scientists should have spent time and trouble, and your scientific institutions have spared no expense, to test the implications of a theory which was perfected and published during the war in the land of your enemies. . . . Let no one suppose, however, that the mighty work of Newton can really be superseded by [relativity] or any other theory. His great and lucid ideas will retain their unique significance for all time as the foundation of our whole modern conceptual structure in the sphere of natural philosophy.

At the end of the article Einstein added this wry comment:

> *Note:* Some of the statements in your paper concerning my life and person owe their origin to the lively imagination of the writer. Here is yet another application of the principle of relativity for the delectation of the reader: today I am described in Germany as a "German savant," and in England as a "Swiss Jew." Should it ever be my fate to be represented as a *bête noire,* I should, on the contrary, become a "Swiss Jew" for the Germans and a "German savant" for the English.

Einstein's words about Newton came from the heart. They were not an exercise in diplomacy, an art at which Einstein, with his instinctive honesty, did not always excel. Among Einstein's papers was found the following undated quatrain, written perhaps in

NEWTON

1942, when the three-hundredth anniversary of Newton's birth was being celebrated with much ceremony and speech-making. Apparently Einstein wrote it not for publication but to give vent to his private feelings:

> Seht die Sterne, die da lehren
> Wie man soll den Meister ehren
> Jeder folgt nach Newtons Plan
> Ewig schweigend seiner Bahn.

It almost defies translation. Here is an indication of its tenor:

> Look to the Heavens, and learn from them
> How one should really honor the Master.
> The stars in their courses extol Newton's laws—
> In silence eternal.

It is now appropriate to look at a document written by the German chargé d'affaires in London some nine months after the appearance there of Einstein's article in *The Times*. On 9 September 1920 the chargé d'affaires reported to the German Foreign Ministry:

The English newspapers have published the violent [verbal] attacks [in Germany] upon the noted physicist Professor Einstein. Today's *Morning Post*° even carries a report that Professor Einstein intends to leave Germany and to go to America. Although, as is well known in England, a prophet is not without honor except in his own country, nevertheless the [verbal] attacks on Professor Einstein [in Germany], and the campaign [there] against the noted [English] scholars . . . leave a very bad impression [here in England]. Particularly at this time, Professor Einstein counts as a cultural factor of the first rank for Germany, since his name is known far and wide. We should not drive such a man out of Germany; we could use him for effective *Kultur* propaganda. If Professor Einstein should really be intending to leave Germany, I should deem it desirable in the interests of Germany's reputation abroad, if the famous savant could be persuaded to remain in Germany.

° In those days an influential Conservative newspaper.

Seht die Sterne, die da lehren
wie man soll den Meister ehren.
Jeder folgt nach Newtons Plan
Ewig schweigend seiner Bahn.

Holograph of Einstein's quatrain about Newton. The minor correction suggests that the quatrain came to Einstein in a flash in essentially final form.

Calculations on the torn sheet on the other side of which Einstein wrote the quatrain about Newton.

Clearly something had happened in Germany. Einstein was indeed under attack there. He had always been sharply outspoken against German militarism, and neither his pacifism nor his socialistic leanings nor his being a Jew—nor his fame—endeared him to the zealots of German nationalism. Desperately needing an excuse for the defeat of Germany, they blamed the pacifists and the Jews. Ugly incidents began to occur. In 1920 a well-financed anti-Semitic campaign was organized in Germany to vilify Einstein and attack his theory of relativity, which was variously described as Jewish and Communist, and as poisoning the wellsprings of pure German science. The organizers spent money prodigally. On 25 August they held a well-advertised mass meeting against relativity in the Berlin Philharmonic Hall, and German newspapers were quick to take up the anti-relativity campaign. Outraged by the meeting, Laue, Nernst, and Rubens tried to combat its irrationality by issuing a joint statement to the press. In it they deplored the personal attacks on Einstein, defended relativity, and pointed out that quite apart from that theory Einstein was an outstanding physicist. And the usually equable Einstein, who had also attended the meeting as a spectator, felt himself goaded into writing a none-too-felicitous public response. The English newspapers had not been exaggerating when, to the dismay of the German chargé d'affaires, they reported the attacks on Einstein.

Professor Lenard now re-enters our story. He had won the Nobel Prize in 1905, the very year in which Einstein had made penetrating use of Lenard's earlier experimental observations of the photoelectric effect. Lenard's regard for Einstein had bordered on idolatry. In 1909, for example, he had written effusively to Einstein, referring to him as a "deep and far-reaching thinker" and confessing that a letter that Einstein had written to him in 1905 had since then always been kept on his desk. But time and events changed Lenard. He became one of the most virulent disparagers of Einstein's works; and his attacks, when they came, were all the more formidable because of his stature as a scientist. He started his attack, together with others, at the Congress of German Scientists and Physicians in Bad Nauheim in 1920, at a session presided over by Planck. Lenard's attack had anti-Semitic overtones but Planck, forewarned, was able to prevent disaster, even though a sharp exchange took place between Lenard and Einstein. Lenard was to become an enthusiastic member of the Nazi Party, and his attacks grew in virulence over the years.

To the official Jewish Community in Berlin Einstein wrote in the fall of 1920 that he would not pay what he owed, saying, "Much as I feel myself a Jew, I feel far removed from the traditional religious forms." He offered instead to make a yearly voluntary contribution to the welfare department of the Community. On being reminded that, as with all religious groups in Germany, each Jew was by law a taxable member of his local Jewish Community, he replied, "Nobody can be compelled to join a religious community. Those times, thank God, are gone forever. I hereby declare once and for all that I do not intend to join . . . but shall remain unassociated with any official religious group." The argument dragged on till February 1924, when Einstein agreed to become a member, having at last realized that he could do so solely in the cultural and not the religious sense.

Meanwhile, with the rapid resurgence of overt anti-Semitism after the war, Einstein had begun to realize that the fame that had come to him brought with it a special responsibility toward the Jews. He could not stand idly by as their suffering and danger increased in Europe. Despite his outspoken aversion to nationalism, he came to feel strongly that he had to give support to Zionism, Theodor Herzl's impossible dream of a Jewish homeland that the war itself had incredibly brought close to actuality. The decision to support Jewish nationalism had not been an easy one for Einstein, but he looked on a Jewish homeland as fulfilling an essential psychological, cultural, and political need for the Jews, focusing their aspirations and giving them a new sense of unity. From England in March 1921 came word, through an intermediary, from Chaim Weizmann, the Zionist leader who was later to become the first President of Israel. Plans had been made for a Hebrew University in Jerusalem, and Weizmann wanted Einstein to join him in a fund-raising visit to America. This was not at all to Einstein's liking and he at once refused, saying that he was no orator and that the Zionists would just be using his name. But his sense of duty intervened and almost in the next breath he consented, even though he would have to miss the forthcoming Solvay Congress—the first since the war.

Einstein in academic procession to receive an honorary degree, Princeton, 1921.

No sooner did the news leak out that Einstein was coming to America than he was deluged with cabled invitations from presidents of academic institutions to lecture, and visit, and receive academic honors. Earlier in 1921 Einstein had lectured to enthusiastic audiences in Prague and Vienna, but neither of these cities was in a country that had been an enemy of Germany during the war. The visit to America marked a new stage in postwar relations. America had fought against Germany. Nevertheless the Americans received the Einsteins with a tumultuous enthusiasm that Einstein found astounding. On 2 April 1921, as the boat was docking, reporters beseiged him on shipboard. The Mayor of New York City gave him an official welcome as if he were an American war hero. President Harding invited him to the White House. And above all, the man in the street took Einstein to heart, captivated by his unpretentiousness. In academic circles he was welcomed warmly. Columbia University awarded him a medal, and Princeton University gave him an honorary degree. Four technical lectures that he gave there were proudly published in English translation by Princeton University Press as a book, *The Meaning of Relativity*, that was to run to six editions and is still being widely bought. At a reception in his honor at Princeton, when asked to comment on some dubious experiments that conflicted with both relativistic and prerelativistic concepts, he responded with a famous remark—a scientific credo—that was overheard by the American geometer, Professor Oswald Veblen, who must have jotted it down. Years later, in 1930, when Princeton University constructed a special building for mathematics, Veblen requested and received Einstein's permission to have the remark inscribed in marble above the fireplace of the faculty lounge. It was engraved there in the original German: "Raffiniert ist der Herrgott, aber boshaft ist er nicht," which may be translated "God is subtle, but he is not malicious." In his reply to Veblen, Einstein explained that he meant that Nature conceals her secrets by her sublimity and not by trickery.

Einstein and Weizmann
on their arrival in the
United States, 1921.

University of London, King's College.

A PUBLIC LECTURE

WILL BE GIVEN ON

THURSDAY, JUNE 9th, at 5.15 p.m.

By PROFESSOR EINSTEIN

ON

"The Development and Present Position of the Theory of Relativity"

Chairman : VISCOUNT HALDANE.

Tickets of Admission   -   -   -   £s 5/-

The Proceeds of the Lecture will be devoted to the Imperial War Relief Fund.

The Lecture will be delivered in German.

ADMIT ONE

Ticket of admission to Einstein's lecture at King's College, University of London, 1921. Note the changed date, the increased price, the announcement that the proceeds would go to the Imperial War Relief Fund, and the warning that the lecture would be given in German.

As for the 1921 fund-raising, Einstein's presence on the platform was everywhere an outstanding asset, and Weizmann and Einstein were able to raise millions of dollars for the Jewish National Fund. As Einstein said in 1921 on returning to Berlin: "Thanks to the untiring energy and splendid self-sacrificing spirit of the Jewish doctors in America, we have succeeded in collecting enough money for the creation of a Medical Faculty, and the preliminary work is being started at once."

The visit to America with Weizmann made a profound impression on Einstein. It reinforced his sense of being a Jew, and confirmed him in his support of Zionism, his open espousal of which embarrassed and alarmed many German Jews who were pinning their hopes on assimilation.

On his way back from America he stopped briefly in England, where he had been invited to lecture at the University of Manchester and at King's College of London University. Feelings in England against Germany still ran high, and no one could tell beforehand what might happen at Einstein's lecture. Einstein spoke in German, the still-hated enemy tongue—and his lectures were received enthusiastically. By the sheer force of his personality, by his naturalness, his simplicity, his humor, his mastery of his subject, and the indefinable aura of greatness that no diffidence of his could hide, he captivated his audiences. All during his stay he was treated as a veritable hero of the mind. Manchester University bestowed on him an honorary doctorate. In London the Einsteins stayed as honored guests in the home of the statesman and philosopher Viscount Haldane. There and elsewhere Einstein met many of Britain's notables. And all in all, as Haldane and Einstein both had hoped, the visit greatly furthered the cause of international reconciliation.

In June 1921 Einstein arrived back in Germany, where shortly thereafter a newly built astronomical observatory came to be called the Einstein Tower in his honor.

Among the scientists who came to Berlin in those days to study with Einstein was a young Hungarian, Leo Szilard, with whom Einstein patented a joint invention of a refrigerating mechanism. We shall be hearing further of Szilard.

In March 1922, largely through the efforts of Paul Langevin, who had to battle strong patriotic French opposition, Einstein lectured at the Collège de France in Paris. It says much for the

Einstein lecturing at the Collège de France, 1922.

strength of the lingering bitterness of the war that this was the earliest that Einstein could lecture in France, and then only with elaborate precautions that, in the event, may or may not have been unnecessary. As he recalled in a letter in 1943: "It was [Walther] Rathenau [the German Foreign Minister] who strongly advised me to accept [the] invitation to Paris, a gesture that was then still considered quite risky." In Paris, where Einstein met with French politicians as well as scholars, he felt that, by his visit, the cause of international reconciliation had once more been served. He had the additional pleasure of seeing his friend Solovine of the Olympia Academy days.

But in Germany something ugly was festering below the surface. On 24 June 1922 it erupted into violence when rightist activists assassinated Rathenau, who was both an internationalist and a Jew. Einstein, too, was an internationalist and a Jew; and in Germany, as in France, his visit to Paris had caused heightened resentment in some quarters. Even among his German scientific colleagues there was nationalist feeling against him. At meetings they hesitated to sit near him, some out of conviction, some out of fear of seeming to be friendly towards him.

The centennial meeting of the annual Congress of German Scientists and Physicians was due to be held in Leipzig in September with Einstein as keynote speaker. But on 5 July 1922 Einstein felt it necessary to write to Planck from Kiel to cancel the lecture, saying:

> . . . A number of people who deserve to be taken seriously have independently warned me not to stay in Berlin for the time being, and especially to avoid all public appearances in Germany. I am assumed to be among those whom the nationalists have marked for assassination. Of course, I have no definite proof but in the prevailing situation it seems quite plausible. If a really important cause were involved, I would not let myself be deterred by such reasons. But the present case involves only a simple formality, and someone (e.g., Laue) can easily take my place. The trouble is that the newspapers have mentioned my name too often, thus mobilizing the rabble against me. I have no alternative but to be patient—and to leave the city. I do urge you to take this little incident calmly, as I do myself. . . .

For a while Einstein heeded the warnings, remaining secluded in Berlin with his regular lectures canceled. But on 1 August he appeared openly at a major Berlin rally against war, and by this bold act he showed that he would not be intimidated, and thereby regained his freedom. Nevertheless he did not give the Leipzig keynote address.

In October 1922, at the invitation of a Japanese publisher, the Einsteins left for a visit to Japan, where they spent some six weeks. In a report to Berlin the German ambassador to Japan likened Einstein's visit to a triumphal procession. Wherever Einstein went enthusiastic crowds gathered spontaneously to catch a glimpse of him. He was received by the Empress. The newspapers vied with one another to report his activities in both factual and fictional detail. He was showered with honors and with all manner of gifts, and he himself was captivated by the picturesque charm of the Japanese. Years later—a tragic quarter-century later—he vividly recalled this visit to Japan, saying, "I loved the people and the country so much that I could not restrain my tears when I had to depart from them." The visit had been a most welcome respite from the tensions in Berlin that had followed the assassination of Rathenau. The German ambassador in Japan, while a little disturbed by Einstein's sometimes inappropriately casual clothes, was much attracted to him, reporting officially to Berlin that despite the outstanding honors bestowed on him Einstein remained modest, friendly, and unpretentious. Evidently Einstein was refreshingly different from other visiting celebrities with whom the ambassador had had to deal.

A few days before the boat bearing Einstein arrived in Japan, the news came that he had been awarded the 1921 Nobel Prize "for his services to theoretical physics and in particular for his discovery of the law of the photoelectric effect." Relativity was not specifically mentioned in the official citation. It was still regarded as too controversial, both scientifically and politically, for it was by no means easy to understand and it had been widely attacked. The daring photoelectric law, because of Millikan's experimental verification, had become an eminently safe reason for awarding Einstein the prize—and in itself an ample reason too.

When a recipient is unable to be present to accept the Nobel Prize in person, it is customary for his country's ambassador to

Einstein in Göteborg, Sweden, on the occasion of his visit there to give his Nobel lecture, July 1923. The fourth person from the left in the front row, sitting in a special chair, is King Gustav V of Sweden.

Sweden to accept it on his behalf. Einstein wanted to have the Swiss ambassador perform this function for him, but the Germans, aware of the honor involved, objected. In the end the problem was solved by a diplomatic maneuver that ended with the Swedish ambassador to Germany personally bringing the diploma and medal to Einstein in Berlin. When Einstein gave his delayed Nobel Prize Lecture in Sweden, he ignored the cautious wording of the citation and spoke on the theory of relativity.

Einstein continued his "triumphal procession" from Japan to Palestine, where his welcome by the Jews had a special quality deepened by the remembrance of tragic millennia. In Jerusalem, on Mount Scopus, the site of the future Hebrew University, he lectured in French and remarked in his travel diary, "I had to begin with a greeting in Hebrew, which I read with great difficulty." He was treated with reverence, being invited at his lecture to speak from "the lectern that has waited for you for two thousand years." He was deeply moved by the aspirations of the Jewish leaders. However, on seeing Jews swaying in anguished prayer at the Wailing Wall, the remnant of the vanished glory of Solomon and his Temple, he wrote in his diary, "Deplorable sight of people with a Past without a Present."

From Palestine he went to Spain, where, to use his own joking phrase, he continued to "whistle his relativity tune." He traveled by rail from Madrid to the French border in the royal coach, which the King had personally put at his disposal. But by the time the Einsteins reached French territory on their way back to Berlin, Einstein had lost all patience with the pomp and fuss that had surrounded his travels, and said to his wife, "*You* can do what you like, but as far as *I* am concerned I shall travel third class."

When they arrived home in the spring of 1923, Europe was showing signs of dangerous strain. The Fascists had seized power in Italy. Poincaré—not Henri the mathematician and physicist but his cousin Raymond, the Premier of France—had sent troops into the German industrial Ruhr to force Germany to pay defaulted war reparations. As a result, Germany was in the throes of a disastrous inflation that was to make the German mark valueless, wiping out the savings of the people and helping to pave the way for the ultimate advent of Nazism.

Yet in these and following years, Berlin was the center of a Golden Age of German art and science, and there, for the most part, Einstein remained. His love of music was well known. When the concert pianist Joseph Schwarz gave a Berlin recital with his son Boris, who was then a youthful violin prodigy, a politician who heard them sent them to Einstein, believing that Einstein would be interested in the young violinist. At the Einsteins' flat on the appointed day, accompanied at the piano by his father, Boris began the Bruch Concerto in G minor. When he reached a lyrical expressive passage in the first movement—one that Boris particularly enjoyed playing—Einstein suddenly burst out, "Ah! One can see that he loves the violin." And at the end of the concerto, Einstein delightedly brought out his own violin and the three of them played trio sonatas of Bach and Vivaldi. Thus began a lasting friendship enriched by many musical sessions.

It is interesting to hear the remarks of a professional violinist about Einstein's playing. Boris Schwarz described his tone as

Exterior of the Einsteins' apartment (indicated by Xs), Haberlandstrasse 5, Berlin. At right is a corner of the music room in the Berlin apartment.

very pure, with little vibrato, saying that Einstein did not like the sensuous, vibrant tone of the nineteenth century. This was in keeping with Einstein's musical preferences. He loved the eighteenth-century music of men like Bach, Vivaldi, and Mozart —especially Mozart. Beethoven, in his passionate C-minor mood, was already, in Einstein's view, too greatly overcharged emotionally. Boris Schwarz added that Einstein was a good sight reader who—and the words are quaintly apt—"played well in time." Einstein played, said Schwarz, with tremendous concentration, leaning forward with his face in the music. In the Berlin days he was a seemingly tireless violinist, ready to continue playing for hours. Indeed, Boris Schwarz tired long before Einstein, and, realizing this, Mrs. Einstein would come to the rescue by bringing in tea.

The Solvay Congresses, interrupted by the war, had been resumed in 1921, but Einstein had not attended because of his trip to America. In the fall of 1923, when plans were made for another Solvay Congress in Brussels, bitterness against Germany

Photograph of Joseph Schwarz, Boris Schwarz, and Einstein, autographed by Einstein. The couplet above the autograph reads:

> Dem Vater und dem Sohne
> Das Spielen war nicht ohne.

To catch something of the highly appreciative and comical effect of the informal double negative of the German, one should read the last two words of the following translation as an admiring, understated exclamation:

> To the father and his lad
> The playing was—not bad!

was still strong in Belgium, whose neutrality the Germans had violated nine years before. Learning that other German scientists would not be invited to Brussels, Einstein insisted, despite pleas of the organizers, that he too not receive an invitation, declaring that he would not attend a scientific congress from which other scientists were excluded simply because they were German.

As the years passed he became increasingly disillusioned about the League of Nations and the prospects of achieving peace through international accord. He realized that powerful forces were already locked in deadly battle and that they could not be deflected by mere debate. Nevertheless, as a member of the Committee on Intellectual Cooperation, under the auspices of the League of Nations, he worked hard with his colleagues of other lands, hoping against hope to achieve something tangible, however inadequate. Of this committee he wrote later, "Despite its illustrious membership, it was the most ineffectual enterprise with which I have been associated."

In 1928, while visiting Switzerland, he was taken ill with an acute heart condition and brought back to Berlin. There, after a few months, he was able to leave his sick bed, but his strength returned only slowly. As before, he gave strong support to the cause of pacifism. For example, in 1928 he wrote publicly:

> No one has the moral right to call himself a Christian or a Jew if he is prepared to commit murder upon the instruction of a given authority, or if he permits himself to be used for the purpose of initiating or preparing such a crime in any way whatsoever.

Nernst, Einstein, Planck, Millikan, and Laue in Berlin, 1931. All are Nobel laureates.

Courtesy of Mrs. Rudolf Ladenburg

Cartoon by Low, 1929.

And in February 1929, shortly before his fiftieth birthday, he was even more forthright and specific in the following statement:

> [In the event of war] I would unconditionally refuse all war service, direct or indirect, and I would seek to persuade my friends to adopt the same position, regardless of how I might feel about the causes of any particular war.

His fiftieth birthday, 14 March 1929, was a world event, and one from which he shrank. Realizing what was likely to happen, he went into hiding to escape the attentions of well-wishers and reporters. The occasion was not without its other bizarre aspects. For example, on the widely heralded day telegrams, cables, and other messages of congratulations poured in on the Berlin apartment from which Einstein had fled, but among the many callers was a minor tax official who bore no gifts: he wished to discuss Einstein's tax return. On being told that he had come on the great man's fiftieth birthday, he was overwhelmed with embarrassment and retired in confusion, offering profuse apologies for his gaucherie. The tax official's blushes must surely rank among the more spontaneous compliments paid to Einstein on that day.

Einstein receiving the Planck medal from Planck, 1929.

Lithograph of Einstein by Emil Orlik, 1928.

Holograph of couplet written by Einstein when asked to comment on the Orlik lithograph. After a false start, Einstein alludes to his girth in the lithograph, writing:

> Die Wissenschaft ist auch was wert.
> Kein Geiger ist so wohlgenährt.

Here is a translation:

> For science *something* can be said.
> No violinist is so well fed.

Again, it was well known that Einstein loved to relax by sailing on the Havel River and its lakes near Berlin, enjoying the warmth of sun and solitude as his mind roamed the universe. Wishing to do him honor, the officials of the City of Berlin voted to give him a birthday present of land and a house on the bank of the Havel. Alas, the house turned out to be occupied and unavailable. When two further attempts to redeem the promise hit other ludicrous snags, the officials asked Einstein to help them solve the problem by selecting a plot of land himself, which the city would then buy for him. Elsa Einstein found a delightful spot amid trees near the Havel in the village of Caputh just beyond Potsdam. The officials approved, and at last a happy ending seemed in sight. But the question of payment by the City of Berlin led to a political hassle that unfortunately began to take on anti-Einstein overtones. By now the birthday gesture had, shall we say, lost some of its luster, and Einstein put an end to the matter by formally declining the nonexistent gift. To fulfill agreements already made, he used his savings to pay for the promised land and the erection thereon of a summer house.

Though this depleted his savings, it nevertheless seemed a good investment. Einstein's notorious love of informality in dress and demeanor was far better suited to this idyllic setting than to the academic circles of Berlin, and the Einsteins spent happy summers in Caputh enjoying the river and the privacy.

They spent the winter of 1930–31, and also the following winter, in the United States, where Einstein was Visiting Professor at the California Institute of Technology in Pasadena, invited by Millikan, who was now its Director. Each spring Einstein returned to his duties in Berlin, and each summer to his retreat in Caputh. But meanwhile calamity had been making giant strides. In the fall of 1929 panic selling hit the New York stock market. It signaled the coming of a worldwide economic depression that was to be long and severe. Established men lost their jobs; young men could not find any. Misery and despair were everywhere, particularly in Germany, where they provided a fertile field for demagogues. Powerful German industrialists, fearing a Communist revolution, gave heavy financial support to the Nazis, whom they mistakenly hoped to control. In America, about this time, two Jewish philanthropists, Louis Bamberger and his sister Mrs. Felix

The Einsteins' house at Caputh.

Einstein's study at Caputh.

Einstein sailing at Caputh with his daughter and son-in-law, Ilse and Rudolf Kayser, ca. 1930.

Einstein at Caputh
on his way to his
sailboat, ca. 1930.

Einstein, his son Albert, and his grandson Bernhard, ca. 1930.

Einstein and his wife Elsa, Pasadena, 1931.

Michelson, Einstein, and Millikan, Pasadena, winter of 1930–31. In the middle of the back row is Walter Mayer, Einstein's collaborator.

Fuld, gave substantial financial support to the educational critic Abraham Flexner so that he could realize his dream of an Institute for Advanced Study. The Institute was conceived as a community of outstanding scholars, amply paid and with no formal duties, who would be able to devote their full energies to their work.

Partly because of the financial aid of the German industrialists, the Nazis gained rapidly in strength. By January 1933 Hitler had become the German Chancellor, and by 23 March he had ruthlessly attained dictatorial power. Freedom of speech, freedom itself—these were now little more than memories in Germany. Terror reigned in their stead.

Meanwhile, in the spring of 1932 Einstein, as on previous occasions, had gone to Oxford. There, as once before in Pasadena, Flexner came to him to discuss the contemplated Institute for Advanced Study. But now a daring thought entered Flexner's mind. Perhaps he could induce Einstein to become a member of the Institute. He ventured to broach the matter. In 1927 Einstein had declined an attractive offer from Veblen of a research professorship at Princeton University, saying that he believed he was too old to be transplanted. But now, foreseeing where Germany was headed, Einstein was inclined to be receptive to Flexner's suggestion, even though he did not wish to forsake his German colleagues.

In the summer Flexner came to Caputh to continue the discussion. Eager to obtain Einstein as his star faculty member, Flexner invited him to name his own salary. A few days later Einstein wrote to suggest what, in view of his needs and his fame, he thought was a reasonable figure. Flexner was dismayed. By American standards it was far too small. He could not possibly recruit outstanding American scholars at such a salary, and to Flexner, though perhaps not to Einstein, it was unthinkable that other scholars at the Institute should outstrip Einstein in salary. This being explained, Einstein reluctantly consented to accept a much higher figure, and he left the detailed negotiations to his wife, Elsa, who was adept at such matters. It was arranged that Einstein would spend part of the year at the Institute and the rest in Germany. But not right away, since he had already agreed to spend a third winter as Visiting Professor in Pasadena. This time, when he sought a visa, a small group of patriotic American women objected loudly to his being allowed to enter the United States, claiming that he was a Communist at heart. His response was caustic:

> Never before [he wrote] have I experienced from the fair sex such energetic rejection of all advances; or if I have, then certainly never from so many at once.
>
> But are they not right, these vigilant lady citizens? Why should one open one's doors to a man who devours hard-boiled capitalists with the same appetite and gusto with which the Cretan Minotaur used to devour luscious Greek maidens, and who in addition is so wicked as to reject every kind of war, except the unavoidable war with one's own wife? Hearken, therefore, to your clever and patriotic womenfolk and remember that the Capitol of mighty Rome was also once saved by the cackling of its faithful geese.

As for his views of Russian Communism at that time, he was not one to accept what was fashionable among certain intellectuals simply because it was fashionable. With Einstein intellectual freedom was a lifelong concern. In June 1932, refusing to endorse an antiwar declaration, he wrote:

> Because of the glorification of Soviet Russia which it includes, I cannot bring myself to sign it. I have of late tried very hard to form a judgment of what is happening there, and I have reached some rather somber conclusions. At the top there appears to be a personal struggle in which the foulest means are used by power-hungry individuals acting from purely selfish motives. At the bottom there seems to be complete suppression of the individual and of freedom of speech. One wonders what life is worth under such conditions. . . .

Partly as a result of the Solvay Congresses in Brussels a remarkable friendship had sprung up between Einstein and King Albert and Queen Elizabeth of the Belgians. An excerpt from a letter that Einstein wrote to his wife, Elsa, telling of a visit to them in 1930 shows this friendship vividly:

International group of scientists in Belgium to make plans for the 1933 Solvay Congress. From left to right: Bohr, Einstein, de Donder, Richardson, Langevin, Debye, Joffe, Cabrera. The photograph was taken on 3 July 1932 by Queen Elizabeth.

. . . I was received with touching warmth. These two people are of a purity and kindness seldom found. First we talked for about an hour. Then [the Queen and I] played quartets and trios [with an English woman musician and a musical lady-in-waiting]. This went on merrily for several hours. Then they all went away and I stayed behind alone for dinner with the [King and Queen]— vegetarian style, no servants. Spinach and hard-boiled eggs and potatoes, period. (It had not been anticipated that I would stay.) I liked it very much there, and I am certain the feeling is mutual.

When Hitler came to power, the Einsteins were in Pasadena. Einstein realized at once that he could not go back to Germany, and in March 1933, in a sharply critical statement, he publicly announced his decision not to return. He went instead to Belgium, to the tiny resort of Le Coq-sur-mer, where for a while, at the

Einstein, 1932.
The photograph was taken
by Queen Elizabeth.

Queen Elizabeth
of Belgium, 1932.

King's behest, he was protected by two bodyguards day and night amid rumors of attempts on his life.

From outside Germany warm offers of academic positions came to him even as the Nazis were loudly confiscating his bank account, and the contents of his wife's safe deposit box, and the beloved house and land in Caputh—the non-gift of the City of Berlin now taken back by the State. Einstein's works joined an illustrious company of writings that the Nazis hurled with glee into book-burning bonfires whose light was the symbol of darkness. When characterizing Einstein's theories as Jewish, the Nazis, in their anti-Semitic frenzy, seemed wholly unaware of the enormous compliment that they were paying the Jews. By Nazi edict, Jews were already being driven from academic positions, debarred from many professions, and hounded into destitution. And Germans who dared to speak out against the totalitarianism of the Nazis risked imprisonment, torture, and death.

On 28 March 1933 Einstein resigned from the Prussian Academy, which, as was later learned, had been about to expel him.

Einstein and King Albert of Belgium, 1933.

He also took steps, for the second time in his life, to renounce his German citizenship; and after he had done so, the Nazis awoke to their lost opportunity and snatched for themselves the immortal distinction of officially revoking Einstein's German citizenship nevertheless. With biting humor Einstein later likened this act to the public hanging of Mussolini's dead body after he had been executed.

The Prussian Academy, when preparing to expel Einstein from membership, charged that in foreign countries he had spread atrocity stories about Germany. When Einstein refuted the charges, they were by implication retracted. The flavor of the letters between Einstein and the Academy at this time comes through in this excerpt from Einstein's letter of 12 April 1933:

> You have also remarked that a "good word" on my part "for the German people" would have produced a great effect abroad. To this I must reply that such a testimony as you suggest would have been a repudiation of all those notions of justice and liberty for which I have stood all my life. Such testimony would not be, as you put it, a good word for the German people; on the contrary, it would only have helped the cause of those who are seeking to undermine the ideas and principles which have won for the German people a place of honor in the civilized world. By giving such testimony in the present circumstances I should have been contributing, even if only indirectly, to moral corruption and the destruction of all existing cultural values.

In those harrowing days many members of the Academy, swayed by nationalism and other emotions, allowed themselves to become infected by the anti-Einstein fever that raged in their country. Laue did not succumb, nor Nernst nor Planck. Indeed, at a plenary session of the Prussian Academy on 11 May 1933, weeks after Einstein had resigned, Planck made the following courageous statement:

> I believe that I speak for my Academy colleagues in physics, and also for the overwhelming majority of all German physicists when I say:
> Mr. Einstein is not just one among many outstanding physicists;

on the contrary, Mr. Einstein is the physicist through whose works published by our Academy, physics has experienced a deepening whose significance can be matched only by that of the achievements of Johannes Kepler and Isaac Newton. . . .

In those perilous times Planck could not lightly have made this affirmation. It ranks therefore as the greatest of the many tributes that Planck in his lifetime paid to Einstein. But even in the era of Nazi dominance Planck spoke the truth as he saw it, and on one occasion this so enraged Hitler that he told Planck face to face that only Planck's age saved him from being sent to a concentration camp.

In April of 1933 Einstein withdrew from the Bavarian Academy, of which he was a Corresponding Member, saying:

> . . . to the best of my knowledge the learned Societies of Germany have stood by passively and silently while substantial numbers of scholars, students, and academically trained professionals have been deprived of employment and livelihood. I do not want to belong to any Society that behaves in such a manner, even if it does so under compulsion.

This was before the days of the extermination camps. But already Einstein was appalled by the Nazi tyranny and the danger to world civilization of a rearming totalitarian Germany bent on war and savage suppression. All his life he had been an outspoken pacifist; we recall in particular his forthright statements of 1928 and 1929, and these are but samples of the many passionate, uncompromising declarations that he had issued on behalf of pacifism and pacifist organizations all over the world. Now in Le Coq-sur-mer he faced a profound moral dilemma, and after much soul-searching he chose what he felt was the lesser of two evils. On 20 July 1933, in response to an appeal to speak out on behalf of two Belgian conscientious objectors, he made his decision known, writing:

> What I shall tell you will greatly surpise you. . . . Imagine Belgium occupied by present-day Germany. Things would be far worse than in 1914, and they were bad enough even then. Hence I must

tell you candidly: Were I a Belgian, I would not, in the present circumstances, refuse military service; rather, I would enter such service cheerfully in the belief that I should thereby be helping to save European civilization. This does not mean that I am surrendering the principle for which I have stood heretofore. I hope most sincerely that the time will once more come when refusal of military service will again be an effective method of serving the cause of human progress.

The pacifists of the world were dismayed. They looked on Einstein as an apostate: he had betrayed their cause. But, as he said in 1935, "In times such as these, any weakening of the democratic countries caused by a policy of refusing military service would actually be tantamount to a betrayal of the cause of civilization and humanity." Despite the bitter criticisms of pacifists all over the world, he continued to express his new views; and other famous pacifists, notably Bertrand Russell, forsook their pacifism too.

In June of 1933 Einstein went to England, where, at Oxford, he gave the Herbert Spencer Lecture. In this lecture, "On the Method of Theoretical Physics," he stressed, with the distilled wisdom of years, that "the concepts and fundamental principles that underlie [theoretical physics] are free inventions of the human intellect," and that they "form the essential part of a theory, which reason cannot touch." After giving other scientific lectures, he returned to Le Coq. In late summer of 1933 he went back to England, staying in relative isolation in Cromer and happily losing count of the days as he worked on his calculations. He was soon to say that the ideal job for a theoretical physicist would be that of a lighthouse keeper. His letters from Cromer show that for him at least this could have been the case. He wrote, "I have wonderful peace here; only now do I realize how driven I usually am," and, "I really enjoy the quiet and solitude here. One can think much more clearly, and one feels incomparably better." While in England, he spoke privately with key people, among them Churchill, about the menace of German rearmament; and on 3 October 1933 he spoke publicly at a huge British rally on behalf of a committee set up by men like Rutherford to aid refugee scholars from Nazi Germany.

Einstein and Churchill at Chartwell, 1933.

And with this his time in Europe came to its end.

With his wife and his secretary and his collaborator Professor Walter Mayer, he left for America. He arrived on 17 October 1933, and his arrival was hailed as a major event. Almost immediately President Roosevelt invited the Einsteins to be overnight guests at the White House, and when the meeting occurred the following January, Roosevelt and Einstein found common ground in their love of sailing, on which they could both speak enthusiastically as experts. But they spoke, too, of growing darkness in Europe.

Flexner had chosen Princeton, New Jersey, as the place for his Institute for Advanced Study. Indeed, until its own buildings were ready for occupancy, the Institute was housed at Princeton

Einstein in Berlin, 1 December 1932. This chance photograph has a particular interest. It was taken by Charles Holdt, a passer-by who recognized Einstein on the street from his pictures. Holdt tells that it was a time exposure because "the sun had already sunk behind the Opera House and the light was very poor." A year or so later, thanking Holdt for sending a copy, Einstein wrote, "The photo was made a few days before I left Berlin forever."

University. The tiny collegiate town of Princeton offered Einstein haven. He continued to speak out strongly against the Nazis, but no special precautions were taken for his personal safety. He roamed the peaceful streets of Princeton without fear. The people were friendly. His utter lack of formality must have surprised them, but they evidently found it endearing. And in this quiet place he was to spend the rest of his days.

10

The Battle and
the Bomb

With Einstein safely in Princeton, we can now go back to tell, all too sketchily, of extraordinary advances that had meanwhile been occurring in atomic theory.

We recall that Einstein, in the Patent Office, had applied Planck's revolutionary idea of the quantum to the theory of light and the theory of inner heat. At the Solvay Congress in 1911, largely because of Einstein's work on heat, it became clear that the quantum had to be taken seriously: and as a result, it also became clear that little else remained clear. The quantum was in outright conflict with Newton and Maxwell both, and there seemed no way of reconciling the new with the old. Science was in deep crisis—deeper than it realized.

Among the select few attending the Solvay Congress in Brussels in 1911 was New Zealand–born Ernest Rutherford, the world's leading atomic physicist. Already a Nobel laureate for his work in Canada on the nature of radioactivity, he was now at Manchester University in England, where he had gathered around him an outstanding group of researchers. As a pioneer himself, he had relished the revolutionary quantum discussions that had tantalized the Solvay conferees, and on his return to Manchester he recounted the arguments so vividly to the young Danish physicist Niels Bohr that Bohr recalled the telling to the end of his days.

The 1913 Solvay Congress. Seated, from the left: Nernst, Rutherford, Wien, Thomson, Warburg, Lorentz, Brillouin, Barlow, Kamerlingh-Onnes, Wood, Gouy, Weiss. Standing: Hasenöhrl, Verschaffelt, Jeans, Bragg, Laue, Rubens, Mme. Curie, Goldschmidt, Sommerfeld, Herzen, Einstein, Lindemann, de Broglie, Pope, Gruneisen, Knudsen, Hostelet, Langevin.

Earlier in 1911 Rutherford had propounded the idea that an atom consists of a tiny, relatively massive nucleus surrounded by planetary electrons—a miniature solar system held together by electrical instead of gravitational forces. Rutherford's fateful discovery of the atomic nucleus was brilliantly founded on experiment. But his model of the atom had a defect. According to Maxwell's theory, it would collapse. The electrons would not stay in steady orbits. They would radiate their energy in the form of electromagnetic waves, and spiral into the nucleus. There was no hope of their being stable, nor of their yielding the sharp spectral lines observed in spectroscopes.

In 1913 Bohr, back in Denmark, came to the rescue. Einstein had already challenged Maxwell. Bohr decided to challenge Maxwell further, and with the same weapon: the quantum—not unmixed with audacity.

Bohr's first concern was to ensure that, in theory, the Rutherford atom would not collapse. Think for a moment of a window shade. When we pull it down an appropriate amount it stays extended. An internal notchedness keeps it from collapsing back into a tight roll. In 1900 Planck had given a quantum notchedness to certain oscillations so that their possible energies were analogous to a series of steps instead of to a smooth, skiddy slope. Quickly realizing the possible universal importance of this quantum notchedness, Einstein, in his theory of inner heat, had extended it in 1906 to other oscillations. And now, early in 1913, Bohr gave a quantum notchedness to the Rutherford atom, to keep it from collapsing.

In defiance of the Maxwellian rules, Bohr flatly declared not only that the electrons *would* remain in steady orbits but also that they would remain in them without radiating. Then, proceeding further along his heretical path, he allowed only orbits of special sizes, forbidding all others. By these high-handed edicts he now had a well-notched Rutherford atom. Almost too well notched, in fact, for how could it give off radiation? Bohr had an answer. He said that light is radiated or absorbed not when an electron is in orbit but when it makes a quantum jump from one permitted orbit to another. He said, too, that the frequency of the light is linked to the change of the electron's energy by Planck's quantum rule, the ratio *energy change/frequency* being equal to Planck's constant *h*. And he showed that from such rules in their more detailed, mathematical form there flowed results in extraordinarily successful agreement with experiment. Above all, though this could be realized only later, he showed the sureness of his intuition by refusing to say what happened during an electron's quantum jump.

Bohr's theory of the Rutherford atom was one of the turning points of physics. It brought Bohr quick scientific fame. Yet, as he himself well realized, his theory was a mishmash of classical and quantum concepts. So much so that important physicists at first dismissed it as nonsense. Concerning those early days. Bohr gently wrote in 1958, "outside the Manchester group [my ideas] were received with much skepticism." Indeed his theory could properly be described as great nonsense. Inspired nonsense. A marvel of intuition. Let Einstein himself tell us of its quality. In the fall of 1913 he spoke of it as "one of the greatest discoveries," and singled out for special admiration Bohr's "enormous achievement" of linking light to quantum jumps of electrons instead of to their oscillations as had been customarily assumed on Maxwellian and even quantum grounds. In his "Autobiographical Notes," written thirty years later and long after Bohr's theory had been superseded, Einstein said of those pre–World War I years:

> All my attempts . . . failed completely. It was as if the ground had been pulled out from under one, with no firm foundation to be seen anywhere upon which one could have built. That this insecure and contradictory foundation sufficed to enable a man of Bohr's unique instinct and sensitivity to discover the major laws of the spectral lines and of the electron shells of the atoms together with their significance for chemistry appeared to me like a miracle—and appears to me as a miracle even today. This is the highest form of musicality in the sphere of thought.

In 1900, when Planck deduced his formula for black-body radiation, he could not avoid mixing quantum and Maxwellian ideas although they were in conflict. In 1916 Einstein found a new quantum approach that basically avoided Maxwellian electromagnetic concepts. The success of Bohr's theory had shown that, so far as internal energy is concerned, an atom is analogous to a series of steps or levels. The existence of these atomic energy levels had in fact been verified by direct experiment, and Einstein realized that whatever the fate of Bohr's theory with its mixture of conflicting concepts, the existence of energy levels would surely survive. He therefore took it as a secure foundation on which to build. Using probability arguments, and without even assuming the existence of photons, he found—the phrase is his own—an "amazingly simple" derivation of Planck's formula for black-body radiation. He found more: for example, a direct link with a basic formula of Bohr's theory. Einstein could scarcely conceal his delight at the way it all fit neatly together. In publishing the work, he wrote, "It commends itself by its simplicity and generality," and he was not exaggerating. It was pure Einstein. He rightly regarded it as among his best work. It had great influence on Bohr, and thus on the whole development of quantum physics. The basic idea is easy to grasp. Einstein considered a gas of atoms all of the same sort. For simplicity let us imagine that they have only two energy levels, and let us speak of particles of light—photons—from the start, even though Einstein did not need to. Further let us imagine that the photons all have energies that just match the difference in these levels. When an atom is at the lower level let us call it "empty," and when it is at the higher level let us call it "full." Thus when an empty atom absorbs a photon it becomes full, and when a full atom emits a photon it becomes empty.

Now let us, with Einstein, make three simple rules, two here and one later, all three being quantum analogues of corresponding Maxwellian processes. An empty atom will remain empty until a photon comes its way. A full atom will sooner or later *spontaneously* emit its photon, without any external stimulus. Lacking adequate data about a full atom's inner processes, we cannot predict when it will emit its photon. So we assume that, if we have many atoms and photons, the emissions take place at random moments, and we write a probability formula for such randomness. It is the type of statistical formula that was used by Rutherford and others in dealing with the radioactive decay of atomic nuclei.

So far, then, we have two processes: empty atoms absorbing photons when photons arrive, and full atoms emitting photons spontaneously at unpredictable moments, this latter process having the technical name *spontaneous emission*. We want the absorptions and emissions to stay in balance. But if we use only the above two rules, we shall not obtain Planck's formula for blackbody radiation. Einstein realized that to obtain it we need a third process. Suppose a full atom encounters a photon. Being full, the atom cannot absorb another photon. We would imagine, therefore, that nothing would happen. But Einstein assumed that, so to speak, the full atom would attempt to absorb the additional photon and as a result lose both, ending up empty. We seem almost to be telling an Aesop fable complete with moral implications, but this third process is of major scientific importance. It is called *stimulated emission,* and we mention here that some three and a half decades later it began to find practical application. It is the basic principle of the laser, the medical and industrial uses of which are already extensive; and it makes possible the military development of a death ray capable of destroying any person, tank, plane, or atomic bomb at which it is directed. This weapon, which may well be used in World War III should that war occur, will have been based on a quantum investigation that Einstein performed in Berlin for aesthetic scientific reasons during World War I.

There are further facets to this particular story. We mention one briefly here. Quickly extending the work in a second paper, Einstein found compelling reasons for regarding light quanta as particles having energy and momentum like bullets—reasons so compelling that he boldly wrote in his article, ". . . radiation in the form of . . . waves does not exist." And indeed the bulletlike behavior of light quanta was strikingly confirmed by experiment in 1923. Yet the evidence for light waves was strong, and as late as 1922, the year in which Bohr was awarded the Nobel Prize, he and others were still reluctant to accept Einstein's idea of particles of light. In a sense, Bohr never did accept it.

Bohr and Einstein first met in 1920 when Bohr was invited to lecture in Berlin on his theory of the atom. Hardly had he arrived when a lively, exhilarating discussion began between him and Einstein that filled every spare moment all the days he was there. This was only to be expected at the first meeting of two such men, for each had the highest respect for the other, and both were fascinated by the staggering problems that enlivened theoretical physics. After Bohr left Berlin, Einstein wrote to him on 2 May 1920, saying, "Rarely in my life has a man given me such joy by his mere presence as you have. I understand now why Ehrenfest loves you so much." And Bohr replied, "It was for me one of the greatest experiences I have ever had to meet you and to speak with you. You do not know how great a stimulation it was for me to hear your views. . . . Never shall I forget our discussions on the way from [Dahlem] to your house. . . ."

By 1922 Bohr was the pride of Denmark, and the Director of an Institute for Theoretical Physics specially set up for him in Copenhagen. It became the world center of atomic theory. Eager young theorists flocked to it from many lands, and later there was much truth in their jesting remark that the official language of the Institute was Broken English.

As for Rutherford, he was now the Director—as Maxwell had once been—of the famous Cavendish Laboratory of Cambridge University. Bohr the theorist and Rutherford the experimenter kept in close touch, and under their inspired leadership atomic physics made fabulous strides.

Yet already in 1922 Bohr's theory was in serious difficulties. Everyone, Bohr especially, had known that it could only be transitional. Bohr had ingeniously extended its range by introducing a "correspondence principle"—remember the phrase—that gave it renewed sustenance from nonquantum physics. But the correspondence principle had all the earmarks of a makeshift. Bohr's theory seemed clearly to be nearing the end of its resources, and since there appeared to be not even a hint of a viable alternative, atomic theorists were in a state of profound frustration.

Then, with explosive suddenness, the barriers to progress were shattered. The hints had been there after all, and in a few bewildering years the whole picture was transformed. Do not struggle to understand what follows. It tells in outline of crowding events and twisting interpretations that strained the intuition of even the greatest scientists. If it proves bewildering, it will at least thereby convey something of the flavor of those convulsive years.

When the French physicist Maurice de Broglie returned from the famous Solvay Congress of 1911, his report excited his young brother, Louis de Broglie, perhaps even more than Rutherford's report of the Congress had excited young Bohr. Haunted by the puzzle of the quantum, and by the conflicting evidence for light as particles and light as waves, Louis de Broglie developed between 1922 and 1924 a seemingly fantastic theory. He regarded light as consisting of particles accompanied and guided by waves. And, what is more important, he also regarded electrons and other particles of matter as similarly accompanied by waves—these waves speeding faster than light. This may well seem unlikely. Indeed, de Broglie's interpretation of his mathematics had to be changed. Yet by means of his waves he was able to give vivid pictorial meaning to Bohr's permitted electron orbits.

One man, Paul Langevin, with rare insight, took de Broglie's ideas seriously. And he told Einstein.

It so happened that shortly before this, Einstein himself had been exercising his powerful physical intuition. He had received a manuscript from an Indian physicist, S. N. Bose, whom he did not know. Before telling about Bose's manuscript, we ask a simple question: if we toss a dime and a quarter, what are the odds that both will come down heads? This elementary problem in probability is easily solved. There are four possibilities, all

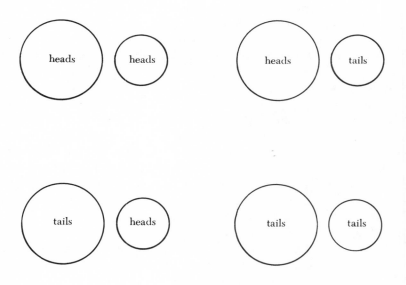

equally likely. Of the four, only one is a pair of heads. Therefore in the long run we expect a pair of heads to come up on the average one-fourth of the time. The odds are one in four. The probability is 1/4.

Suppose we now toss two newly minted dimes. Obviously the odds for a pair of heads must still be one in four. There are essentially the same four cases, but two now seem alike: one dime heads and one dime tails. This tempts us to argue that there are only the following three different cases: both dimes heads, one heads and one tails, and both tails. As a result we are likely to

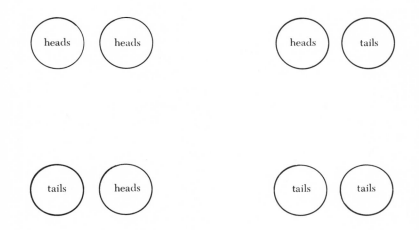

come to the false conclusion that the odds for a pair of heads are not one in four but one in three. If we do make such an error we need not feel ashamed—unless we are professionals. In the early days of the theory of probability great mathematicians fell into this sort of trap. The way to avoid it is to imagine the dimes marked so that they can be told apart.

We now return to Bose. He treated light quanta not electromagnetically but simply as particles and applied to these particles the statistical methods used in the theory of gases. Like newly minted dimes, light quanta of equal energy would be indistinguishable. What if one could not tell them apart? What if one could not put distinguishing marks on them? What if one therefore deliberately made the sort of counting error described above? What then? Why then, as Bose showed, one had a new way of deriving Planck's famous black-body radiation formula. If one did the counting "correctly," one did not obtain Planck's formula.

Sensing the importance of Bose's idea, Einstein personally translated the manuscript into German and arranged for its publication in a German scientific journal. That was not all. With what proved to be prophetic intuition—indeed, the concept came to be known as the Bose-Einstein statistics—Einstein extended the idea of Bose by applying his method of probability counting to the case of a gas of indistinguishable particles of matter. Thus when Einstein saw de Broglie also treating light and matter in a unified way he was at once attentive. And although, as Einstein remarked to Born shortly afterwards, de Broglie's ideas looked "crazy," Einstein sensed that they were important. Accordingly, in 1925, in his second paper extending the ideas of Bose, Einstein not only brought in de Broglie's idea but also commended the work of de Broglie to the attention of physicists.*

Einstein knew that his word carried enormous scientific weight, yet even he could hardly have anticipated the swift, spectacular effect of his recommendation of de Broglie's ideas. As a result of it, early in 1926 at Zurich University, the Austrian physicist Erwin Schrödinger began publishing a highly successful atomic theory. Closely linked to Newtonian equations, it nevertheless treated matter not as particles, nor yet as particles accompanied by waves, but solely as waves—perfectly smooth waves not in everyday space but in abstract mathematical spaces that could have many dimensions.

Meanwhile, in June 1925, a twenty-three-year-old German physicist, Werner Heisenberg, had already initiated an equally successful atomic theory along vastly different lines. He renounced electron orbits as unobservable, and he refused to picture in any such terms what goes on in the world of the atom. Adopting an austere, abstract approach, he found, in long-known facts about atomic spectra, reasons for the following extraordinary conclusion: that atomic theorists, while keeping close to Newtonian equations, should use mathematical entities such that x times y is not the same as y times x.

---

* There is something strange in this sequence of events that goes beyond the manifest strangeness of the concepts. It happens that Bose's method of statistical counting was not wholly new. It had been adumbrated in connection with Planck's formula as early as 1911 by Ehrenfest, among others. One would have thought that Einstein, of all people, with his overwhelming interest in both Planck's formula and light quanta, would have seized on the embryonic idea of 1911, and perhaps even have applied it at once to particles of matter in a gas without having to wait for the stimulus of Bose's paper. It may well be that Einstein was unable to assimilate the 1911 hints right away into his scheme of things because he had a psychological need to think of his revolutionary light quanta as particles. Even in 1924 he conceded only reluctantly that the statistical procedures used by Bose and himself robbed the particles of their individuality, and thus blurred the physical concept of a particle. This psychological need of Einstein's, if indeed it existed, is worth bearing in mind when we come to subsequent developments described in this chapter.

Fortunately Heisenberg was Born's assistant at Göttingen University, and Born had the insight to take Heisenberg's idea seriously. Born and his collaborator Pascual Jordan vigorously developed Heisenberg's concepts, and by November the three men had brought the theory to a definitive form. So too, independently and more neatly, had a young English physicist, Paul Dirac, at Cambridge University. Like Heisenberg, he too was twenty-three. In June 1926 Born made a major advance for which, much later, he received the Nobel Prize. He reinterpreted Schrödinger's theory—to Schrödinger's chagrin and distress. Taking a hint from an early attempt by Einstein to reconcile the wave and particle aspects of light, Born proposed that Schrödinger's waves were not, as Schrödinger had thought, waves of matter. Rather, they were waves of probability* associated with particles of matter.

At this utterly confused stage let us pause to ask where de Broglie and Heisenberg found the inspiration to conceive their extraordinary ideas, and the courage to develop them mathematically. It is no easy thing, emotionally, to be a pioneer. One needs great faith and fortitude. For example, when Heisenberg had almost finished his basic calculations, he seriously wondered whether he should not throw them into the fire. Admittedly, atomic theory was ripe for heroic measures. But desperation was only the spur. In itself it gave little guidance.

The ideas of de Broglie grew directly from Einstein's idea of light quanta, and even more immediately from his special theory of relativity. That theory was important for Heisenberg, too. Its bold denial of absolute simultaneity was what gave him the courage to deny the unobserved orbits. Moreover, a clue had developed from Einstein's work of 1916—the work that ultimately led to the laser. But paramount was the influence of Bohr. Heisenberg had just spent an inspiring year at the Copenhagen Institute, and his idea was a direct outgrowth of the correspondence principle with which Bohr had extended the range of his own ailing theory. In its death throes it gave birth to the theory of Heisenberg, and this can well be regarded as the greatest of its many triumphs.

The ideas of de Broglie and Heisenberg were of extraordinary

---

* More strictly, waves of what are called "probability amplitudes," but we need not be that strict.

originality. Yet so neatly did de Broglie's work grow out of relativity and the concept of light quanta that one almost wonders how Einstein could have missed taking the decisive step himself; and in a comparable way, so neatly did Heisenberg's work grow out of Bohr's correspondence principle that one almost wonders how Bohr could have missed taking this equally decisive step himself. But we must not let hindsight diminish the luster of dazzling achievements. De Broglie and Heisenberg deservedly received the Nobel Prize, as too did Schrödinger.

Even so, we may look on this in another way. The de Broglie-Schrödinger concepts are a tribute to the intuition of Einstein; and the Heisenberg theory is a tribute to the intuition of Bohr. It is fitting that this should be so, since Bohr and Einstein, the two masters, were destined to engage in a prolonged battle over the interpretation of the new theory.

We deliberately say theory rather than theories. For Schrödinger—and he was not the only one—discovered a mathematical link that showed them to be substantially equivalent. And with the probability interpretation, Dirac, and independently Jordan, soon found that they were different aspects of a single, more general theory. It goes by the name *quantum mechanics,* and is essentially the theory used today.

Waves of probability in multidimensional spaces? x times y not the same as y times x? And now the two ideas linked together? What is the world—the quantum world—coming to? The physicists of those turbulent days had little chance to catch their breath. They were caught in the climax of a scientific revolution that had been smoldering since 1900. If we are to share something of what they felt, buffeted by staggering events that crowded in on them, we may not be leisurely here. We must press urgently on. Like them, we have further jolts to face. In 1927, inspired once more by the manner in which Einstein had conceived the special theory of relativity, Heisenberg enunciated a far-reaching principle that gave pictorial vividness to the strange mathematical implications of quantum mechanics.

To see, for example, a cat, we have to let light shine on it. That is to say, we must bombard it with light quanta. And these photons will jolt it. When we view objects of everyday size, the jolts are, in general, utterly negligible. Not so in the microscopic realm of the atom. Take, for example, an electron. It is far too small to see. But if, in imagination, we use light to observe it clearly, we have to use photons that, relatively speaking, come at it like bullets and jolt it by unknowable amounts. Heisenberg concluded that, because of such unavoidable quantum jolts of observation, we cannot at the same time know precisely both where a particle is and how it is moving. The more accurately we observe its location, the less accurately we can observe its momentum, and vice versa. This, in bare outline, is Heisenberg's principle of indeterminacy. Perhaps it does not seem very radical. But see what follows from it.

If, at a particular time, we cannot know with precision both the position and momentum of a particle, we are deprived of data needed for predicting where it will be later on. The future is thus indeterminate: causality has become a quantum casualty.

This is far more shattering than Einstein's denial of absolute simultaneity. It undercuts traditional science far more deeply. Indeed, if the future is indeterminate, we may well wonder how there can be any such thing as traditional science. But all is not chaos. A remnant of determinacy remains, though it is not of a sort that is likely to give us a sudden warm glow of comprehension. Here is one way of describing the remnant: between observations the waves of probability progress in a deterministic manner. Because of this we can predict probabilities. And for everyday objects these probabilities amount to virtual certainties so that in the motions of planets, shrapnel, and the like the indeterminacy escapes our notice.

Scientists conceived these various ideas in desperation, startled by the success of a mathematically beautiful and highly successful quantum mechanics that seemed riddled with physical contradictions. What are we to think of it all? What sort of sense, if any, can we make of it? In 1927 Bohr gave an answer that became, with the ideas of Born and Heisenberg, the basis of what is now known as the Copenhagen interpretation. Bohr invoked a concept of what he called *complementarity*. What follows does not pretend to be more than a rough sketch of this subtle concept, on the details of which there does not seem to be general agreement. We note first—and by now the point needs no stressing—that the quantum world of the atom is not easy to visualize in everyday terms. Bohr boldly proposed that there *is* no simple everyday way of visualizing it. When we make quantum experiments, we begin by setting up apparatus, which we usually adjust by some such method as turning knobs and reading dials; and we end by making other such mundane readings. Thus we begin and end in the everyday, nonquantum world. We have to. We cannot avoid it. Yet from such experiments, doubly anchored in the familiar, we try to envisage the strange quantum world of the atom. So remote, argued Bohr, is that world from our ordinary experience that, if we wish to visualize it, a single everyday picture will not suffice. We are reduced to using pairs of conflicting complementary images. Never mind that the wave and particle images are contradictory. We need them both. They merely complement one another. They do not imply an actual physical contradiction. Much as there is no actual conflict in the conflicting appearance of the sky at noon and night, so too is there no actual conflict when some experiments show us electrons behaving like waves, and other experiments of different type show us electrons behaving like particles. The conflict is only in our minds because we seek a single simple everyday picture that does not exist. In our pictures not only do we need wave and particle but also such things as position and momentum despite their seeming Heisenbergian conflict. Again, when we seek a sharp image in terms of space and time, we have to give up strict determinism, and vice versa. We must learn, said Bohr, to live with this all-pervasive complementarity. We cannot escape it—and in this very realization lies our escape.

What of Einstein in all this? He did not like it. It went counter to all his scientific instincts. Ever since, as a young man, he had extended Planck's pioneering work of 1900, he had tried strenuously to make physical sense out of the light quantum that he had himself introduced. We can only guess at the number of attempts he made and discarded in his lifetime. The problem was always on his mind. It gave him no rest. How could individual photons behave like particles when hitting atoms, yet travel with wavelike properties as if each could be in many places at once? De Broglie had aggravated the wave-particle puzzle by spreading it to matter as well as light, so that it pervaded physics. This Einstein accepted. The pervasiveness was itself a form of unity.

Bohr had concluded that we must be content to live with wave and particle as complementary images. But here Einstein's instinct rebelled. On 12 December 1951, near the end of his life, he wrote these words to his old friend Michele Besso, with whom, in those far-off days at the Patent Office, he had discussed his emerging ideas: "All these fifty years of conscious brooding have brought me no nearer to the answer to the question 'What are light quanta?' Nowadays every Tom, Dick, and Harry thinks he knows it, but he is mistaken."

Einstein had been in the thick of the struggle to interpret the new quantum mechanics. He had immediately argued with Born over the probabilistic interpretation of Schrödinger's theory. But his main antagonist was Bohr.

Late in 1927, at the fifth Solvay Congress, the battle flared into the open. Born and Heisenberg argued that the indeterminacy is unavoidable: that because of the absence of strict causality, the probabilities tell all there is to tell. Bohr agreed. But Einstein did not. He was unwilling to accept what his instinct rejected. He felt

The 1927 Solvay Congress. First row, from the left: Langmuir, Planck, Mme. Curie, Lorentz, Einstein, Langevin, Guye, Wilson, Richardson. Second row: Debye, Knudsen, Bragg, Kramers, Dirac, Compton, de Broglie, Born, Bohr. Third row: Piccard, Henriot, Ehrenfest, Herzen, de Donder, Schrödinger, Verschaffelt, Pauli, Heisenberg, Fowler, Brillouin.

Bohr and Einstein in deep thought: a study in contrasts. The photograph was taken by Ehrenfest.

A second such photograph taken by Ehrenfest. (Both were reproduced from negatives restored by William R. Whipple.)

Einstein and Bohr. The photograph was taken by Ehrenfest.

that the theory was incomplete. And he brought forth a succession of ingenious arguments in support of his views. Never before had the new quantum mechanics been subjected to so formidable and penetrating an attack. But Bohr and his allies, hard pressed, stood their ground. Refining their concepts in the heat of battle, they defeated the objections of Einstein one by one, and Einstein, for all his ingenuity, had to retreat. The unknowable jolt of observation could not be avoided. Every scheme that Einstein proposed for measuring a jolt involved a new observation with a jolt of its own. To measure this new jolt, one needed another jolting observation, and so on in a succession that offered no visible hope of victory. Indeterminism had survived Einstein's attack. Immediately after the Congress Bohr and Einstein continued the battle at the home of the Ehrenfests, and Ehrenfest, who worshiped both Einstein and Bohr, was bewildered to see one of his heroes unwilling to accept the emerging Copenhagen interpretation. A few months later, in May 1928, Einstein wrote to Schrödinger, saying in part: "The Heisenberg-Bohr tranquilizing philosophy—or religion?—is so delicately contrived that, for the time being, it provides a gentle pillow for the true believer from which he cannot very easily be aroused."

In 1930, at the Sixth Solvay Congress—the last that Einstein was destined to attend—he offered a new proposal for circumventing Heisenberg's indeterminacy principle. This time Bohr was staggered. The argument seemed impregnable. He could see no weak spot in it. Yet if there were none, then the whole quantum theory, which was now more successful than ever, must be fundamentally deficient. This Bohr could not concede. Yet Einstein's argument stood implacably before him, demanding surrender. Bohr tried to destroy it this way and that, but it withstood his attacks. He could not sleep. Too much was at stake. Far into the night he struggled with the problem. And by morning he had the solution: Einstein's argument failed because of Einstein's own principle of equivalence, and thus because of Einstein's own general theory of relativity. Discovering this was a stupendous feat. Einstein was forced to concede the round. And to concede that Heisenberg's principle of indeterminacy was valid. But he still did not give up the fight.

In Belgium in 1933, just before leaving Europe forever, he mentioned a new idea. Two years later he published it with his collaborators Boris Podolsky and Nathan Rosen at the Institute for Advanced Study. Here is the gist of the argument, shorn of all mathematics. It is deceptively simple. In imagination, we bounce two electrons, A and B, off one another and wait until they are so far apart that neither can significantly affect the other. There is

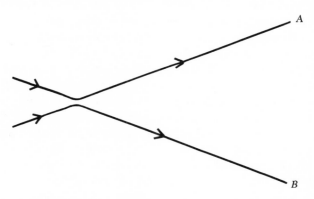

cunning in this. For by making measurements on A, we can draw conclusions about B, and nobody will be able to argue that our observation of A jolted B or affected B in any way. According to the quantum theory itself, if we observe the precise position of A we can at once infer the precise position of B; and if, instead, we observe the precise momentum of A we can at once infer the precise momentum of B. Is the strategy clear? We are going to observe A, but to talk about B, which is unaffected by our observation of A.

For vividness, let us suppose that the bounce occurs on Sunday and that the distances are such that we can wait till a week later before making our observation of A. According to Heisenberg, we cannot precisely determine at the same time both the position and momentum of an electron. But we do have a choice as to which quantity to measure. So on Monday we decide that we will measure the precise position of A. But on Tuesday we change our mind and decide that we will measure the precise momentum of A instead. On Wednesday we decide that we will measure the position of A after all. On Thursday we switch again to the momentum of A. On Friday we are back with the position of A. On

Saturday with the momentum of A. And on Sunday, unable to make up our mind, we flip a coin and perform on A the measurement that the coin indicates.

Suppose the coin told us to observe the position of electron A. Then by observing it we should at once also know the position of the other electron, B, *without affecting B in any way.* The quantum theory itself guarantees this. Suppose instead that the coin told us to observe not the position but the momentum of A. Then by observing that we should at once know the momentum of B, again without influencing B in any way.

Surely we cannot seriously imagine electron B changing chameleon-like in step with our changes of mind, having precise position but not momentum on Monday, precise momentum but not position on Tuesday, precise position but not momentum on Wednesday, precise momentum but not position on Thursday, and so on right up to the last moment, at which time it somehow matches the decision selected by the coin—with B all this while isolated physically from A and from us and our coin. Surely, argued Einstein and his collaborators, the precise position and precise momentum of B must both have physical reality at the same time. But Heisenberg had shown that the quantum theory forbids our knowing both at once. Therefore the quantum theory does not give a complete description of physical reality. It is an incomplete theory.

How would you answer this argument? Would you surrender? Bohr did not. Soon we shall tell how he met it. But meanwhile a breathing spell will be welcome and we take the opportunity to mention a few other matters.

Some of our remarks about Maxwell's theory must have made it seem like a relic of bygone days. But in 1927 Dirac showed how to rejuvenate it. He gave it a quantum transfusion. Then, using the Bose-Einstein method of statistical counting, he derived from the rejuvenated Maxwell theory not only Planck's formula for black-body radiation but also all the results obtained quite differently by Einstein in his "laser" work of 1916. And, despite inherent problems, the rejuvenated theory of Maxwell went on to become by far the most accurately verified physical theory that we have today.

Having made our amends to Maxwell, let us not forget Newton.

Bohr and Heisenberg and Schrödinger had all built on Newtonian foundations; and Dirac, in a particularly felicitous way, had shown that the new quantum mechanics was essentially Newtonian mechanics with a quantum transfusion. Having said this, let us not forget Einstein. In 1928 Dirac brilliantly applied the special theory of relativity to the quantum theory of the electron, an achievement as remarkable for its mathematical beauty as for its spectacular success. In view of these and other achievements, it will come as no surprise that he was awarded the Nobel Prize.

In Einstein's long battle over the interpretation of quantum mechanics one theme recurred again and again: his instinctive dislike of the idea of a probabilistic universe in which the behavior of individual atoms depends on chance. As was his custom when facing deep problems of science, he tried to regard things from the point of view of God. Was it likely that God would have created a probabilistic universe? Einstein felt that the answer must be no. If God was capable of creating a universe in which scientists could discern scientific laws, then God was capable of creating a universe wholly governed by such laws. He would not have created a universe in which he had to make chance-like decisions at every moment regarding the behavior of every individual particle. This was not something that Einstein could prove. It was a matter of faith and feeling and intuition. Perhaps it seems naive. But it was deep-rooted, and Einstein's physical intuition, though not infallible, had certainly stood him in good stead. All science is based on faith. The many strange developments that we have already seen—Bohr's own initial theory among them—should have convinced us by now that great science is not built on cold logic.

Einstein summed up his intuitive feeling about the quantum theory in the picturesque phrase "Gott würfelt nicht," which he used in various forms on many occasions. It can be ploddingly translated "God does not play dice." But here is a translation by the poet Jean Untermeyer that has something of the magic and majesty that one finds in great art and great science:

> "God casts the die, not the dice."

Bohr, too, gave a translation of Einstein's phrase. Mistrustful of

Dr. Marcial Dc

Statue of Einstein erected in 1930 in Montevideo, Uruguay. The rear view of the statue shows that Einstein faces the Parque Hotel, part of which houses a gambling casino—where men play dice.

arguments in which one ascribes attributes to God in everyday language, Bohr translated the word "Gott" not as "God" but as "the providential authorities." Perhaps we see in this an indication of the difference between the outlooks of Bohr and Einstein on matters of science. Yet in a letter written in 1945 to an inquirer about his religious beliefs Einstein himself said, "It is always misleading to use anthropomorphical concepts in dealing with things outside the human sphere—childish analogies." This would seem to agree with Bohr's mistrust of arguments about a God who did not play dice. However, in a letter written to a freethinker in 1953 Einstein explained that by this God who did not play dice he meant "not Jahwe or Jupiter but Spinoza's immanent God." And in the 1945 letter previously quoted Einstein had gone on to say, as he often said: "We have to admire in humility the beautiful harmony of the structure of this world, as far as we can grasp it. That is all." Thus it would seem that for Einstein the harmony of the universe would be marred if, to use his metaphor, God played dice. When an Einstein uses an argument in physics, it carries enormous weight even if expressed in terms of a metaphor. Despite his many statements, we do not know what Einstein wholly meant by the word God. In Einstein's scientific work God was the governing concept—an ill-defined concept, for who can define God?—but a symbol not only of Einstein's passion for wonder and beauty but also of that intuitive sense of communion with the universe that was the hallmark of his genius—another word that defies our attempts at definition.

Let us look now at Bohr's reply to the argument of Einstein, Podolsky, and Rosen in which by observing electron A one could in theory obtain information about electron B without influencing B. We recall the daily changes of mind as to whether to observe the position or momentum of electron A, and the conclusion that the precise position and precise momentum of electron B must both have physical reality at the same time, from which it followed that the quantum theory is incomplete. The argument caused Bohr deep concern. It proved far more subtle than he first thought, and only after probing analysis did he hit on an answer. He had to retreat a little by not invoking the jolt of the act of observation. As we shall amplify later, he had to regard an experiment as a single whole—a "single phenomenon" as he later called it—necessarily beginning and ending in the everyday world. And now his point was this. Suppose we signed a contract beforehand binding ourselves to measure, say, position. Then there would be no new problem since there would be no changes of mind. Right from the start the experiment would be designed to measure position and not momentum. If, instead, we signed a contract beforehand binding ourselves to measure momentum, we should be making *a quite different experiment*, in which, in this case, position would not be involved. Thus two different "physical phenomena" in Bohr's sense of the phrase enter the discussion. Now, argued Bohr, so far as the actual physical phenomenon, or complete experiment, is concerned, it makes no difference whether we sign a contract beforehand or change our mind from day to day and end by tossing a coin. What counts is the complete experiment we actually made, not the different one that we did not make, nor the details of when and how we decided which one to make. The two experiments are mutually exclusive physical phenomena. If we make one we cannot make the other at the same time. Therefore, said Bohr, we may not confront the experiment we actually made—whichever it was—with the one we did not make. Thus there is no actual conflict, and no valid ground for deducing that quantum mechanics is incomplete.

Einstein had to concede that Bohr's position was logically unassailable. But this was because Bohr had retreated to an impregnable position. He had denied Einstein the right to make his conceptual confrontations, and Einstein likened Bohr's overall attitude to solipsism.° People who reject solipsism cannot do so on logical grounds. Nevertheless they reject it. In much the same sense Einstein rejected the Copenhagen interpretation of quantum mechanics—not on the basis of logic but of instinct and belief.

But, with few exceptions, other scientists did not reject it. When they saw that it held together and withstood searching criticism, they were eager to accept it. Immersed in the heady delights of making exciting applications of the new theory, they had little desire to be disturbed anew by doubts about its foundations. The paper by Einstein, Podolsky, and Rosen caused momentary qualms; and a sigh of relief went up when Bohr answered it. He was not the only one to respond. Lesser scientists also wrote to refute it, but as Einstein wryly remarked, their refutations were all different.

Before this, the Copenhagen interpretation had already acquired almost the force of dogma. Anyone daring to question it

---

° A solipsist is a person who believes that he alone exists, everything being what he thinks and feels. It is no use our trying to convince him by slapping his face that we also exist. He merely says that we and the slap are products of his imagination. There is no way at all in which he can be proved wrong.

risked ridicule and loss of reputation. Few could withstand the pressure to conform. Planck disliked the Copenhagen position. De Broglie quickly surrendered to it, though he did so against his better judgment and later sought to escape it. Schrödinger, after momentary distress, argued strongly and vividly against it. And Einstein, as we know, would not accept it. But the objectors were few. The vast majority of quantum physicists were of the Copenhagen persuasion and brusquely dismissed objectors as die-hards. This phase lasted some twenty years, but then new voices were raised in doubt, and although most quantum physicists today still accept the Copenhagen interpretation in one form or another, it no longer commands quite the allegiance it did in its heyday. Not that there is any agreement on an alternative. But significant defections from strict orthodoxy betray a more than passing unease.

That the situation presents problems is often denied. Yet Dirac, for example, writing in 1963, was aware that they exist. He did not envisage a return to classical determinism. But, foreseeing developments as yet unknown, he said, "Perhaps it is impossible to get a satisfactory picture for [the present transitional] stage." The present quantum mechanics, in its Copenhagen interpretation, has consequences that, like those of relativity, outrage common sense. Here is a vivid example proposed by Schrödinger in 1935. It will help us recapitulate. By way of preface we remark that according to the Copenhagen interpretation it is impossible to predict the moment of radioactive decay of an atomic nucleus. This has a familiar ring. Did not Einstein himself use this sort of idea in 1916 in his "amazingly simple" derivation of Planck's formula? Did not Einstein have atoms emit photons spontaneously at unpredictable times? Indeed, Bohr had been greatly influenced by this work of Einstein's and had found in it confirmation of the idea of quantum processes that are spontaneous, uncaused, and unpredictable. Are, then, such things as radioactive decay and other spontaneous emissions instances, to use Einstein's vivid phrase, of God playing dice? Yes, according to Copenhagen. No, according to Einstein. For Einstein had regarded the theoretical unpredictability as due to the incompleteness of the theory, which he regarded as transitory: the fault was in ourselves, not in our atoms. But the Copenhagenists insisted that the quantum equations told the whole story, forbidding *in principle* the prediction of the precise moments at which such spontaneous processes would occur: only probabilities could be known beforehand.

With this in mind, let us look at Schrödinger's example. Place a cat in a closed room with a vial of cyanide. Place a potentially radioactive atom in a detector in such a way that if the atom undergoes radioactive decay the detector will trigger a mechanism that breaks the vial and thus kills the cat. Suppose that the atom is of a type that has a fifty-fifty chance of undergoing radioactive decay in an hour. At the end of the hour is the cat dead or alive?

It must be one or the other—or so we would think. But according to a standard Copenhagen interpretation of the mathematics of quantum mechanics, the cat at the end of the hour is in a limbo state, with a fifty-fifty chance of being alive and a fifty-fifty chance of being dead. Of course, we could look and see whether the cat is alive or dead at the end of the hour. The mere act of taking a peek could hardly kill the cat, and if it were dead could surely not bring it back to life. Common sense thus tells us that here the looking is inconsequential: the cat is either definitely alive or else definitely dead, whether we look or not. Yet according to the above-mentioned interpretation, the looking causes a drastic alteration in the mathematical description of the state of the cat, changing the state from its limbo character either to one in which the cat is definitely alive or else to one in which it is definitely dead, whichever the case happens to be.

Suppose we accept the mathematics as giving a complete description of the relevant aspects of the physical situation. Then the fact that merely looking at the cat should cause so drastic a change in the mathematical description and thus in the physical situation is certainly not easy to accept. Bohr avoided the quantum awkwardness by insisting that we have to consider the total physical phenomenon as a single entity, beginning and ending in the nonquantum, everyday world, with the cat observed at the end as either definitely alive or else definitely dead. We may not stop short in the realm where the quantum holds sway and expect to make everyday sense of an uncompleted physical phenomenon.

This subtle doctrine is impregnable—on its own terms. It denies us the right to form everyday pictures of the intermediate quantum stages between the nonquantum start and the nonquantum finish of a total phenomenon. If we rebel and, with Einstein, regard quantum mechanics as giving an incomplete description of physical reality, we can look on such awkwardnesses as temporary, even though we cannot come up with a better theory. Einstein freely conceded the extraordinary accomplishments of quantum mechanics. In his "Autobiographical Notes," choosing his words with care, he spoke of it as "the most successful physical theory of our era." He did not equate its success with acceptability. He still mistrusted its probabilistic nature. He still disliked its inherent indeterminism. And in answering his critics in the same book that contained his "Autobiographical Notes," he summarized the case for his views in a way that one finds persuasive or not according to one's predilections. It is too early to guess what the outcome will be of the battle between Bohr and Einstein —too early to guess whether the instinctive misgivings of Einstein will in the long run prove to have been in a significant, if unexpected, way well founded. The verdict belongs to the unpredictable future.

The immediate verdict, however, had been strongly against Einstein. He had extended Planck's concept of the quantum when all others, including Planck himself, had feared it; his pioneering ideas on the quantum had been the decisive factor in its initial acceptance; he had welcomed the revolutionary concepts of de Broglie that inspired Schrödinger; he had been in the forefront of scientific fashion; he had been the far-sighted creator of new trends of fashion when the future was shrouded in darkness; and now he came to be widely looked upon by quantum physicists as an outmoded conservative—a has-been battling in vain against an inescapable revolution in the very fundamentals of science.

This attitude of the quantum physicists is understandable. Einstein's daring quantum innovations had been absorbed into the new quantum mechanics, and with the advent of that theory his quantum role had become solely that of a critic. It was easy for eager believers to hold his criticisms against him and to forget how important those very criticisms had been for the refinement of the Copenhagen interpretation. Einstein's general theory of relativity had placed him in the exalted class of Newton. But unlike the special theory of relativity, the general theory gave atomic physicists no aid. Its few applications were to the heavens rather than the laboratory, and the more Einstein immersed himself in this theory and its further generalization, the farther it took him from the immediate concerns of the atomic physicists. His departure from Europe in 1933 for the Institute for Advanced Study, and the relative isolation that he deliberately sought in Princeton, increased his remoteness from the mainstream of physics. Yet even as his influence among physicists dwindled, he remained for the public the supreme symbol and oracle of science.

Meanwhile in Europe other major events, both scientific and political, were building toward a climax. In 1919, while still at Manchester, Rutherford had discovered that violently colliding nuclei of helium and nitrogen could change into nuclei of hydrogen and oxygen: familiar, nonradioactive nuclei, hitherto considered unchanging, had been transmuted. Obviously, this was important. Yet it seemed harmless enough. It was on a microscopic scale, the experiments involving individual atoms, and it attracted far less public attention than that other major scientific event of 1919, Eddington's eclipse verification of Einstein's general theory of relativity.

As the years passed, Rutherford's discovery mushroomed. Other allegedly stable atomic nuclei were also found to be transmutable. In 1932 at the Cavendish Laboratory in Cambridge, where Rutherford was director, individual nuclear transmutations yielded the first clear-cut verification of Einstein's formula $E = mc^2$—a quarter of a century after Einstein had propounded it in 1907. In 1933 an even sharper verification was found, with mass in this case being not partially but totally converted into energy.*

There was now no doubt that Einstein's intuition had been sound, and that mass is an enormous reservoir of energy. We do not extract much energy when we burn an ounce of coal. We cannot even burn an ounce of sand. Yet in a single ounce of coal,

---

* This convenient wording, though customary, can be misleading. When "mass is converted into energy," there is just as much mass after the conversion as before. Initially there is mass of a resting, captive sort. Afterwards some or all of this mass is released and becomes mass in the form of energy of motion or radiation. The 1933 experiment was particularly significant. It verified, albeit for a particular case, not so much Einstein's proposal of 1905 that all energy has mass, but rather his even bolder and much more important realization of 1907 that *all mass* is equivalent to energy.

or sand, or anything else, there resides energy equivalent to that obtained by burning literally tons of coal. Several tons. A hundred thousand or so, in fact. Could this reservoir of energy be tapped for practical purposes? It is interesting that Rutherford and Einstein both said no. Extracting energy from nuclear mass was extremely wasteful: one had to squander much more energy than one extracted.

Yet in 1932, the same year that saw the first sharp confirmation of $E = mc^2$, nuclear transmutations studied in Germany and France had led James Chadwick at the Cavendish Laboratory to discover the neutron, an electrically neutral particle of about the same mass as a hydrogen nucleus. And with the discovery of the neutron the whole situation was changed, though, with one exception, nobody yet realized it. The exception was Einstein's former student Szilard, a refugee in England, who foresaw with startling clarity what the neutron might bring forth. These events of 1932 and 1933 occurred around the time Hitler came to power and scholars began to flee Germany. Schrödinger, for example, who was not a Jew, left his professorship in Berlin, going ultimately to Dublin, while Born left Göttingen and ultimately took a professorship in Edinburgh. Germany's supply of brains was gravely depleted.

In 1934, in Fascist Italy at the University of Rome, Enrico Fermi led his team of collaborators in bombarding atomic nuclei with neutrons which, being electrically neutral, could approach the nuclei without being electrically repelled. The results obtained, which were to earn Fermi the Nobel Prize, need not concern us. Of particular interest for our story is his gentle bombardment of the heaviest and most highly charged nuclei known, those of uranium. He thought that he might have created a hitherto unknown element—we now call it neptunium—but he could not be sure.

What he did not know was that he had done something far more momentous: he had caused uranium nuclei to split. This fact lay all unsuspected, a deadly time bomb biding its time as political tensions mounted. Nazi Germany was rearming while the democracies stood by in seeming paralysis. In March 1936 the Nazis, not yet ready for war, reoccupied the Rhineland in a colossal bluff, and met with no resistance. In that same year Bohr proposed a theory of atomic nuclei in which he showed that they had many of the characteristics of drops of liquid. And meanwhile in Berlin at the Kaiser Wilhelm Institute, the institute with which Einstein had once been associated, the German chemists Otto Hahn and Fritz Strassmann and the Austrian physicist Lise Meitner had together been repeating Fermi's neutron bombardment of uranium and seeking by exhaustive chemical means to determine whether he had produced the new element or not.

In March 1938, as Europe trembled, Nazi Germany took over Austria by military threat without firing a shot. Lise Meitner, who was Jewish, was now in danger. Only her being a foreigner had so far saved her from the harsh anti-Semitic laws of Nazi Germany. Now that Austria, the land of her birth, was part of Germany, she was a foreigner no more, and being a citizen she had to flee. With Bohr's aid she found haven at the Nobel Institute in Sweden, where she was once more a foreigner and once more safe.

In September of 1938 came the Munich Pact, a futile act of appeasement: seeking to stave off war with Germany at any cost, and perhaps to lead Hitler into war with Russia, the demoralized democracies betrayed their ally Czechoslovakia and effectively handed it over to the dictators; and in England the voice of Churchill was raised in protest—Churchill who held no power.

In that same month of September Mussolini, aping Hitler, instituted anti-Semitic laws in Italy, where hitherto there had been no anti-Semitism of consequence. And Fermi, already wary of totalitarianism, quietly began to make plans to leave. For his wife was Jewish.

In November 1938, in a week of organized violence and terror, the Nazis waged war on the Jews of Germany. In December Fermi went to Sweden with his family to receive his Nobel Prize, and from there they went permanently to America, where a professorship was awaiting him at Columbia University in New York City. With World War II less than a year away, Fermi's uranium time bomb began to reveal its secret. Just before Christmas 1938 Hahn and Strassmann completed a technical paper showing that when uranium nuclei are bombarded by relatively slow neutrons, they can yield nuclei of barium, which are only about half as massive as those of uranium. The uranium nuclei must have been split—something that seemed physically out of the question. Flabbergasted, Hahn sent the details to Lise Meitner, who discussed the problem with her nephew Otto Frisch—also a refugee from the Nazis—and, using Bohr's idea of nuclei behaving like drops of liquid, they solved the problem in a few days. Because of the powerful electrical repulsions within a uranium nucleus, it could, as a drop, be so close to the verge of instability that the entry of a single neutron might well cause it to split into two smaller drops—two smaller nuclei. But wait. Because of their mutual electrical repulsion, these nuclei would have to fly violently apart. Where could so much violent energy possibly come from? The answer was Einstein's $E = mc^2$. Without the mass belonging to the energy of the violent motion, the combined mass of the two smaller nuclei would be significantly less than that of the original uranium nucleus and neutron. With the missing mass reappearing as energy of motion, the whole picture was clear. Uranium nuclei had indeed been split into almost equal halves—a process that Meitner and Frisch named *fission*. But even more spectacular was the prediction that the fission must be accompanied by the release of what, on an atomic scale, was a staggering amount of energy.

Events now moved fast. In Copenhagen Frisch made the crucial experiment confirming the existence of the predicted bursts of energy. But before this he hastened to tell the theory to Bohr, who was about to leave for a stay at the Institute for Advanced Study in Princeton. Bohr brought the sensational news to American physicists in January 1939, and uranium fission was widely confirmed there even before Frisch's experiment was published. Fermi was one of the first to realize that among the fragments of a split uranium nucleus there might happen to be further neutrons. If so, as Szilard had foreseen half a dozen years earlier, these neutrons could cause further uranium splittings and there would thus be a remote chance that the process could cascade as a chain reaction, producing a cataclysmic outpouring of energy.

At the end of March 1939, with Czechoslovakia seized and Poland threatened, the British and French decided to stand firm, declaring that if Poland was attacked by Germany they would come to its defense. But the firmness came too late to deflect the world from its headlong rush toward tragedy. In the meantime

Sketch of Einstein by Leonid Pasternak, the father of Boris
Pasternak.

Fermi, and Szilard, and others at Columbia University had taken
a further step toward the atomic bomb by confirming that neutrons are indeed produced in uranium fission.

Nobody could yet tell whether an atomic bomb was feasible.
The odds seemed strongly against it. But among foreign physicists

in the United States, many of them refugees from totalitarianism, there was growing alarm. They could guess all too easily what would happen to civilization if the dictatorships won the race to make atomic bombs. Things would be bad enough even if the democracies won it. But that risk had to be taken, and in April Fermi tried to alert the United States Navy. He elicited little more than a polite expression of interest.

With a mounting sense of foreboding, Szilard enlisted the aid of his Hungarian-born friend Eugene Wigner, professor of theoretical physics at Princeton University. In mid-July they went to see Einstein, who was vacationing on Long Island at remote Nassau Point, near the village of Peconic—enjoying his sailing, and apparently unaware of the possibility of a nuclear chain reaction. To pause at this desperate moment and repeat that Einstein enjoyed playing the violin will seem strangely irrelevant. Yet his love of music is part of a chain reaction of its own, for it had cemented the friendship between him and Queen Elizabeth of Belgium—now the Queen Mother. Who could have foreseen the unlikely events that would emerge from the quartets played at the palace? Who could have dreamed at the time that they would one day be linked to the fact that the Belgian Congo was the world's main source of uranium ore? When Szilard and Wigner came to see Einstein, they told him about the danger of a possible nuclear chain reaction, their initial intention being to urge him to use his influence with the Queen Mother to ensure that uranium ore from the Belgian Congo not reach the Nazis. But events quickly took a different turn, partly because the indefatigable Szilard had been in touch with an influential economist, Alexander Sachs, who proposed something far more ambitious: a direct approach to President Roosevelt. There was a further visit to Nassau Point by Szilard—this time accompanied by the Hungarian-born physicist Edward Teller. Einstein helped draft and later signed a letter to Roosevelt that has become famous. It is dated 2 August 1939, bears the peaceful address of Nassau Point, and reads in part as follows:

> Some recent work by E. Fermi and L. Szilard, which has been communicated to me in manuscript, leads me to expect that the element uranium may be turned into a new and important source

of energy in the immediate future. Certain aspects of the situation seem to call for watchfulness and, if necessary, quick action on the part of the Administration. I believe therefore that it is my duty to bring to your attention the following. . . . it is conceivable . . . that extremely powerful bombs of a new type may . . . be constructed. A single bomb of this type, carried by boat or exploded in a port, might very well destroy the whole port together with some of the surrounding territory. However, such bombs might very well prove to be too heavy for transportation by air. . . . I understand that Germany has actually stopped the sale of uranium from the Czechoslovakian mines which she has taken over. That she should have taken such early action might perhaps be understood on the ground that the son of the German Under-Secretary of State, von Weizsäcker, is attached to the Kaiser Wilhelm Institute in Berlin, where some of the American work on uranium is now being repeated.

It is doubtful that Einstein would have signed this letter had he not already tempered his pacifism in the face of an evil that he regarded as greater than war. One would have expected the effect of the letter—coming from none other than Einstein—to have been spectacular. Yet it was curiously blunted.

Nazi Germany and Communist Russia had long been preaching hatred of one another. Late in August 1939 these unlikely bedfellows signed a nonaggression pact, upon which, on 1 September, Germany attacked Poland, and, in effect, World War II, long simmering, had officially begun.

But the letter of 2 August had still not reached Roosevelt. Sachs did not deliver it till 11 October 1939, three weeks after the Nazi defeat of Poland. True, Roosevelt at once formed an Advisory Committee on Uranium and it made a promising start, but by March 1940, it seemed to have accomplished so little that Szilard and Sachs asked Einstein to write a letter to Sachs that could be shown to Roosevelt. Therefore on 7 March, with the aid of Sachs, Einstein wrote a second letter, this one if anything more urgent than the first. It reached Roosevelt quickly, and in April Einstein was invited to attend an enlarged meeting of the Committee. On 25 April 1940 Einstein wrote to its chairman declining the invitation but stressing the need for urgency.

In May 1940 the Nazis overran both Holland and Belgium, and by 22 June France had surrendered. In the ensuing Battle of Britain, fought in the air, the British prevailed by the slimmest of margins. But they prevailed and the tide of Nazi victory was stemmed. Germany next turned to the east, and on 22 June 1941, despite the nonaggression pact, invaded Communist Russia. And still the uranium project remained in low gear.

Back in February 1939, working in Princeton with the American physicist John Wheeler, Bohr had predicted on the basis of his liquid-drop theory that not all uranium but only a rare form of it would be readily split by neutrons. This prediction, widely doubted at the time, had now been verified, and it implied two things: that a bomb made out of this rare uranium would have a fair chance of working, and that because of the difficulty of extracting this uranium, the construction of the bomb would require an industrial complex of formidable dimensions.

In England, early in 1940, Meitner's nephew Frisch, whom we have already met, and Rudolf Peierls, another refugee from Nazi Germany, had already alerted the British to the probable feasibility of the bomb. Building on the liquid-drop work of Bohr and Wheeler, they had actually computed the approximate amount—unexpectedly small—of the rare uranium that would be needed to cause an explosion. Their work changed the initially skeptical attitude of the British and prompted significant developments in England that influenced major American decisions. Thus, what with the initial American delays, it is possible that, in the United States, even if Einstein had not written his letters of 1939 and early 1940 the bomb would still have been made when it was. For the ultimate decision to go all out on its manufacture did not officially come until 6 December 1941.

And in the Pacific early next morning, the Japanese, all unaware, attacked Pearl Harbor.

The rest of the story of the war and the bomb has been told too often to need retelling here. While armies fought, and millions of defenseless people—men, women, and children, Jewish and non-Jewish—were tortured and murdered in concentration camps, British, American, and refugee scientists, fearful of a possible Nazi monopoly of nuclear weapons, joined forces in the United States to speed the construction of the bomb. On 2 December

1942 in Chicago Fermi, at the head of a team of scientists, produced the first self-sustaining nuclear chain reaction—the first
man-made nuclear fire. In 1943 Bohr, being half Jewish, had to
flee Denmark to escape the Nazis, who had marked him for arrest
and deportation to Germany—a chilling intimation of the fate
that might have been Einstein's had he fallen into Nazi hands.
After adventurous journeys Bohr reached England and from there
went to America, spending much time in Los Alamos, where
J. Robert Oppenheimer was leading a team whose intricate task
it was to design the bomb.

Bohr was among the first to take a long-range view of the
appalling consequences of a successful bomb. In 1944 he spoke
with both Roosevelt and Churchill about the potential political

Einstein and Szilard.

problems of an atomic bomb, but with consequences that were none too fortunate. Indeed, at one stage Churchill, mistakenly believing that Bohr was giving hints to the Russians, spoke seriously of having him arrested. Szilard was another of those who early foresaw the perils that faced mankind. Lacking Bohr's influence, he spoke guardedly to Einstein, and on 25 March 1945, Einstein wrote Szilard a letter of introduction to Roosevelt. Armed with this, Szilard would now be able to present a detailed memorandum to the president.

This he did. But not to Roosevelt. For on 12 April Roosevelt died. Had he lived but a few weeks longer he would have known of the suicide of Hitler, whose dreams of world conquest had been reduced to ashes.

As Germany crumbled, investigators found that the Nazis had, after all, made no significant military nuclear progress. But in America plans were too far advanced to be stopped by this news, and on 16 July 1945 the bomb was tested in a desolate part of New Mexico, producing the first of the mushroom clouds that have cast a pall over the outlook for man.

Of Einstein's letters concerning the possibility of the bomb we already know. During World War II he acted at times as a consultant to the United States Navy. Moreover, in November 1943, when asked to aid a war-bond rally by donating the manuscript of two of his papers, he readily agreed. One of the requested manuscripts was that of his famous paper on relativity, written in Bern in 1905. But in those far-off days Einstein had not been in the habit of keeping his manuscripts once the articles appeared in print. He therefore offered the next best thing. He rewrote the article in his own handwriting as his secretary read it to him from the printed version. It makes a piquant picture: Einstein taking dictation from his secretary. At one point Einstein looked up in surprise and exclaimed, "Did I say that?" On being assured that he did, he said, "I could have said it much more simply." Alas, we do not know what part of the paper he was referring to. When on 3 February 1944 the handwritten copy of the famous paper was offered for auction in Kansas City, it brought in some six million dollars for the war effort. The other manuscript, that of a paper in process of publication, fetched five and a half million. Both manuscripts now reside in the United States Library of

Congress. As for the manuscript of the general theory of relativity, it is now in the library of the Hebrew University in Jerusalem.

But we are shirking what cannot be shirked: on 6 August 1945 an atomic bomb was exploded over Hiroshima.

Einstein's secretary heard the news on the radio. When Einstein came down from his bedroom for afternoon tea she told him. And he said, *"Oh weh,"* which is a cry of despair whose depth is not conveyed by the translation "Alas."

The Einsteins in Japan, ca. 1923.

I I

A Broader Canvas

From World War II we return to World War I. In 1917, with the eclipse expeditions still in the future, Einstein, in Berlin, applied his fledgling general theory of relativity to the universe as a whole. Not really to the universe with all its mysteries. Not to its detail and rich variety. Not to people and their dreams and frustrations, nor to the flower-filled meadows of the earth, nor the earth itself, nor the inconsequential sun that looms so large in our lives, nor the individual stars strewn in the heavens. Just to a bare, abstract, and thoroughly smoothed-out model of the whole, much as we represent the teeming, warring, nonspherical earth by a placid, unfeeling globe.

From the start, Einstein had intended his theory to apply universally. But he had applied it first to the solar system. Now when he sought to apply it to infinite space he found unexpected problems. Try as he would, he could not make it fit at infinite distances. Oh, it could easily fit mathematically. But Einstein was a physicist and for him the neat mathematical fit was a physical misfit. His way of avoiding the misfit was not easily come by. In presenting it in his paper of 1917 that inaugurated the subject of relativistic cosmology, he wrote of "rather a rough and winding road" that he had had to travel to reach his drastic solution of the problem.

To prepare his readers, he began by discussing known difficulties in Newton's theory if one takes the stars to be distributed more or less uniformly throughout infinite space. One can avoid the difficulties by imagining the stars to form a sort of diffuse island in infinite space, being ever more sparse at ever greater distances from the central cluster. But such an islandlike solution to the Newtonian problem did not commend itself to Einstein. He listed simple yet penetrating arguments against it. For example, if, on a gigantic scale, one regarded the stars as particles of a gas, then ultimately, according to the theory of gases, this diffuse island of stars could not exist at all: it could contain no matter. A related argument, also based on the theory of gases, put the situation this way: by a process akin to evaporation, stars would overcome the gravitational ties binding them to the central concourse and escape into the vastness of infinite space, never to return.

Such arguments were more than Newtonian warming-up exercises. Einstein applied them, with others quite different, to the general theory of relativity in a broad-based attack on the problem of relativistic cosmology. We need not pursue the details. Following Mach, Einstein argued that an object acquires inertia only because of the presence of all the other matter in the universe. He spoke of this as the relativity of inertia. His whole approach hinged on it, and on an observational fact: that the relative speeds of the stars among themselves were, on the whole, so small that the universe could be treated as essentially static. This last severely limited the possibilities, and after a considerable struggle Einstein found himself forced to conclude that infinite distances caused relativistic and Machian trouble. What was to be done?

Obviously, if there were no infinite distances they could not cause trouble. So Einstein decided to banish them. It was as simple as that.

But actually it was not as simple as that. It was a desperate remedy, used only as a last resort after all the others that Einstein tried had failed. And to achieve his aim—to be rid of infinite distances without emptying the static universe or leaving it with a gaping wound—Einstein found that he had to make a slight change in his gravitational field equations, thereby, in his eyes, contaminating the purity of their beauty. He added to them a simple term multiplied by an extremely small quantity that he denoted by the symbol λ—the Greek letter lambda.

All very well. But how did Einstein rid himself of the infinite distances? As before, the geometers had already provided the theoretical means. In his new model of the universe Einstein conceived of space, with its three dimensions, as of finite extent yet without boundaries. We can visualize its essence if we think of space as having two dimensions instead of three. Consider first a flat surface of infinite extent. If we want to be rid of its infinite distances we can encircle a region and declare all the rest off-limits; or we can cut most of it away, leaving something with edges—like this page, for example. In contrast to this, consider now the surface of a ball. It is finite. It does not extend to infinite distances. Yet on it there are no edges, no boundaries, no off-limit regions. Indeed, all places on it are similar. It has nothing corresponding to a center.

Nothing corresponding to a center? Surely that is false.

But it is not. Admittedly, the ball has a center; but the center is not on the surface. Remember: for the sake of visualization we are thinking here in terms of two dimensions, not three; and we have to be consistent. We have to imagine here not just space but also the stars and ourselves—everything—as spatially two-dimensional and inhabiting just the two-dimensional *surface* of the ball. The surface is all the space there is. What we normally regard as its interior and exterior we must regard as simply not there—and this is by no means easy to do.

Nevertheless, suppose it done. Then we have envisaged a two-dimensional space—the surface of the ball—that is of finite extent yet has neither boundaries nor center nor off-limit regions. Let us not struggle to visualize the next step, the jump to three dimensions. Like the geometers, Einstein dealt with the problem by formal mathematical analogy. He used a three-dimensional cosmic space lacking center and boundaries yet having only finite extent, and he grafted to it a fourth dimension, time, uncurved and of infinite extent.

By thus banishing infinite spatial distances Einstein brilliantly solved his immediate cosmological problem. But in so doing he apparently introduced others. His smoothed-out universe, taken as a whole, had absolute rest, absolute time, and absolute simultaneity. For he had built it on the approximate assumption that the stars were at rest among themselves. They could thus, as a group, play the scandalous role of a cosmic reference frame at absolute rest, and the simultaneity in this reference frame could therefore qualify as absolute.

It undoubtedly comes as a surprise to see Einstein himself reintroducing absolute rest and absolute simultaneity in this way. In solving his immediate cosmological problem, he apparently subverted his whole previous structure. But he knew what he was doing. It was no more catastrophic than his previous transition from the special theory of relativity to the general where he gave up the constancy of the speed of light. In noncosmological applications his previous work stood firm. As for the absolute cosmic time and absolute cosmic rest, they were a price he dared to pay in order to treat the universe as a whole. And people who later extended his work paid a comparable price.

But why should he and they have to pay a price at all? Because we have only one universe. General principles, no matter how valid, inevitably become special when applied only to a single case. What makes them general is precisely their applicability to a variety of situations. When we dare to make the object of our study the universe as a whole, where can we find a variety of specimens?

Not in our stars, but in ourselves. There turned out to be too great a variety of model universes for aesthetic comfort. Einstein did not know this at the time. Nor did he know that the stars had misled not only himself but all others and that what had been regarded as a fact of observation was to turn out to be false. With the aid of his λ, and his idea of a spatially finite universe uniformly filled with matter at rest, he was led by his calculations to a single basic type of model of the universe. Its size and its mass were both determined by the value of λ. Once this value was fixed by astronomical observation, he would indeed have a unique model for a unique universe. It was a majestic concept. And before we proceed we must stress the importance of Einstein's paper of 1917. For, as we shall see, it was flawed. But we must not let subsequent discoveries diminish its luster in our eyes. It was an outstanding event, and a fruitful one. It set a whole new course. It took an enormous initial step that opened up a path that was to prove unexpectedly tortuous—far too much so to be treated other than sketchily here. Let us tell just a few of the highlights.

Barely had Einstein taken his pioneering step when in 1917

in neutral Holland de Sitter discovered a different solution of Einstein's cosmological equations. This was embarrassing. It showed that Einstein's equations did not lead to a unique model of the universe after all. Moreover, unlike Einstein's universe, de Sitter's was empty. It thus ran counter to Einstein's belief, an outgrowth of the ideas of Mach, that matter and space-time are so closely linked that neither should be able to exist without the other.

De Sitter's universe had confusing properties. For example, it was intended as a static universe—whatever that might mean, considering that it was empty. But if one were to sneak in a few specks of dust, thus leaving its emptiness essentially undisturbed, one could say that these specks would fly apart with ever-increasing speed. In this sense, it was an expanding universe and thus contrary to the prevailing astronomical evidence.

Important progress came in 1922 and again in 1924 when the Russian mathematician Alexander Friedmann found new cosmological solutions of Einstein's equations. Unlike de Sitter's universe they were not empty; unlike Einstein's universe they were not static. Friedmann had discovered the relativistic possibility of nonempty universes, some expanding, others contracting, and yet others passing from expansion to contraction. Moreover, although these could each be of finite spatial extent, they could also be spatially infinite, with space either flat or uniformly curved. It was an unexpectedly rich haul. Yet Friedmann's mathematical discoveries had little immediate impact. Even Einstein did not appreciate them at the time. In fact, his instinctive first impression was somewhat negative.

But shortly before this, the astronomers had begun to agree on a new picture of the universe. They had long realized that our solar system is a peripheral and relatively microscopic part of a vast congregation of stars forming a nebula. We call this nebula our galaxy because to the naked eye it is vaguely visible in the heavens as the wispy Milky Way, the word galaxy being derived from the Greek word for milk. A decisive measurement in 1924 by the American astronomer Edwin Hubble confirmed the view that not all nebulae are relatively close to our galaxy, and soon the picture grew of a universe in which the stars cluster by the billions into islandlike nebulae distributed more or less uniformly throughout space. In terms of nebulae rather than stars, Einstein's supposition of a uniform distribution of matter in space was still acceptable.

But his assumption of a static universe was not. The astronomers, notably Hubble, had been studying, with the aid of the famous one-hundred-inch telescope atop Mount Wilson in California, the distances and motions of the nebulae. And in 1929 Hubble published persuasive evidence not only that distant nebulae were receding, but that their recessions were orderly. The greater the distance the greater the speed of recession, the ratio of speed to distance being more or less the same for all nebulae then studied. This ratio came to be called Hubble's constant. For the most distant of the nebulae studied, the speeds of recession were impressive, rising to some seven thousand miles per second. Considering the enormous mass of a nebula—billions of times that of the sun—such speeds are staggering. Nevertheless, later evidence indicated that they were greatly exceeded by the recessional speeds of yet more distant nebulae.

Had Einstein known all this in 1917, it is possible that he would have sought an expanding, rather than a static, model of the universe: that he would have thought of space as the three-dimensional analogue not of the surface of a ball but of the surface of an expanding balloon. For suppose we think of the nebulae as analogous to nonexpanding spots on a uniformly expanding balloon. Our first thought is likely to be that, since the expansion is uniform, all the spots will recede from one another at the same speed along the surface. But we quickly see that this is not so. Take the simple case of a row of spots, A, B, C, D, each an inch from its neighbor, and imagine that in one second each inch

grows to two. Then, although AB has increased by 1 inch in that

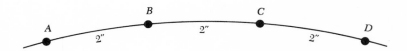

second, AC has increased by 2 inches and AD by 3. Thus the speed of recession increases in proportion to the distance apart, a result in neat accord with Hubble's observations of the nebular recessions.

But in 1917 scientists believed that the stars had only small relative motions, and this had thrown Einstein off. Nevertheless it was not Einstein who linked the new observations of nebular recession to Friedmann's discovery of expanding universes as consequences of Einstein's equations. Nor was it Friedmann. In 1927 the Belgian Abbé Georges Lemaître, unaware of Friedmann's work, proposed on the basis of Einstein's equations a universe that started out as an Einstein universe but then expanded in a Friedmann manner to become, after infinite time, a universe of the de Sitter type. This work, too, might have gone unnoticed— it was published in an obscure journal—had not Eddington in 1930 hailed it enthusiastically and arranged to have it reprinted in English translation in the leading British journal of astronomical research, where it appeared in 1931. Now at last the idea of an expanding universe came into its own, and ultimately Friedmann's work received belated recognition.

That Einstein's equations should have contained within them the possibility of an expanding universe was certainly gratifying. But there were problems. Friedmann had shown that the equations permitted an extraordinary assortment of basically different types of universes. Indeed, in 1931 Lemaître switched his preference to one that started explosively from a tiny, incredibly massive globule that he called a primeval atom. But Einstein's dream of uniqueness was shattered, and he was far from pleased by the many possibilities. Almost from the start, he—and de Sitter too— had looked on the added λ term as an aesthetic blemish. As early as 1919, by an ingenious method, Einstein had tried to be rid of it while retaining his closed static universe, saying that the λ term was "gravely detrimental to the formal beauty of the theory." Indeed, he had warned about λ in his basic paper of 1917, in which, at the very end, he wrote:

> In order to arrive at this consistent view, we admittedly had to introduce an extension of the field equations of gravitation that is not justified by our actual knowledge of gravitation. It is to be

emphasized, however, that a positive curvature of space is given by our results even if the supplementary [λ term] is not introduced. That term is necessary only for the purpose of making possible a quasi-static distribution of matter, as required by the fact of the small velocities of the stars.

When this "fact" became no longer a fact, the λ term lost its *raison d'être* for Einstein. From then on he refused to have anything to do with it. By banishing it he did more than restore the beauty of the gravitational equations. He also reduced the number of possible types of Friedmann universes to three, only one of which was closed and thus finite. In 1931 Einstein treated this unique universe as the adult version of his brainchild of 1917. We can think of this so-called oscillating universe as expanding explosively from a compact, fiery globule whose far-flung fragments slow down in their flight, reined in by gravitation, and then fall back to form once again a compact globule.

But if the λ term was missing, the age of the universe came to a billion years or so°—a long time compared with the age of a man, and even with the age of man, but not long enough for the estimated age of the earth. And the universe could hardly be younger than that.

If one kept the λ term—as Lemaître, for example, did—one could extend the theoretical age of the universe, and also have leeway to match the astronomers' estimates of its average density. Pointing to the observational data, cosmologists argued that the λ was needed. But Einstein was adamant. In his view, beauty and logical simplicity were paramount. He trusted his gravitational field equations, unsullied by λ, more than he trusted the astronomical data with which they were in conflict. And as a result he came once more to be regarded as a has-been—this time by cosmologists who felt that his sense of beauty in its unworldliness had here led him grievously astray.

In 1945, for the second edition of his book *The Meaning of Relativity*, Einstein wrote an Appendix in which he summed up his views on cosmology. A dozen years earlier he had concluded with de Sitter that the question of spatial finiteness was something

---

° We use here the numerical situation as it existed a decade or so later. The difference, although of historical interest, does not alter the essentials.

to be decided by observation. In the Appendix he left the question open. But on the banishment of λ he was adamant. He offered no alibis. He said bluntly:

> The age of the universe . . . must certainly exceed that of the firm crust of the earth as found from the radioactive minerals. Since determination of age by these minerals is reliable in every respect, the cosmological theory here presented would be disproved if it were found to contradict any such results. In this case I see no reasonable solution.

Three years later, partly because of the problem of the age of the universe, a fascinating theory was proposed in which the universe had no beginning or end but was in a steady state with matter continually created in space to compensate the attenuation caused by the perpetual expansion.

Yet just before Einstein wrote the 1945 Appendix there had already begun a significant observational development, and in the next quarter-century or so the universe aged by billions of years. Or, to put it more prosaically, the astronomers' estimates went from a billion or so years to something like ten billion, and even more. The age problem was thus eased. But cosmologists preferred to let observation rather than seeming whim decide the numerical value of λ. At first the observational data indicated that λ was not zero. But by the early 1970s the data were more favorable to the possibility that λ is zero and that in a highly smoothed-out sense the universe is of the simple oscillating type that Einstein had favored in 1931. Many cosmologists now follow Einstein's lead in banishing λ. But there are others who regard this action with scorn.

Were Einstein alive, he would be looking on with quiet amusement, steadfast in his rejection of λ and biding his time, convinced that his aesthetic sense would one day be fully vindicated. Let us be patient too.

Back in 1916, even before his cosmological adventure, he had begun considering gravitational waves. It is not surprising that the general theory of relativity—a field theory—should imply the existence of such waves. But by the very nature of the theory, they had to be waves of space itself—ripples of curvature traveling with the speed of light. Or, in four-dimensional terms, frozen corrugations of space-time acquiring for us the aspect of motion because of our passage through time.

It is possible that the American physicist Joseph Weber has actually detected gravitational waves. If his results are confirmed, his feat will tower as a dazzling achievement. Among other things, it could provide one of the most important verifications of the general theory of relativity—a verification differing decisively from all others so far known.

Whatever the outcome, we are reminded of Maxwell, whose prediction of electromagnetic waves was not confirmed till after his death. Maxwell's waves were to play an unexpected relativistic role. For, after long delay, they gave rise to a new breed of sky-watchers, the radio astronomers, who use not optical but radio telescopes. And their observations have led to the active involvement of relativists. It would take us too far afield to tell of the quasars, the pulsars, and other discoveries that have flowed from their observations and brought this about. Or to tell how the experimenters, refining their techniques of measurement, are invading the realm of the general theory of relativity and subjecting it to increasingly sophisticated and delicate tests too numerous to mention.

What the future will bring remains to be seen. But already the discovery of the pulsars has confirmed the theoretical prediction of burned-out stars exploding in gravitational collapses that lead to neutron stars—as massive as the sun yet only a dozen or so miles across. And there remains the theoretical prediction of even more catastrophic gravitational collapses leading to "black holes" whose gravitation is so great that even light striving outwards from them can only fall inwards. Do the black holes exist or are they figments of the relativistic equations? Time may tell. The search is on.

This at least can be said: that as of the early 1970s, more than fifty years after its advent, the general theory of relativity has met all experimental tests, and that after decades of being before its time it is coming richly into its own amid the excitement and hurly-burly of current cosmic research.

1 2

All Men Are Mortal

Once more we defy the strict order of time and return to an earlier era. With his arrival in Princeton, Einstein entered the final phase of his life, and soon we shall tell of autumnal things, some with the bright glow of early fall, but others tinged with the somber hue that comes with the chill of winter.

Let Einstein's own words set the mood. It is the war-weary year 1918. The bending of light is still unverified. World fame has not yet made its intrusion. Einstein is happy in his work. Scientists already recognize his greatness. Yet the exaltation that he expresses has an undertone of sadness. He is speaking of Planck at an official celebration of Planck's sixtieth birthday, but the words reveal something of Einstein himself:

> I believe with Schopenhauer that one of the strongest motives that leads men to art and science is escape from everyday life with its painful crudity and hopeless dreariness, from the fetters of one's own ever-shifting desires. A finely tempered nature longs to escape from personal life into the world of objective perception and thought; this desire may be compared with the townsman's irresistible longing to escape from his noisy, cramped surroundings into the high mountains, where the eye ranges freely through the still, pure air and fondly traces out the restful contours apparently built for eternity.
>
> With this negative motive there goes a positive one. Man tries

to make for himself in the fashion that suits him best a simplified and intelligible picture of the world: he then tries to some extent to substitute this cosmos of his for the world of experience, and thus to overcome it. This is what the painter, the poet, the speculative philosopher, and the natural scientist do, each in his own fashion. Each makes this cosmos and its construction the pivot of his emotional life, in order to find in this way the peace and security that he cannot find within the all-too-narrow realm of swirling personal experience. . . .

The supreme task of the physicist is to arrive at those universal elementary laws from which the cosmos can be built up by pure deduction. There is no logical path to these laws; only intuition, resting on sympathetic understanding, can lead to them. . . . The longing to behold [cosmic] harmony is the source of the inexhaustible patience and perseverance with which Planck has devoted himself . . . to the most general problems of our science. . . . The state of mind that enables a man to do work of this kind is akin to that of the religious worshiper or the lover; the daily effort comes from no deliberate intention or program, but straight from the heart.

In 1921 Einstein had written to a friend: "Discovery in the grand manner is for young people . . . and hence for me a thing of the past." Yet in the years between 1917 and 1931 he had not been idle. We already know of his role in the tumultuous emergence of quantum mechanics, and the isolation that resulted from his battle over its interpretation. In 1918 the outstanding German mathematician Hermann Weyl—then a professor at the Zurich Poly—proposed an extension of the general theory of relativity that was so natural and ingenious that it deserved a better fate than the one that befell it. Because of the curvature of space-time in Einstein's theory, and the consequent lack of straight lines, direction played strange tricks. To appreciate the effect of curvature on direction, let us consider the curved, two-dimensional surface of the earth. Imagine two ships far apart starting out from the equator and sailing due north. We would surely tend to agree that they were parallel when they started, and that since they were both going due north each was traveling directly ahead, veering neither to right nor to left. Yet as the ships travel northward along lines of longitude they become more and more inclined toward each other. This being the case, we would surely deny that they remain parallel.

It occurred to Weyl that—to stay with our ship analogy—not only the directions but also the sizes, though not the shapes of the ships might change as a result of travel,* and he introduced this sort of change of size as a possibility in curved space-time thus making a fundamental alteration in its geometrical structure. Our first impression is likely to be that if a superb mathematician wishes to play with such ideas it is his privilege to do so. But Weyl had something more in mind. He showed that with this new geometrical structure of space-time he could, in a natural way, link Einsteinian gravitation with Maxwellian electrodynamics. This at once excites our interest. For when Einstein treated gravitation as curvature he was unable to give electromagnetism a correspondingly fundamental geometrical role. But Weyl, with his changes of lengths, had made electromagnetism too an aspect of geometry—a geometrical partner of gravitational curvature. He had thus constructed what we call a *unified field theory.*

Mathematically and aesthetically, Weyl's theory was a considerable achievement. But Einstein, ever the physicist, quickly saw that it was unacceptable. While others gazed in admiration at what Weyl had wrought, Einstein put his finger on its physical flaw: namely, that it implied that the lengths of objects would depend on their pasts. In space-time, "lengths" can refer to lengths of time as well as space. Atoms emit light whose pulsations mark off well-defined lengths of time, as is shown by the existence of quite sharp spectral lines. If the atoms had had widely different pasts, they would, according to Weyl's theory, mark off discrepant lengths of time, thus giving rise *en masse* not to spectral lines but rather to spectral smears. It follows that we may not tamper with lengths in the manner proposed by Weyl. Such was Einstein's official argument against Weyl's theory. It shows a master physicist in action, instinctively sensing the central issue. But it leaves something hidden. Here is an excerpt from a letter to Weyl in 1918 that shows a deeper Einstein objection:

---

* In a manner having nothing at all to do with the FitzGerald-Lorentz contraction.

Could one really accuse the Lord God of being inconsistent if he passed up the opportunity discovered by you to harmonize the physical world? I think not. If he had made the world according to your plan [I would have said] to him reproachfully: "Dear God, if it did not lie within Thy power to give an objective meaning to the [equality of sizes of separated rigid bodies] why hast Thou, Oh Incomprehensible One, not disdained . . . to [preserve their shapes]?"

Here indeed we see the master physicist in action.

Reluctantly, Weyl withdrew his theory from the realm of gravitation, finding a niche for part of it in the realm of the quantum, where it did link up satisfactorily with electromagnetism. In those days only two main fundamental "forces" were known, the gravitational and the electromagnetic. Weyl had made people realize that to treat the one but not the other as an aspect of geometry was inartistic. The search was now on for a new type of geometry that would satisfactorily encompass both, and it was to occupy Einstein to the end of his days. If we tell here of a few of the unified field theories that were proposed by him and others it is partly because they betray a pattern amid their variety. As for Weyl, he was appointed to a professorship at Göttingen, but with the coming to power of the Nazis he left for the United States, where he became a colleague of Einstein at the Institute for Advanced Study.

Eddington built a unified field theory similar to but more general than Weyl's. On a globe, when we make a journey by the shortest route, we find ourselves traveling along the straightest route allowed by the curvature of the surface. This link between "shortest" and "straightest," which survived in Einstein's curved space-time, was broken by Weyl; and it remained broken in the theory of Eddington, which he proposed in 1921.

But in that same year T. Kaluza, in Germany, took a quite different tack. Introducing a somewhat atrophied fifth dimension, he wrote down Einstein's gravitational equations unchanged—but for five dimensions instead of four. And behold, they linked gravitation and electromagnetism without further ado.

In 1923 Einstein extended Eddington's work. Soon, however, he became dissatisfied with what he had constructed, and in 1925

produced a different unified field theory. This time he was enthusiastic, writing in his introductory paragraph, "After an unremitting search during the past two years I now believe I have
found the true solution." His theory rested in major part on the
following arithmetical coincidence. In one of the customary ways
of describing electromagnetism six field quantities are used. The
metrical tensor $g_{\mu\nu}$ has a certain symmetry. Remove that symmetry
and it will automatically contain not ten but sixteen field quantities. Use ten combinations of these for gravitation and there will
be six left over—just the number of field quantities with which to
represent electromagnetism. This idea of Einstein's is worth re-
membering in view of later developments.

We pass now to 1928, the year of the death of Lorentz, whom
Einstein revered. Speaking beside the grave, Einstein eulogized
Lorentz not only as a "genius" but also as "the greatest and noblest
man of our times, [who] shaped his life like an exquisite work of
art down to the smallest detail." Coming, as they did, from a usually ebullient nonconformist, these were heartfelt words. Years
later Einstein was to say:

> Whatever came from this supreme mind was lucid and beautiful
> as a good work of art. . . . If we younger people had known H. A.
> Lorentz only as a sublime mind, our admiration and respect for him
> would have been unique. But what I feel when I think of H. A.
> Lorentz is far more than that. He meant more to me personally
> than anybody else I have met in my lifetime.

Einstein said this in 1953, a quarter-century after the death of
Lorentz in 1928.

In that same year 1928, as we know, Einstein himself had been
gravely ill. But he continued to work. It was his medicine—his
very life. He had given up his unified field theory of 1925 despite
his initial enthusiasm. He had worked on the theory of Kaluza
with its puzzling fifth dimension for which there seemed no physical counterpart. And now, in 1928, he embarked on a new approach to a unified field theory. His new theory, involving what he
called "distant parallelism," was in a way the reverse of Weyl's.
We recall that Weyl, seeing parallelism disturbed, had decided to

disturb lengths too. In contrast, Einstein, seeing lengths undisturbed, decided to introduce a comparably undisturbed parallelism, the trick being to do this without giving up the curvature of
space-time. By early 1929 he had solved the main problems involved in writing down field equations for his unified field theory.
On the day of official publication of the third of a formidably
technical series of nine articles on the theory that were compre-
sensible only to specialists, excited headlines appeared in foreign
newspapers throughout the world. A paper in New York City
scored an absurd journalistic scoop by printing an English translation of the whole abstruse article, complete with formulas, cabled
direct from Berlin. In this frenzied, unscientific atmosphere, Einstein's new theory was hailed in the press as an outstanding scientific advance. Yet Einstein had stated in his article that it was still
tentative; and soon he found that he had to abandon it.

112 Mercer Street, Einstein's house in Princeton.

Lotte Ja

By the end of 1930 he and his collaborator Mayer had sent in for publication a quite different theory, designed to retain the essence of Kaluza's five-dimensional idea while remaining in four dimensions. This attempt, too, Einstein ultimately abandoned. And when he arrived at the Institute for Advanced Study in 1933, he and Mayer were still seeking new geometrical structures for possible use in the quest for unification.

We spoke earlier of a pattern amid the variety of unified field theories. What was this pattern? What did the theories have in common? We should ask, rather, what they lacked in common. In his earlier search for the general theory of relativity, Einstein had been guided, for example, by his principle of equivalence linking gravitation with acceleration. Where were the comparable guiding principles that could lead to the unique construction of a unified field theory? No one knew. Not even Einstein. Thus the search was not so much a search as a groping in the gloom of a mathematical jungle inadequately lit by physical intuition.

Often in the Princeton years Einstein was to think that he had at last achieved the unification he sought, only to find by further calculation that his equations had unacceptable consequences. Yet he continued undaunted. Ernst Straus, who worked with him at the Institute for Advanced Study, gives this vivid picture:

> The first theory on which we worked when I came to be his assistant he had worked on alone for over a year, and we continued working on it for about nine months more. Then, one evening I found a class of solutions to the field equations which in the light of the next morning seemed to show that the theory could not have physical significance. We turned it over and over all morning but the conclusion was inevitable. So we left for home one-half hour early. I must say that I was quite dejected and I was wondering: if the pick-and-shovel man feels so badly about the collapse of the edifice, how badly must the architect feel! But when I came to work the next morning Einstein was eager and excited: "You know, I've been thinking last night and the proper approach seems to be . . ." This was the start of an entirely new theory, also relegated to the trash heap after half-a-year's work and mourned no longer than its predecessor.

Straus tells too that "often when [Einstein] noted a satisfactory feature he would exult, 'This is so simple God could not have passed it up.' "

For a while the search for a unified field theory became a mathematical fad indulged in by many people, famous and not, who produced an enormous number of competing geometrical theories. When the fad began to die down, Einstein continued. But still he could find no physical guidance, no magical insight, and because of this, many physicists looked upon his long search with barely concealed contempt. But Einstein could recall the ten arduous years of unremitting labor—with a similar resolute discarding of seemingly promising ideas—that had taken him from his special to his general theory of relativity. In his search for a unified field theory, all he could build on was his unparalleled lifetime experience and his profound conviction that there *ought* to be such a theory—that, as the ancient Hebrews put it, the Lord is one. This was enough to sustain him in his quest for more than thirty years through disappointment after disappointment. True, he had not been able to keep abreast of the latest developments in physics. True, his inspiration was flagging. True, ideas came far less torrentially than when he was younger. But they came nevertheless, and his search for a unified field theory was characteristic of the indomitable ferocity and tenacity with which he pursued his ideas throughout his life.

In 1936 he was saddened by the death, after a long, wasting illness, of Marcel Grossmann, without whose faithful friendship the genius of Einstein might never have flowered. Ties with the past were breaking. Moreover, the initial excitement about the general theory of relativity had long since died down, and among physicists the theory was in eclipse. Nevertheless Einstein worked on. And in 1937, with the Polish physicist Leopold Infeld and the author as collaborators, he sent in for publication a major discovery—a consequence of his general theory of relativity that enhanced its already extraordinary beauty and revealed an aspect of it unmatched by other theories. Independently and essentially by a different method that used additional assumptions about matter, the Russian physicist Vladimir Fock in 1938 sent in for publication what amounted to the same discovery. In the case of Einstein the discovery had its roots in work he had done ten years before with J. Grommer, but now the idea had matured in Einstein's mind into a concept of magnificent subtlety. So complex and extensive were the new calculations that only their outline could be published, the complete calculations being deposited in the library of the Institute for Advanced Study, where specialists could consult them. Yet the essence of the work lends itself to simple description.

The gravitational field equations restrict the curvature of space-time. Some types of curvature are permitted, others are not. A crude analogy is a sheet of paper, which, though it can curl in many ways, cannot bulge. Consider, now, a gravitating astronomical body. Alone, it would be associated with a characteristic space-time curvature, which we may indicate diagrammatically like this:

But suppose we had several gravitating bodies. If each preserved its characteristic space-time curvature unchanged, the curvatures would clash, like this:

Obviously we have to modify them if we want them to merge smoothly like this:

How do we find the right way to do this smoothing? We consult the field equations. But the field equations prove stricter than we expect. They allow the curvatures to be joined smoothly only if the world lines of the gravitating bodies spiral around one another according to certain rules; or, in everyday language, only if the gravitating bodies move in certain highly restricted ways.

What are these ways? Perhaps you have guessed. They are, substantially, the ways permitted by Newton's theory of gravitation. Not precisely, of course. There are deviations. And these reflect the difference between the gravitational theories of Newton and Einstein.

This is clearly a major result. But if we stop at this point we shall miss its deeper significance. Newton's theory had two distinct parts: a law of gravitation and laws of motion. Maxwell's similarly: field equations of electromagnetism plus Newton's laws of motion —with, as go-between, an extraneous formula expressing what is called the Lorentz force. Einstein's theory had hitherto also seemed split: gravitational field equations and a "shortest-path" rule for the planetary motions—a makeshift rule, with the planets treated as specks having no gravitational space-time curvature of their own. But now one could see that Einstein's theory was in fact not split in this way. The gravitational field equations them-selves controlled the motion, and they did so not for just specks but for massive gravitating objects with curvatures of their own. The field equations needed no supplementary rules. They were self-sufficient. The structure of the theory thus had a greater economy of rules, a greater simplicity, a greater homogeneity, a greater artistry, than even Einstein had imagined when he had constructed it some twenty years before.

What if one placed Maxwell's field equations into a general-relativity setting? Then Einstein's motional magic worked even more powerfully than before. From the self-sufficient field equa-tions the Lorentz force, no longer an interloper, emerged auto-matically along with the motion.

In the course of the intricate calculations there were unpleasant surprises. Things did not always work out as expected. At times the situation seemed so hopeless that Einstein's collaborators be-came despondent. But Einstein's courage never faltered, nor did his inventiveness fail him. He had been working on the problem a decade and more, and for him a setback was merely a setback, not a defeat. To his despondent, new-come collaborators he said with a laugh that if the world had already waited all these years for the idea to come to fruition, a few extra months of waiting would make little difference; and if, in the end, the idea did not work, that would be no tragedy, provided one had tried.

Corresponding to the three dimensions of space, three equa-tions are needed for the motion of a particle. But the self-sufficient gravitational field equations, being four-dimensional, would surely give four equations per particle. To Einstein's collaborators this loomed as a major threat to the success of the project. But not to

Einstein. He saw in it a wonderful possibility: the extra equation would allow only certain orbits in the manner of Bohr's theory of 1913. Imagine the irony, after the battle with Bohr, if Bohr's early quantum theory and analogous quantum effects should prove to be contained in Einstein's general theory of relativity. Alas, it did not work out that way. The fourth equation imposed no limitations. But this unfulfilled hope reveals the persistence and roving breadth of Einstein's striving for physical oneness.

Sometimes in the course of the work there came utter bafflement. On those occasions, when excited discussion failed to break the deadlock, Einstein would quietly say in his quaint English, "I will a little tink"—he could not pronounce the *th*. Then, in the sudden silence, he would pace slowly up and down or walk around in circles, all the time twirling a lock of his hair around his forefinger. There was a dreamy, far-away, yet inward look on his face. No sign of stress. No outward indication of intense concentration. No lingering trace of the previous excited discussion. Only a placid inner communion—Einstein working at his highest pitch. Minutes would go by. Then, quite suddenly, he would return to the world, a smile on his face, and an answer to the problem on his lips, but not so much as a hint of the reasoning—if such it was—that had led him to the solution.

On 20 December 1936, only three years after leaving Europe for Princeton, Einstein's wife Elsa died. Ashen with grief, Einstein insisted on continuing the work, saying that now he needed it more than ever. At first his attempts to concentrate were pitiful. But he had known sorrow before and had learned that work was a precious antidote.

Long before the outbreak of World War II Einstein, like Bohr and other such men, had done what they could to help people escape from Nazi Germany. Elsa Einstein, too, had been active. In this connection violinist Boris Schwarz, whom we have already met, has an interesting story to tell. Bureaucracy acts in ways too complex to be made wholly comprehensible in a book about Einstein. Boris Schwarz and his parents, all born in Russia, had become naturalized German citizens. Nevertheless the Nazis, on coming to power, canceled the Schwarzes' citizenship—after all, were they not Jews? This cancellation made the Schwarzes stateless persons, and as such they were somewhat less vulnerable than

German-born Jews. Within Germany they were not allowed to give concerts, except to Jewish groups. But they were issued stateless passports that gave them the opportunity to go abroad—provided they could obtain visas. To obtain a visa, however, the Schwarzes first had to have a German re-entry permit. Although the Nazis had revoked the Schwarzes' citizenship, they did not withhold the re-entry permits, and the Schwarzes were thus able to earn a living by giving concerts abroad.

But it was becoming increasingly clear that the future in Germany offered them little but danger and possible violent death. In desperation they approached the pastor of the American Church in Berlin. He wrote to the Einsteins, and as a result the Schwarzes received from America a warm letter, dated 25 August 1935, from "Elsa Alberti," a pseudonym that they had no difficulty in deciphering. Nowhere in the letter was there mention of the dangerous name *Einstein*. Further letters followed, although Elsa Einstein was already seriously ill.

Meanwhile Einstein had been using his influence, and early in 1936 Boris Schwarz unexpectedly received word from the American Embassy in Berlin that a United States entry visa was awaiting him there. Entry visas to America were in great demand and in short supply. To arrange for this one to be granted, Einstein had had to do more than just use his influence. He had had to sign an affidavit guaranteeing that if Boris Schwarz came to America he would not become a public charge. This Einstein did, offering, as on several other occasions, his own financial resources as guarantee. But in the case of someone who was not a relative, a single affidavit was not enough. So Einstein induced a wealthy American investment banker to join him in vouching for Boris Schwarz. Even so, all was not plain sailing. When Schwarz went to the United States Embassy, he was asked to give proof that he indeed knew Einstein. For there was no telling whether he—or for that matter Einstein—was telling the truth in saying that they were known to each other. The times were desperate and the entry rules stringent. The embassy staff could little afford to take chances, but Einstein could as little bring himself not to. Fortunately quite striking evidence existed. Schwarz showed the officials photographs of Einstein and himself and his father playing music together. As a result the visa was granted, and Schwarz was able to enter the United States, where Einstein had already approached the conductor Eugene Ormandy and others to ease the search for a position. Ormandy, feeling greatly honored by Einstein's request, gave unstinting aid and then ventured to make a request of his own—a photo of Einstein.

Once Boris Schwarz was admitted, the parents were quickly able to follow, and the Berlin trio were thus happily reunited. When they played music together in Princeton, Einstein's enjoyment must have been greatly enhanced by the knowledege that he had saved them from almost certain death in the Nazi gas chambers.

The Schwarzes were lucky. Their story was not typical of the fate of Jews under the Nazis. We have told it in some detail so that it can stand as an epitome of the untiring efforts of Einstein to help friends and former colleagues and even strangers to escape the Nazi persecution. Indeed, so recklessly did he write affidavits that for a while they underwent a form of inflation that significantly reduced their value. Nevertheless, one way or another, many men owed their lives to Einstein's intervention.

Although the case of Infeld does not come within the same category, it is somewhat related. For Infeld, despite his gifts as a physicist, despite the joint work on the equations of motion, and despite Einstein's own efforts on his behalf, was unable to find a position in America. To help him, Einstein collaborated with him on a book, *The Evolution of Physics,* that was published in 1938. It described for the layman the majestic development of physical science as seen by the man who had revolutionized scientific thought while maintaining a striking continuity with the broad sweep of the past. The book was an immediate success, and with its success Einstein said to Infeld, "You are a made man." Undoubtedly the book played no small part in Infeld's obtaining a position in Canada.

We have already told of Einstein's letter of 2 August 1939 to Roosevelt warning of the possibility of a uranium bomb. A week later, on 9 August, we find Einstein writing earnestly to Schrödinger. About the bomb? No. But about that other disturbing problem, the interpretation of quantum mechanics. After congratulating Schrödinger on his argument concerning the cat in a limbo quantum state, neither definitely alive nor definitely dead,

Einstein speaks of "the mystic"—he means Bohr—"who forbids, as being unscientific, an inquiry about something that exists independently of whether or not it is observed, i.e., the question as to whether or not the cat is alive at a particular instant before an observation is made." Twice in the letter Einstein says that he is "as convinced as ever" that quantum mechanics gives an incomplete description of reality. And toward the end comes this passage, which seems to refer not only to the problems of the quantum but also to his hopes of solving them by means of a unified field theory: "I write this to you," says Einstein, and we have to remember that he is writing to one of his staunchest supporters, "not with any illusions that I shall convince you, but with the sole intention of letting you understand my point of view, which has driven me into deep solitude."

Three days later Einstein wrote to the Queen Mother of Belgium. About uranium? No. But about his nostalgia for Europe, his summer enjoyment of sailing and chamber music, and the advantages of solitude.

In 1935 the Einstein household had gone briefly to Bermuda to re-enter the United States with permanent visas. On 22 June 1940, after the necessary five-year waiting period, Einstein, his daughter Margot, and his secretary took the examinations for United States citizenship. On 1 October they were sworn in as citizens. With the Battle of Britain at its height and the survival of civilization in doubt, the world situation was bleak. A few months before, France had surrendered to the Nazis—it happened on the day of the citizenship examinations. A year later, to the very day, the Nazis invaded Russia, and it seemed as if Nazism was on the verge of victory. But, as we know, the tide had already turned, and it is appropriate to tell here of an erroneous and little-known theory that Einstein put forward three years later.

The war in Europe by then was nearing its end. On 6 June 1944, while the Russians attacked in the east, the Americans, British, and Canadians crossed the English Channel in a giant amphibious operation that created a beachhead in Normandy and spelled the doom of Hitler's dream of enslaving the world. By November the German armies were in serious trouble, retreating rapidly on both fronts. Then, on 16 December 1944, the Germans launched a surprise counterattack in the west that almost broke

Einstein and others at the Copernican Quadricentennial, 1943, in Carnegie Hall, New York City. Since France was under Nazi occupation at the time, Einstein symbolically wore academic regalia of the Sorbonne.

through the allied lines; it developed into what came to be called the Battle of the Bulge. On hearing of the attack, Einstein became seriously alarmed. He reasoned as follows: All the evidence pointed to the fact that the Nazis had already lost the war. Why, then, should they waste lives by launching a counterattack that could ultimately gain them nothing? They must have had a good reason. Einstein theorized that they had produced what he referred to as "the radioactive bomb" and were spending lives to buy time to enable them to use it. He could not know that they had no bomb and that the attack had been personally ordered by Hitler as a last desperate gamble.

From the failure of the Nazi counterattack and the failure of the Nazis to make use of nuclear explosives, Einstein may well have inferred that the Nazis had after all not succeeded in creating a workable atomic bomb. But the danger of an American bomb still existed, and when the bomb was exploded over Hiroshima his worst fears were realized. His horror of the bomb, whether in dictatorial or democratic hands, weighed heavily on his conscience. Not because he had written urgently to Roosevelt in 1939, when he feared that the Nazis would develop the weapon first and thus control the world. Not because, in all innocence, he had propounded the formula $E = mc^2$ in 1907. Not for these reasons, but because as a man in a position of unique public esteem, he felt a profound moral obligation to use his influence to the utmost to try to save mankind from horrors that, despite Hiroshima and Nagasaki, it did not yet comprehend.

Whenever he could, and his chances were many, for he was much in the public eye, he warned of the danger and fervently preached the cause of world government. When leading scientists banded together in 1946 to form an Emergency Committee of Atomic Scientists, they asked Einstein—the Einstein whose quantum-mechanical views they spurned and whose search for a unified field theory they derided—this Einstein, the most famous of them all, they asked to be their chairman; and he unhesitatingly accepted. For they needed to capture the earnest attention of the public and of influential public figures. And they needed funds to carry out the colossal educational task of making people realize elementary things, such as that America had no inviolable monopoly of the "secret" of how to make the bomb, that other nations would inevitably discover it for themselves, and that the political structure of the world was now outmoded. By the sheer magic of his name Einstein was able to call forth financial aid and to provide a special prestige that commanded attention.

He threw himself unsparingly into many such activities, and he urged with fervor the creation of a supranational military force to preserve peace among nations. This idea was, to most, a forlorn hope. It had been proposed before in less dangerous times, but to no avail. What chance was there that it would be accepted now, even under the threat of extinction? Nevertheless, without some such form of world authority Einstein could see no hope for mankind.

And yet, behind his impassioned efforts to warn of disaster if the world remained disunited there were ghosts that would not be still. Einstein who had ardently preached reconciliation after World War I, Einstein who had been impatient with those on both sides of that conflict who clung to their bitterness against their enemies, this very Einstein—a different Einstein—never forgave Germany its Nazi atrocities against the Jews. Even in 1933, at the time of his resignation from the Prussian Academy, which had leveled false charges against him, he had written to Planck:

> . . . in all these years I have only enhanced Germany's prestige and never allowed myself to be alienated by the systematic attacks on me in the rightist press, especially those of recent years, when no one took the trouble to stand up for me. Now, however, [and this, remember, was back in 1933] the war of annihilation against my fellow Jews compels me to employ, in their behalf, whatever influence I may possess in the eyes of the world.

And when in 1946, after the defeat of Nazi Germany, he was invited to rejoin the Bavarian Academy, he refused, saying, "The Germans slaughtered my Jewish brethren; I will have nothing further to do with the Germans. . . ." In 1949, when he was asked to renew official ties with the Kaiser Wilhelm Institute, renamed the Planck Institute, he refused, saying:

> The crime of the Germans is truly the most abominable ever to be recorded in the history of the so-called civilized nations. The conduct of the German intellectuals—seen as a group—was no better than that of the mob. And even now there is no indication of any regret or any real desire to repair whatever little may be left to restore after the gigantic murders. In view of these circumstances I feel an irrepressible aversion to participating in anything that represents any aspect of public life in Germany. . . .

In 1951, after firmly rejecting many other invitations, he refused to rejoin, mark you, the Peace Section of a Prussian organization, writing:

> Because of the mass murder that the Germans inflicted upon the Jewish people, it is evident that a self-respecting Jew could not

Einstein and Otto Nathan, May 1947.

possibly wish to be associated in any way with any official German institution. . . .

And to the end of his days he did not relent.

Yet, although part of him must have been haunted by the past—and haunted, too, by the atomic future—he still found joy and contentment in life, and an inner peace in his struggle to create a satisfactory unified field theory. We have already described some of his attempts. Let us pass over others and tell of a theory on which he had published a paper in 1945. On this theory, which underwent various modifications, he worked for the remaining years of his life. It was a close cousin of his theory of 1925, the one with an unsymmetric $g_{\mu\nu}$ containing sixteen quantities, ten combinations of which were used for gravitation and six for electromagnetism. Thus for Einstein there had been something prophetic after all in his words of 1925: "I now believe I have found the true solution."

Einstein in his study at 112 Mercer Street, ca. 1946.

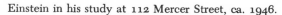

H. Landshoff

No satisfactory way exists to explain this final theory in simple terms. No pictures come to our aid. It is intensely mathematical, and over the years, with helpers and alone, Einstein surmounted difficulty after difficulty only to find new ones awaiting him. Various researchers, Infeld included, showed that the field equations led to manifestly incorrect motions: electrically charged particles would move as if they had no charge. Despite this, Einstein kept his faith in the theory. The field equations were not necessarily in final form. Besides, Einstein had for a long time been seeking a deeper unity—a unity of field and matter. For these, though linked, had hitherto been things of basically different sorts. In the general theory of relativity the pure field equations were adulterated at the places occupied by matter. As Einstein pointed out, there seemed no way of retaining the general theory of relativity without the concept of a field. And he argued that if one believed wholeheartedly in the basic idea of a field theory, matter should enter not as an interloper but as an honest part of the field itself. Indeed, one might say that he wanted to build matter out of nothing but convolutions of space-time. In his new theory, therefore, he looked for pure field equations that would remain pure even at those places where there was matter, and he hoped that matter would then manifest itself as a sort of lumpiness of the field. He hoped too that by insisting on solutions of the pure field equations—the technical term is solutions free of singularities—automatic restrictions would appear corresponding to the existence of atoms and quanta. To most physicists it seemed a remote chance at best, even in principle. In practice the mathematical difficulties were staggering. Suppose Einstein did succeed in finding appropriate field equations. How would he go about finding the desired solutions free of singularities? He knew that there was no standard practicable method. Nevertheless he struggled on, saying despairingly, "I need more mathematics."

In Zurich, in 1948, his first wife, Mileva, died, severing yet another link with the past. Einstein's own health was causing serious concern, and at the year's end he underwent an abdominal operation. In the words of a close associate: "It was an exploratory one and—at that time to our immense relief—'only' an enlargement of the abdominal aorta was discovered."

Despite convalescence in Florida, Einstein remained frail, but

Einstein, his daughter Margot, and his secretary, Helen Dukas, May 1947.

Maja Winteler-Einstein,
ca. 1940.

Lotte Neustein

he returned as quickly as possible to Princeton, in part to be near his sister, Maja. For Maja, who had visited him there in 1939, had remained when war broke out; and in May 1946 she had suffered a stroke that led to increasing paralysis. Death did not come to her quickly. She lingered on till June of 1951, and shortly thereafter Einstein wrote to a cousin:

> During the last years I read to her every evening from the finest books of old and new literature. Curiously, her intelligence had barely suffered in spite of her progressive illness, although near the end she could hardly speak audibly. Now I miss her more than one can imagine. But I am relieved that she has it behind her. . . .

The years of nightly reading of great works to his dying sister were a sad echo of the joyful Olympia Academy, where, too, great books had been read. In 1953, on a visit to Paris, Habicht met with Solovine. It was 12 March, two days before Einstein's seventy-fourth birthday. Moved by their memories of the wonderful days in Bern half a century before, the two aging men sent Einstein a picture postcard of Notre Dame addressed in French "To the President of the Olympia Academy, Albert Einstein, Princeton, New Jersey, U.S.A.," and of course it reached him. Crowded into the cramped space of the card were these two nostalgic messages in German:

> To the Right Reverend, incomparable President of our Academy:
> In your non-presence despite the reserved seat, there was held today a sad-solemn session of our world-famous Academy. The reserved seat, which we always keep warm, *awaits*, yes *awaits* and *awaits* your coming. Habicht.

The nostalgic "Olympia Academy" postcard sent to Einstein from Paris by Habicht and Solovine, 12 March 1953.

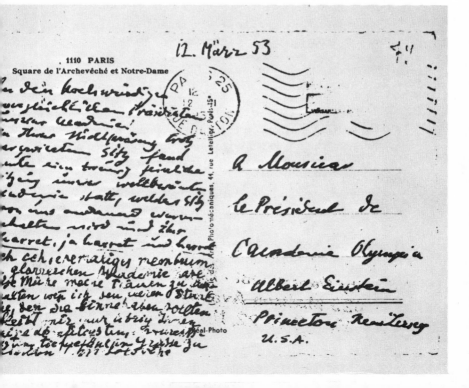

I also, erstwhile member of the glorious Academy, have great
difficulty holding back my tears when I see the empty chair that
you should have occupied. There remains for me only to convey
to you my most humble, most reverent, and heartfelt greetings.
M. Solovine.

Although in frail health, Einstein had not lost his impishness.
With a mock-solemnity that could not hide his own nostalgia, he
replied on 3 April 1953:

To the immortal Olympia Academy!
In your short active life, dear Academy, you took delight, with
childlike joy, in all that was clear and intelligent. Your members
created you to make fun of your long-established sister Academies.
How well their mockery hit the mark I have learned to appreciate
fully through long years of careful observation.
We three members have, at least, all proved durable. Even if
[we] have become somewhat decrepit, a glimmer of your bright,
vivifying radiance still lights our lonely pilgrimage. For, unlike
[us], you did not grow old and become like an overgrown head of
lettuce.
To you our fidelity and devotion till the last learned gasp!
A.E.—now only a corresponding member.

The years were taking their inevitable toll. Already, on 6 January 1951, Einstein had written to the Queen Mother of Belgium:

Much as I should like to, it will probably not be given to me to
see Brussels again. Because of a peculiar popularity that I have
acquired, anything I do is likely to develop into a ridiculous comedy. This means that I have to stay close to my home and rarely
leave Princeton.
I am done with fiddling. With the passage of years, it has become more and more unbearable for me to listen to my own playing. I hope you have not suffered a similar fate. What has remained
is the relentless work on difficult scientific problems. The fascinating magic of that work will continue to my last breath.

On 6 June 1952, a year and a half later, he wrote to his cousin:
"As to my work, it no longer amounts to much: I don't get many

ALL MEN ARE MORTAL

results any more and have to be satisfied with playing the Elder
Statesman and the Jewish Saint, mainly the latter." And, indeed,
less than half a year later, on the death of Chaim Weizmann,
Einstein was asked to succeed him as President of the State of
Israel. Although deeply moved, Einstein gently declined, saying
that he lacked the necessary aptitude and experience, and adding:
"I am the more distressed . . . because my relationship to the Jewish people has become my strongest human bond, ever since I
became fully aware of our precarious situation among the nations
of the world."

In 1954 he was to write to the Queen Mother of Belgium: "I
have become an *enfant terrible* in my new homeland because of
my inability to keep silent and to swallow everything that happens
here."

In part this was because Senator Joseph McCarthy, who was
ultimately censured by the Senate, had been branding people as
subversives, destroying careers, and, by his demagogic cry of
"Communist," reducing even courageous political leaders to spine-
lessness. In this fevered atmosphere Einstein had spoken up boldly
against the threat to intellectual freedom. Because of his espousal
of unpopular causes, he was himself bitterly attacked by some
Americans. When Infeld, who had had no part in the making of
the bomb, accepted an important professorship in his native
Poland, the press cried out irrationally that Infeld was somehow
about to convey atomic secrets to the Communists; and this, too,
was twisted in twisted minds into something somehow to Einstein's discredit.

In 1965–67 the Russians brought out the complete scientific
works of Einstein in four volumes. It was the only such collection.
But in earlier days Communist officialdom had never quite known
what line to take about Einstein's theory of relativity. In 1952
a Soviet Academician attacked it as being contrary to Dialectical
Materialism, the philosophical basis of Marxism, and he chided
certain Soviet scientists for supporting Einstein's theory. On receiving a letter about this, Einstein replied in lighthearted vein
saying that it had cheered him up considerably. Nevertheless,
long troubled by the limitations on freedom of thought and utter-
ance in Russia, he then wrote the following aphorism, which was
published in 1953: "In the realm of the seekers after truth there

is no human authority. Whoever attempts to play the magistrate there founders on the laughter of the Gods." In addition he wrote these biting stanzas, hitherto unpublished:

> *Wisdom of Dialectical Materialism*
> By sweat and toil unparalleled
> At last a grain of truth to see?
> Oh Fool! to work yourself to death.
> *Our* party makes truth by decree.
>
> Does some brave spirit dare to doubt?
> A bashed-in skull's his quick reward.
> Thus teach we him, as ne'er before,
> To live with us in sweet accord.*

In America, amid the fear and oppression of the McCarthy era, a teacher entangled in the investigatory meshes of the House Committee on Un-American Activities sought Einstein's aid. And on 16 May 1953 the ailing Einstein wrote him these ringing words:

> The problem with which the intellectuals of this country are confronted is very serious. Reactionary politicians have managed to instil suspicion of all intellectual efforts into the public by dangling before their eyes a danger from without. Having succeeded so far, they are now proceeding to suppress the freedom of teaching and to deprive of their positions all those who do not prove submissive, i.e. to starve them out.
>
> What ought the minority of intellectuals to do against the evil? Frankly, I can only see the revolutionary way of non-cooperation in

---

* *Weisheit des Dialektischen Materialismus*
Durch Schweiss und Mühe ohnegleichen
Ein Körnchen Wahrheit zu erreichen?
Ein Narr, wer sich so kläglich schinden muss
Wir schaffen's einfach durch Parteibeschluss.

Und denen, die zu zweifeln wagen
Wird flugs der Schädel eingeschlagen.
Ja, so erzieht man, wie noch nie,
Der kühnen Geister Harmonie.

the sense of Gandhi. Every intellectual who is called before one of
the committees ought to refuse to testify, i.e. he must be prepared
for jail and economic ruin, in short, for the sacrifice of his personal welfare in the interest of the cultural welfare of his country.

. . . this refusal to testify must [be based] on the assertion that
it is shameful for a blameless citizen to submit to such an inquisition and that this kind of inquisition violates the spirit of the
Constitution.

If enough people are ready to take this grave step they will be
successful. If not, then the intellectuals of this country deserve
nothing better than the slavery that is intended for them.

In those days there was danger even in writing a private letter
of this sort. But Einstein added a postscript saying, "This letter
need not be considered 'confidential.' " And by so doing—but only
by what and who he was—he converted it into a public manifesto
that resounded throughout the world.

Of what and who he was we have by now an inkling. Admittedly, the triumphs of modern quantum mechanics far surpass in
number and precision those of the general theory of relativity.
But, though quantum mechanics was the product of many minds,
Einstein's own part in its development was in itself momentous.
Moreover the special theory of relativity plays an outstanding role
in modern quantum research. And as for the monumental general
theory of relativity, it was, in an important sense, the creation of
one man, and thus ranks among the greatest scientific achievements of all time. Whatever the future may hold, Einstein's theory
of relativity will be secure. For although all theories are mortal,
the great ones, like all masterpieces of art, retain their greatness
forever.

In his "Autobiographical Notes," when speaking of the theory,
Einstein had to tell of difficulties in the Newtonian system.
Abruptly he stopped and addressed himself directly to Newton,
saying:

Enough of this. Newton forgive me. You found the only way that,
in your day, was at all possible for a man of the highest powers of
intellect and creativity. The concepts that you created still dom-

inate the way we think in physics, although we now know that they must be replaced by others farther removed from the sphere of immediate experience if we want to try for a more profound understanding of the way things are interrelated.

What manner of man addressed Newton thus across the timeless centuries? A man of humility and profound simplicity who preserved the wide-eyed wonder of a child. Einstein's sense of the mysterious and the tragic lies barely concealed in these words that he wrote to the Queen Mother of Belgium in 1939: "I am grateful to destiny for having made life an exciting experience so that life has appeared meaningful." *Appeared* meaningful—it is Einstein speaking.

But we must not let such somber thoughts conceal the sense of sheer fun that found expression in his booming laugh, his love of amusing mechanical gadgets, his ready resort to doggerel, and his impish sense of mischief. For example, when sending a copy of the photograph appearing as the frontispiece of this book to a long-time friend, Einstein wrote these irreverent lines:

> Here's what the old guy looks like now.
> You feel: this Horror my peace will shatter.
> Think: what's important is inside.
> And anyway—what does it matter?*

He was by nature a rebel who enjoyed being unconventional. Whenever possible he dressed for comfort, not for looks. Externals meant little to him. They were irrelevant complications and encumbrances. In everything he sought simplicity. Science was his passion, and next to science music. His sister tells that when playing the piano he would suddenly stop and exclaim: "Well, now I have found it"—a solution to a scientific difficulty. His violin, like his science, was his constant companion, accompanying him

---

* Here is the original German:

> So sieht der alte Kerl jetzt aus
> Du fühlst: O jeh! es ist ein Grauss
> Denk: auf das Innre kommt es an
> Und überhaupt—was liegt daran?

This photograph of Einstein was taken in Philadelphia on an occasion for which he had changed only reluctantly from his usual comfortably casual home attire. The inscription reads:

Hier sitz ich und streck meine Füsse raus
Und doch sieht man deutlich, es war nicht zuhaus.

Here is a translation:

Although I sit here and stretch my feet out,
It wasn't at home; of that there's no doubt.

on all his journeyings. No matter what he was doing, science was always present in his mind.

When stirring tea, he noticed the tea leaves congregating at the center and not the circumference of the bottom of the cup. He found the explanation and linked it to something unexpectedly remote: the meandering of rivers. When walking on sand, he noted with wonder what most of us have known unthinkingly: that damp sand gives firm footing although dry sand and sand immersed in water do not. Here too he found a scientific explanation.

He looked on music as he looked on science, seeking above all a natural, simple beauty. Mozart was his ideal. When someone sug-

These silhouettes of Einstein, his wife Elsa, and his daughters Ilse and Margot were made from life by Einstein himself in 1919. They were pasted on the first page of a popular German children's classic, *Peterchens Mondfahrt* (*Peterkin's Journey to the Moon*), sent as a Christmas present to the small son of friends. Einstein was extremely proud of his accomplishment. The silhouettes took him two hours to make.

Peterchens Mondfahrt.

Einstein in winter.

gested to him that Beethoven was a greater composer, he would have none of it. He said that Beethoven created his music, but Mozart's music was so pure that it seemed to have been ever-present in the universe, waiting to be discovered by the master. On another occasion, contemplating the devastation that would result from atomic war, Einstein said that people would no longer hear Mozart. At first this seems a strangely irrelevant remark. Yet what could more deeply convey in so few words the destruction of civilization?

He looked on his worldwide fame as a solemn trust—a gift of fate—to be used for the common good. He knew how great was the weight of his name. He spoke out passionately for the cause of human freedom, and his conscience made it difficult for him to turn down requests for aid to worthy causes.

Many anecdotes are told about him that show his human side. Straus tells that Einstein's cat was miserable when it rained and Einstein said to it apologetically, "I know what's wrong, my dear, but I really don't know how to turn it off." And when the Strauses' cat had kittens, Einstein was eager to see them. Let Straus continue the story:

> [Einstein] came home with us in a detour on his walk home. He was dismayed when he saw that our neighbors were all people from the Institute and said: "Let's walk quickly. There are so many people here whose invitations I've declined. I hope they don't find out that I came to visit your kittens."

He had the gift of putting visitors immediately at their ease— not so much by his words as by his attitude. He had no need to dominate them, nor any desire to do so. He treated them as equals, and such was his naturalness and innate humility that the visitor had no chance even to feel flattered, for flattery was clearly not involved. There was no trace of condescension such as often lurks behind the studied friendliness of other men. He was not as other men. He had his human frailties, but there was about him a greatness that shone all the more brightly because of his simplicity.

On public issues he spoke out simply and fearlessly, like the biblical prophets, for he was deeply concerned about his fellow man. Yet he wrote:

> My passionate sense of social justice and social responsibility has always contrasted oddly with my pronounced lack of need for direct contact with other human beings and human communities. I am truly a "lone traveller" and have never belonged to my country, my home, my friends, or even my immediate family with my whole heart. In the face of all these ties I have never lost a sense of distance and a need for solitude—feelings that increase with the years.

He wrote this in 1930. It remained true all his life.

Nevertheless he found pleasure not only in his work but also in its recognition by scientists. To the Royal Astronomical Society of London, which had awarded him its 1925 Gold Medal, he wrote:

> He who finds a thought that lets us penetrate even a little deeper into the eternal mystery of nature has been granted great grace. He who, in addition, experiences the recognition, sympathy, and help of the best minds of his time, has been given almost more happiness than a man can bear.

He left us further clues to his inner self, but we can interpret them only in the light of our own experiences, not his. For example, he wrote, "The most beautiful experience we can have is the mysterious. It is the fundamental emotion that stands at the cradle of true art and true science." Even if we have known for ourselves the ecstasy of the creative artist or the religious mystic, we can sense only obliquely what Einstein felt. Behind his words is a transcendental experience that is uniquely his. He was at heart an artist, employing the medium of science. And he was a man possessed. Often when seized by an idea, he would work on it to the point of imminent collapse. If the idea proved recalcitrant, he would return to it again and again, year after year, with savage persistence. He scoffed at those who thought that such intellectual work was unadulterated joy, saying, "Whoever knows it does not go tearing after it."

Joy there was, and of the most intense sort, but he worked because he could not do otherwise. He was helpless in the grip of an inexorable compulsion. Thanking a lady who had sent him a poem on his seventy-first birthday, he wrote in 1950:

Einstein at the seventieth-birthday symposium in Princeton, 19 March 1949, with (from left to right) H. P. Robertson, Eugene P. Wigner, Hermann Weyl, Kurt Gödel, I. I. Rabi, Rudolf Ladenburg, J. Robert Oppenheimer, and G. M. Clemence.

An uneasy feeling comes over me when the inevitable birthday nears. All year long the Sphinx stares at me in reproach and reminds me painfully of the Uncomprehended, blotting out the personal aspects of life. Then comes that accursed day when the love shown me by my fellow man reduces me to a state of hopeless helplessness. The Sphinx does not let me free for a moment, and meanwhile I am troubled by a bad conscience, being unable to do justice to all this love because I lack inner freedom and relaxation.

On another occasion he used a different metaphor. Thanking Hermann Broch in 1945 for a copy of his book on the poet Vergil, Einstein expressed himself in Faustian terms: "I am fascinated by your *Vergil*—and am steadfastly resisting him. The book shows me clearly what I fled from when I sold myself body and soul to Science—the flight from the I and WE to the IT."

Howard Schrader, Princeton University

He tried to describe his method of thought, saying that the essential part was a "rather vague" nonlogical playing with "visual" and "muscular" signs, after which explanatory words had to be "sought for laboriously."

But how much can we learn from this? Are we not like tone-deaf people striving to comprehend a symphony? For example, on 19 March 1949 an intimate symposium was held in Princeton in honor of Einstein's seventieth birthday. In Einstein's presence, outstanding scientists in various fields gave detailed accounts of his achievements. But the most vivid tribute came unrehearsed, made eloquent by its very ineloquence. Among the speakers was the Nobel laureate I. I. Rabi. As he gave his prepared lecture, he suddenly seemed to realize the impossibility of conveying even to experts the special magic of Einstein's genius. With a gesture of helplessness, he paused in midsentence, pointed at his wrist

The last photograph of Einstein, made on his seventy-sixth birthday, 14 March 1955.

watch, and in a tone of mingled awe and surprise blurted out, "It all came from this!"

Let us now hear from Einstein. To Solovine, who had written congratulating him on his seventieth birthday, he wrote in reply on 28 March 1949, saying in part:

> You imagine that I look back on my life's work with calm satisfaction. But from nearby it looks quite different. There is not a single concept of which I am convinced that it will stand firm, and I feel uncertain whether I am in general on the right track.

There was no false modesty in this. Einstein knew that his work was important. But he knew too the frailty of all theories. Indeed, who should know it better than he, who had upset the foundations of even the mighty conceptual edifice of Newton? We are reminded of Newton's own words near the end of his life:

> I do not know what I may appear to the world; but to myself I seem to have been only like a boy playing on the sea-shore, and diverting myself in now and then finding a smoother pebble or a prettier shell than ordinary, whilst the great ocean of truth lay all undiscovered before me.

For a while near the end of 1954 Einstein was ill and weak. He knew that he had not many years left to live. More than once he spoke of death as a release, as he did in a letter written on 5 February 1955, adding, "I have come to look upon death as an old debt, at long last to be discharged." Yet before he died he was to experience yet one more sorrow. In March of 1955 his friend Michele Besso died—Besso whom he had thanked in 1905 at the end of the paper on relativity. To Besso's surviving son and sister he wrote on 21 March 1955:

> The foundation of our friendship was laid in our student years in Zurich, where we met regularly at musical evenings. . . . Later the Patent Office brought us together. The conversations during our mutual way home were of unforgettable charm. . . . And now he has preceded me briefly in bidding farewell to this strange world.

A late painting of Besso, made by Paul Winteler, son of Jost Winteler and brother-in-law of both Besso and Einstein.

This signifies nothing. For us believing physicists the distinction between past, present, and future is only an illusion, even if a stubborn one.

Besso indeed preceded him only briefly. In but a few weeks Einstein himself would be making his farewell. Meanwhile, however, there was important work to be done. Alarmed by the atomic arms race, Bertrand Russell in England was preparing a statement that he hoped would be signed by a select group of leading intellectuals of the world to warn of the peril that lay ahead. He turned to Einstein for aid, which Einstein gave willingly. On 2 March 1955 Einstein wrote of the project to Bohr in a letter that began with the revealing words: "Don't frown like that! This letter has nothing to do with our old controversy on physics; but rather

concerns a matter on which we are in complete agreement." Near
the end of the letter came these equally revealing words:

> In America things are complicated by the likelihood that the most
> renowned scientists, who occupy official positions of influence, will
> hardly be inclined to commit themselves to such an "adventure."
> My own participation may exert some favorable influence abroad,
> but not here at home, where I am known as a black sheep (and not
> merely in scientific matters).

The long Russell-Einstein statement, published after Einstein's
death, asked bluntly: "Shall we put an end to the human race; or
shall mankind renounce war?" It was signed by eleven men. Bohr
was not one of them. He and others, perhaps with more realism
than Russell and Einstein, tended to regard it as a futile gesture.
Yet in the days remaining to him Einstein could not remain silent.
And, because of the statement, scientists and others were to meet
in a series of international conferences that were not without influence on the all-too-inadequate attempts to control the prolifer-
ation of atomic weapons.

The signing of the statement was Einstein's last completed
public act. With the seventh anniversary of the founding of the
State of Israel a month away, he had been asked to prepare a
cultural and scientific statement to be broadcast there as part of
the official celebration. He preferred instead to try to influence
world opinion by touching upon Arab-Israeli relations in the larger
context of world peace. On 11 April 1955, and again on 13 April,
although unwell, he conferred with Israeli officials. Later on the
thirteenth he was seized with severe abdominal pains and other
alarming symptoms. By Friday, 15 April, he was in such agony
that he was taken to Princeton Hospital. He knew death was near.
To a close associate he spoke chidingly yet gently through his pain,
saying in effect, "Don't look so upset. Everybody has to die some
day." He asked if the process of dying would be horrible, but the
doctors could make no prophecy. Under treatment in the hospital
his pain was lessened. On the Saturday he asked for his glasses, and
on the Sunday for his calculations and his notes for the statement
for Israel. His daughter, Margot, temporarily a patient in the
hospital, had been brought in to visit with him, and at first she did
not recognize him, so ravaged was his face by pain and pallor. His

The last page of calculations made by Einstein.

older son had come from California to his bedside. His long-time friend and trusted counselor the economist Otto Nathan came to be with him during his last few days and hours.

Two years before, Einstein had written to the Queen Mother of Belgium: "'The strange thing about growing old is that the intimate identification with the here and now is slowly lost; one feels transposed into infinity, more or less alone, no longer in hope or fear, only observing." Nine months later, in words that recall the beliefs of an early atomic speculator, the Roman poet Lucretius, Einstein had written to an inquirer:

To think with fear of the end of one's life is pretty general with human beings. It is one of the means nature uses to conserve the life of the species. Approached rationally that fear is the most unjustified of all fears, for there is no risk of any accidents to one who is dead or not yet born. In short, the fear is stupid but it cannot be helped.

But now that his time had come he faced death unafraid, and even with a jest. He was serene, untroubled in spirit, and ready for the last great adventure. He spoke calmly and with his customary humor of personal matters and of science, and more sadly of America and of the dimming hope of world peace. And in this way he spent his last waking hours. On the Sunday evening he fell asleep, and on 18 April 1955, little more than an hour after midnight, the aneurism burst and the beat of his heart was stilled.

Two centuries and more before, when Newton died, his body lay in state as the world mourned, and his ashes were enshrined with regal ceremony in Westminster Abbey, in the heart of London, near the ashes of the greatest of England's sons. When Einstein died, there was worldwide mourning too. But Einstein had asked that there be neither funeral service, nor grave, nor monument. Quietly, in the presence of a few who had been close to him, he was cremated near Trenton, New Jersey. By his own desire, the manner of disposal of his ashes was kept secret from the world so that there would be no place, however humble, that might become a shrine. But the river of Time flowed on and bore his ashes, wherever they were, toward the great ocean on whose shore Newton too had played.

ALBERT EINSTEIN

Ulm, 14 March 1879—Princeton, 18 April 1955

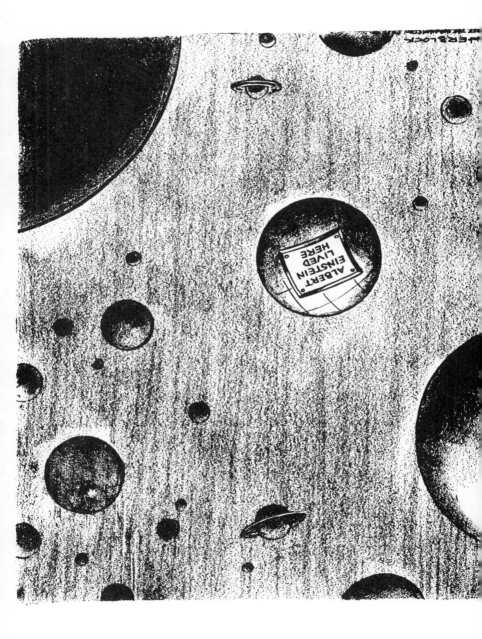

ALBERT
EINSTEIN
LIVED
HERE

Index

Aarau, Switzerland, 27, 28, 29
Acceleration, relativity of, 105–107,
  108, 110
"Aclab," 108–10, 114, 117
Adler, Friedrich, 88
Advisory Committee on Uranium, 206
Albert, King of Belgium, 164–65, 167
Ampère, André Marie, 45
Annalen der Physik, 32, 33, 34–35, 39,
  41, 50, 51, 55, 57, 60, 69, 79, 80,
  83, 84
Anti-Semitism, 144, 202. *See also*
  Nazism
Aristotle, 61
Astronomy, radio, 220
Atomic bomb, 204, 205, 207, 208, 209,
  210, 236
Atomic theory, 173, 179, 182, 183, 184,
  185; Bohr's, 175, 176, 179, 183,
  201–202; de Broglie's, 179, 183, 184;
  Heisenberg's, 182, 183, 184;
  Rutherford's, 174, 175, 177;
  Schrödinger's, 182
Avogadro's number, 56

Bach, Johann Sebastian, 152, 153
Bamberger, Louis, 159
Barium, 202
Barrow, Isaac, 88
Bavarian Academy, 169, 237
Beethoven, Ludwig van, 153, 252

Belgium, 154, 165, 169, 190, 207
Berkeley, George, 63
Berlin, Einstein in, 101, 104, 120, 150,
  152, 153, 159, 172
Berlin Physical Colloquium, 83
Berlin University, 136
Bern University, 86, 87
Besso, Michele, 27, 39, 41, 42, 55, 78,
  79, 80, 87, 88, 187, 257, 258
Black-body radiation, 48, 51, 56, 176,
  177, 181, 192
Black holes, 220
Bohr, Niels, 165, 173–79 *passim*, 184,
  193, 198, 208, 209, 231, 258, 259;
  and complementarity principle,
  185–86, 187; and Einstein, 178, 187,
  188, 189, 190, 192, 193, 194, 195,
  196, 199, 234; liquid-drop theory of,
  203, 207
Boltzmann, Ludwig, 41, 48, 51, 56, 57
Bolyai, Wolfgang, 126
Born, Max, 6, 135, 136, 137, 182, 183,
  187, 201
Bose, S. N., 180, 181, 182 and *n.*, 192
Bragg, William L., 174, 187
Brillouin, L. M., 97, 174, 187
Britain, Battle of, 207, 234
Broch, Hermann, 254
Broglie, Louis de, 179–87 *passim*, 197,
  199
Broglie, Maurice de, 97, 174, 179

Brown, Robert, 58
Brownian motion, 58, 59, 84
Bulge, Battle of, 235

Calculus, tensor, 117, 119, 122, 125
California Institute of Technology, 159
Cambridge University, 42, 179, 183, 200, 201
Caputh, Einstein at, 159, 160, 161, 163
Causality, 119, 120; and indeterminacy principle, 185, 187
Cavendish Laboratory, 179, 200, 201
Chadwick, James, 201
Chain reaction, nuclear, 208
Chaplin, Charles, 3
Chavan, Lucien, 85
Christoffel, Elwin, 126
Churchill, Winston, 170, 171, 202, 208, 209
Clemence, G. M., 254
Clifford, William, 126
Columbia University, 145, 202, 204
Committee on Intellectual Cooperation, 154–55
Communism, 164, 245
Compass needle, magnetic, 9, 11, 45, 47
Complementarity, 185–86, 187
Compton, A. H., 187
Congress of German Scientists and Physicians, 89, 93, 143, 149
Copenhagen interpretation of quantum mechanics, 185, 190, 196, 197, 198, 199
Copernican Quadricentennial (1943), 235
Copernicus, Nicolaus, 60
Correspondence principle, Bohr's, 179, 183
Cosmology, relativistic, 211, 212
Covariance, general, principle of, 116, 117, 120, 123, 124, 127
Curie, Marie, 97, 98, 174, 187; quoted, 98–99
Curvature tensor, 126
Czechoslovakia, 202, 203, 206

Debye, Peter, 165, 187
"Development of Our View of the Nature and Constitution of Radiation, The" (Einstein), 93
Dialectical materialism, 245, 246
Dirac, Paul, 183, 184, 187, 192, 193, 197
Donder, T. de, 165, 187
Doppler effect, 110n.
Dyson, Frank, 129

Economic depression, 159
Eddington, Arthur, 129, 131, 200, 217, 224; quoted, 133
Ehrenfest, Paul, 95, 96, 100, 124, 135, 137, 138, 178, 182n., 187, 190
Einstein, Abraham, 8
Einstein, Albert: on atomic theory, 176, 177, 180; "Autobiographical Notes" by, 8, 9, 10, 11, 12, 22, 31, 58, 176, 199, 247; and Avogadro's number, 56; in Berlin, 101, 104, 120, 150, 152, 153, 159, 172; at Bern Patent Office, 34, 35, 36, 37, 39, 41, 42, 50, 60, 82, 84, 85–86, 87, 88; and Bohr, 178, 187, 188, 189, 190, 192, 193, 194, 195, 196, 199, 234; on Brownian motion, 58, 59, 84; on capillarity, 32; at Caputh, 159, 160, 161, 163; childhood of, 9, 13, 14, 16, 17, 18, 19, 20, 21, 22, 24; on Communism, 164, 245–46; and compass-needle incident, 9, 11, 47; at Congress of German Scientists and Physicians, 93; on cosmic reference frame, 213–14; death of, 261; education of, 18–22, 25, 27, 30, 31; in England, 147–48, 163, 170; equation $E = mc^2$ propounded by, 81, 82, 84, 105, 109, 200, 201, 203, 236; on equivalence, principle of, 107, 108, 109, 110, 113, 119, 124, 127, 129, 190; on experience of the mysterious, 253; at fiftieth birthday, 57; in France, 148–49; Gelegenheitsarbeit of, 6, 7, 43; on general covariance, principle of, 116, 117, 120, 123, 124, 127; on gravitation, see Gravitation; infinite distances rejected by, 212, 213; at Institute for Advanced Study, 171–72, 200, 227; intuition of, 72, 105, 113, 119, 121, 123, 124, 127, 128, 180, 181, 184, 193, 195, 200, 222; in Italy, 26; in Japan, 150; lambda (λ) rejected by, 218, 219; on light quanta, 51, 52, 53, 54, 69, 72, 100, 101, 178; and mathematics, 8, 22, 24, 116, 125; on motion, 105–107; as music-lover, 7, 20, 152, 248, 250, 252; on Nazi Germany, 237; on Newton's greatness, 139, 141, 142, 247–48; Nobel Prize awarded to, 7, 54, 150–51; as pacifist, 155, 157, 169; in Palestine, 151; Ph.D. acquired by, 55; and phrase "Gott würfelt nicht," 193; Planck medal

received by, 157; popular acclaim of, 133, 134, 145–47, 148, 150–52; in Prague, 94, 95, 96, 98, 99, 145; as *Privatdozent*, 87; and professorship, election to (1909), 88; on public issues, 252–53; on quantum concepts, 51, 52, 53, 54, 69, 72, 84, 187, 190, 192, 193, 195, 196, 199, 222, 233, 234, 247; on quantum law of photochemical processes, 96; quoted, 8, 10, 11, 12, 15, 20, 22, 25, 31, 32, 36, 58–59, 79, 86, 95, 98, 116, 117, 124, 135, 138–39, 149, 155, 157, 164, 165, 168, 169, 170, 176, 205–206, 217–18, 219, 221–22, 224, 225, 237, 238, 242, 244, 246–47, 248, 252, 254, 257, 258, 259, 261; on relativity, *see* Relativity; religious beliefs of, 94; and Roosevelt, letter to, 205–206, 233, 236; Royal Astronomical Society's Gold Medal awarded to, 135, 253; and Russell on atomic arms race, 258; at seventieth birthday, 254, 255, 257; at Solvay Congresses, 96, 97, 98, 190; in Spain, 152; sugar paper by, 55–56, 57; on Supreme Being, 95; in Sweden, 151; as Swiss citizen, 31, 137; and thermodynamics, papers on, 41; and unified field theory, 225, 226, 227, 228, 234, 239, 240; in Vienna, 145; violin played by, 7, 20, 152, 153, 248; on visits to United States, 145–47, 159; and wonder, sense of, 9, 11, 18, 20, 94, 195; during World War I, 103–104, 178, 221; during World War II, 206, 209; Zionism supported by, 144, 147; in Zurich, 27, 30, 31, 32, 85, 94, 100

Einstein, Bernhard, 162
Einstein, Eduard, 39, 102
Einstein, Elsa, 134, 159, 162, 163, 164, 231, 232, 250
Einstein, Hans Albert, 39, 40, 102, 162
Einstein, Hermann, 6, 12, 15, 18, 25, 26; quoted, 33–34
Einstein, Hindel, 8
Einstein, Ilse (married Kayser), 134, 161, 250
Einstein, Jakob, 15, 18, 20, 25, 27
Einstein, Maja. *See* Winteler-Einstein, Maja
Einstein, Margot, 134, 234, 241, 250, 259
Einstein, Mileva (née Maric), 28, 39, 40, 102, 103, 134, 240
Einstein, Pauline, 6, 18, 135

Einstein, Rudolf, 134
Einsteinstrasse, 15
Einstein Tower, 148
Electromagnetism, 47, 93, 225; and gravitation, 223, 224, 225, 239; Maxwell's theory of, 30, 34, 45, 47, 52, 53, 65, 230
Electrons, in atomic theory, 174, 175, 176, 179, 185, 186, 191, 192
Elizabeth, Queen of Belgium, 164–65, 166, 205
Emergency Committee of Atomic Scientists, 236
Energy: and inertial and gravitational mass, 109; and mass, equivalence of, 81, 84, 200 and *n*.
Energy/frequency ratio, and quanta, 49, 51, 53, 175
England, Einstein in, 147–48, 163, 170
Entropy, 41, 51, 56
Equivalence, principle of, 107, 108, 109, 110, 113, 119, 124, 127, 129, 190
Ether, 64, 66, 67, 69, 71, 77; superfluity of, 72, 84
Euclid, 24, 126
Evolution of Physics, The (Einstein and Infeld), 233
Expanding universe, 215, 216, 217, 218

Faraday, Michael, 45, 46
Fermi, Enrico, 201, 202, 203, 204, 205, 208
Field, concept of, 45
Field equations: gravitational, 119, 120, 121–24, 126, 212, 217, 218, 229; sought for unified field theory, 226, 240
Fifth dimension (Kaluza), 224, 225, 227
Finlay-Freundlich, Erwin, 111, 133
Fission, nuclear, 203
FitzGerald, G. F., 66, 67, 77
FitzGerald-Lorentz contraction, 66, 67, 77, 223n.
Flexner, Abraham, 163, 171
Fock, Vladimir, 228
Foundations of the General Theory of Relativity (Einstein), 130
Four-dimensional space-time, 89, 90, 92, 119
Fowler, R. H., 187
France, Einstein in, 148–49
Frank, Philipp, 95
Franz Josef, Emperor, 94

Fresnel, Augustin, 44, 47, 52, 64, 65, 66, 67
Friedmann, Alexander, 215, 217, 218
Frisch, Otto, 203, 207
Fuld, Mrs. Felix, 159
Galileo, 60, 106, 107, 108
Gandhi, Mahatma, 247
Gas constant and probabilistic formula for entropy, 56
Gauss, Karl, 118, 126
General covariance, principle of, 116, 117, 120, 123, 124, 127
General theory of relativity, 5, 6, 84, 96, 100, 104, 116, 117, 125, 128, 129, 190, 199, 211, 212, 219, 220, 222; eclipse observations in support of, 5, 6, 111, 129, 131, 132, 133, 200; equivalence principle in, 108, 113; and gravitational red shift, 111, 128, 129; and gravitational waves, 220; and perihelion motion of Mercury, 124, 125, 128, 129
Geodesics, 120, 121
Geometry, 126; non-Euclidean, 126; and unified field theory, 224
"Geometry and Experience" (Einstein), 70
"Geometry book, holy," 22, 23, 25, 125
German Physical Society, 50
Germany: Einstein attacked in, 141, 143–44, 167, 168; Einstein unforgiving toward, 237–38; Nazi, 51, 163, 167, 168, 169, 170, 201, 202, 206, 231, 237; after World War I, 135ff., 152
Gibbs, Willard, 41
Gödel, Kurt, 254
Göttingen University, 84–85, 88, 183
Gouy, M., 58, 174
Gravitation, 9, 104, 107, 113, 114, 119, 229; as curvature of space-time, 120; and electromagnetism, 223, 224, 225, 239; field equations of, 119, 120, 121–24, 126, 217, 218, 229, 230; light deflected by, 109, 111, 128, 129, 131, 133; Newton's law of, 45, 61, 113, 119, 230; time warped by, 111, 115
Gravitational potential, 113, 121
Gravitational red shift, 111, 128, 129
Gravitational waves, 219, 220
"GravLab," 108, 109, 110, 111, 114
Grommer, J., 229

Grossmann, Marcel, 30, 34, 35, 36, 55, 86, 98, 116, 117, 119, 120, 126
Guye, E., 187
Habicht, Konrad, 37, 38, 39, 42, 51, 55, 57, 60, 79, 243
Hahn, Otto, 202, 203
Haldane, Viscount, 148
Hale, George, 111, 112, 133
Haller, Friedrich, 34, 36
Harding, Warren G., 145
Havel River, 159
Heat, internal, theory of, 47–48, 53, 57, 96, 173, 175
Hebrew University (Jerusalem), 144, 151, 210
Heisenberg, Werner, 182, 183, 184, 185, 187, 190, 191, 192, 193
Henriot, E., 187
Herbert Spencer Lecture, 170
Hertz, Heinrich, 47, 52, 54
Herzen, E., 97, 174, 187
Herzl, Theodor, 144
Herzog, Albin, 27
Hiroshima, bombing of, 210, 236
Hitler, Adolf, 163, 165, 169, 201, 202, 209, 235
Holdt, Charles, 172
"Holy geometry book," 22, 23, 25, 125
House Committee on Un-American Activities, 246
Hubble, Edwin, 215, 216, 217
Hubble's constant, 216
Huygens, Christiaan, 44
Indeterminacy, principle of, 185, 187, 190
Inertia, relativity of, 114, 212
Infeld, Leopold, 228, 233, 240, 245
Institute for Advanced Study (Princeton), 163, 171, 191, 200, 203, 224, 227, 229
Institute for Theoretical Physics (Copenhagen), 178, 183
Interference, wave phenomenon of, 44
Israel, 144, 245, 259
Italy, 25, 26, 27; Fascist, 152, 201, 202
Jahrbuch der Radioaktivität, 81
Japan, Einstein in, 150, 210
Jeans, James, 97, 98, 174
Jewish National Fund, 147
Jordan, Pascual, 183, 184
Judaism, 16, 94
Kaiser Wilhelm Institute, 100, 202, 206, 237
Kaluza, T., 224, 225, 227

Kamerlingh-Onnes, Heike, 33, 97, 98, 137, 138, 174
Kant, Immanuel, 24, 126
Kayser, Ilse. See Einstein, Ilse
Kayser, Rudolf, 10, 161
Kepler, Johannes, 60, 169
Kleiner, Alfred, 35, 55, 87, 88
Knudsen, M. H. C., 97, 174, 187
Koch, Jette, 13
Kramers, Hendrick, 187

Ladenburg, Rudolf, 254
Langevin, Paul, 97, 98, 138, 148, 165, 174, 180, 187
Langmuir, Irving, 187
Larmor, Joseph, 68
Laser, 178, 183, 192
Laue, Max von, 84, 143, 149, 155, 168, 174
League of Nations, 154, 155
Leibniz, Gottfried, 63
Leiden, Netherlands, 99, 100, 129, 138, 139
Lemaître, Georges, 217, 218
Lenard, Philipp, 52, 53, 143, 144
Lengths: mutual contractions of, 77; in space-time, 223
Library of Congress, 209–10
Light: deflection of, 109, 111, 128, 129, 131, 133; particle theory of, 44, 51, 52, 64, 71, 178; particle-wave theory of, 179, 186; quanta of, 51, 52, 53, 54, 100, 101, 178, 181, 182n., 183, 184, 186 (see also Photons); speed of, 67, 70–71, 72, 73, 89, 109, 113, 117, 121; wave theory of, 44–45, 47, 51, 52, 54, 64, 71, 178
Lindemann, F. A., 97, 174
Lobachevski, Nikolai, 126
London University, 147, 148
Lorentz, Hendrik Antoon, 64–68 passim, 78, 79, 84, 97, 98, 100, 131, 137, 174, 187, 225
Lorentz force, 230
Lorentz transformation, 68, 77, 78
Lucretius, 261
Luitpold Gymnasium, 19, 25, 26

McCarthy, Joseph, 245
Mach, Ernst, 59, 63, 78, 94, 105, 123, 212, 215
Manchester University, 147, 148, 173
Marxism, 245
Mass: and energy, equivalence of, 81, 84, 200 and n.; equality of inertial and gravitational, 113

Mathematics, and Einstein, 8, 22, 24, 116, 125
Matter: as curvature of space-time, 126, 127; particle-wave theory of (de Broglie), 186; and radiation, 51; and unified field theory, 240; wave theory of (Schrödinger), 182, 183
Maurer, Professor, 112
Maxwell, James Clerk, 30, 34, 45, 46, 47, 48, 51, 52, 53, 54, 65–69 passim, 79, 93, 104, 127, 173, 174, 179, 192, 220, 230
Mayer, Walter, 162, 171, 227
Meaning of Relativity, The (Einstein), 146, 218
Meitner, Lise, 202, 203
Mercury: calculation of perihelion motion of, 124, 125, 128, 129
Metrical tensor, 118, 119, 126, 225
Michelson, Albert, 66, 162
Michelson-Morley experiment, 66, 67, 68, 69, 117
Milan, Italy, 26, 33
Millay, Edna St. Vincent, 24
Millikan, Robert, 54, 150, 155, 159, 162
Minkowski, Hermann, 84, 85, 88, 89, 92, 93, 123
Morley, E. W., 66
Motion: Newton's laws of, 61, 63, 64, 106, 114, 230; relativity of, 105–107, 113
Mozart, Wolfgang Amadeus, 7, 20, 153, 250, 252
Munich, Germany, 16, 18, 25, 26, 134
Munich Pact (1938), 202
Mussolini, Benito, 168, 202

Nagasaki, bombing of, 236
Nathan, Otto, 238, 261
Nazism, 15, 152, 159, 163, 167, 168, 169, 201, 202, 233, 234. See also Anti-Semitism
Nebulae, 215, 216; recessions of, 216, 217
Neptunium, 201
Nernst, Walther, 96, 97, 98, 100, 143, 155, 168, 174
Neustätter, Otto, 26, 27; quoted, 27–28
Neutrons: atomic nuclei bombarded by, 201, 202, 203; discovery of, 201
Newton, Isaac, 7, 42, 44, 45, 52, 63, 64, 67, 70, 79, 88, 91, 104, 107, 108, 120, 123, 127, 140, 169, 173, 192, 211, 229, 261; on absolute space and time, 61, 63, 89, 90; Einstein on

greatness of, 139, 141, 142, 247–48;
and gravitation, law of, 45, 61, 113,
119, 230; and motion, laws of, 61,
63, 64, 106, 114, 230; as President
of Royal Society, 132; quoted, 104,
257

Nicolai, Georg, 103, 104
Nobel Institute, 202
Nobel Prize, 6, 7, 32, 48, 54, 65, 66,
84, 143, 150, 173, 178, 183, 184, 193,
201, 202, 255
Non-Euclidean geometry, 126

Olympia Academy, 37, 38, 242, 243,
244
"On the Dynamics of the Electron"
(Poincaré), 68
"On the Electrodynamics of Moving
Bodies" (Einstein), 60
"On the Method of Theoretical Physics"
(Einstein), 170
Oppenheimer, J. Robert, 208, 254
Orlík, Emil, 158
Ormandy, Eugene, 233
Ørsted, Hans Christian, 45
Oscillating universe, 218, 219
Ostwald, Wilhelm, 32, 33, 34, 59

Palestine, Einstein in, 151
Parallelism, distant, 225
Paris, Einstein in, 148–49
Pasadena, California, 159, 162, 163, 165
Pasternak, Leonid, 204
Patent Office, Bern, 34, 35, 36, 37, 39,
41, 42, 50, 60, 82, 84, 85–86, 87, 88
Pauli, Wolfgang, 187
Peierls, Rudolf, 207
Perrin, Jean Baptiste, 97, 98
Photoelectric effect, 52, 53, 54, 117,
143, 150
Photons, 54, 177, 185, 186, 197;
spontaneous emission of, 177, 197;
stimulated emission of, 177. See
also Light, quanta of
Piccard, Auguste, 187
Planck, Max, 48–53 passim, 56, 59, 83,
93, 96, 97, 98, 100, 103, 138, 143,
149, 155, 168, 169, 173, 175, 187,
197, 199, 221, 222; formula of, for
black-body radiation, 48, 51, 56, 176,
177, 181, 182n, 192; quoted, 83–84,
168–69
Planck Institute, 237
Planck's constant (h), 49, 50, 175
Plato, 61
Podolsky, Boris, 191, 195, 196

Poincaré, Henri, 67, 68, 78, 84, 92, 97,
98; quoted, 99
Poincaré, Raymond, 152
Poland, 203, 206, 245
Pope, W. J., 174
Prague, German University in, 94
Princeton, New Jersey, 171–72, 242,
243, 259; symposium in (1949), 255
Princeton University, 145, 146, 163,
171–72, 205
Principe island, 129, 130
Principia (Newton), 61, 62, 63, 105
Probabilistic universe, 193
Probability, waves of, 183, 184, 185
Prussian Academy of Science, 100, 124,
167, 168, 237
Pulsars, 220
Pythagorean theorem, 20–21, 91, 92,
125

Quantum, 5, 49–54 passim, 56, 97–98,
173–79 passim, 181
Quantum mechanics, 184, 185, 186,
187, 190, 191, 192, 193, 195–99
passim, 222, 233, 234, 247
Quasars, 220

Rabi, I. I., 254, 255
Radiation: black-body, 48, 51, 56, 176,
177, 181, 192; entropy of, 51; and
matter, 51
Radioactivity, 81, 173, 197, 198
Radio astronomy, 220
Radium, 81
Rathenau, Walther, 149, 150
Red shift, gravitational, 111, 128, 129
Reference frame, cosmic, 213–14
Relativity, 3, 5, 28, 60, 68, 69, 84, 85;
general theory of, see General theory
of relativity; principles of, 67, 70–72,
73, 74, 76, 77, 78; Soviet attitude
toward, 245; and space-time, 89, 90,
92; special theory of, see Special
theory of relativity
"Reminiscences" (Einstein), 117
Rest, absolute, in cosmic reference
frame, 213, 214
Ricci, Gregorio, 117
Richardson, O. W., 165, 187
Riemann, Bernhard, 126, 127
Robertson, H. P., 254
Roosevelt, Franklin D., 171, 205, 206,
208, 209, 233, 236
Rosen, Nathan, 191, 195, 196
Royal Astronomical Society, 132, 135,
253